Cyber-Security and Threat Politics

Myriam Dunn Cavelty posits that cyber-threats are definable by their unsubstantiated nature, sharing with other 'new', post-Cold War threats an unknowable quality. Despite this, they have been propelled to the forefront of the political agenda. Using an innovative theoretical approach, this book examines how, under what conditions, by whom, for what reasons, and with what impact cyber-threats have been moved on to the political agenda. In particular, it analyses how governments have used *threat frames*, specific interpretive schemata about what counts as a threat or risk, and how to respond to this threat. The findings point to a change in the nature and logic of security: the maintenance of 'business continuity' for an individual, corporate, or local actor is often regarded as equal in importance to national or even international security in the realm of cyber-threats. By looking at the foundations and formation of these practices from a security studies angle, this book closes a gap between practical and theoretical academic approaches. It also contributes to the more general debate about changing practices of national security and their implications for the international community.

This book will be of much interest to students of security studies, information warfare, and International Relations theory.

Myriam Dunn Cavelty is Lecturer and Head of the new risks research unit at the Center for Security Studies (CSS), ETH Zurich.

CSS Studies in security and international relations
Series Editors: Andreas Wenger and Victor Mauer
Center for Security Studies, ETH Zurich

The *CSS Studies in Security and International Relations* examines historical and contemporary aspects of security and conflict. The series provides a forum for new research based upon an expanded conception of security and will include monographs by the Center's research staff and associated academic partners.

War Plans and Alliances in the Cold War
Threat perceptions in the East and West
Edited by Vojtech Mastny, Sven Holtsmark and Andreas Wenger

Transforming NATO in the Cold War
Challenges beyond deterrence in the 1960s
Edited by Andreas Wenger, Christian Nuenlist and Anna Locher

US Foreign Policy and the War on Drugs
Displacing the cocaine and heroin industry
Cornelius Friesendorf

Cyber-Security and Threat Politics
US efforts to secure the information age
Myriam Dunn Cavelty

Cyber-Security and Threat Politics

US efforts to secure the information age

Myriam Dunn Cavelty

LONDON AND NEW YORK

First published 2008
by Routledge
2 Park Square, Milton Park, Abingdon, Oxon OX14 4RN

Simultaneously published in the USA and Canada
by Routledge
270 Madison Ave, New York, NY 10016

Routledge is an imprint of the Taylor & Francis Group, an informa business

© 2008 Myriam Dunn Cavelty

Typeset in Times by Wearset Ltd, Boldon, Tyne and Wear
Printed and bound in Great Britain by TJI Digital, Padstow, Cornwall

All rights reserved. No part of this book may be reprinted or reproduced or utilised in any form or by any electronic, mechanical, or other means, now known or hereafter invented, including photocopying and recording, or in any information storage or retrieval system, without permission in writing from the publishers.

British Library Cataloguing in Publication Data
A catalogue record for this book is available from the British Library

Library of Congress Cataloging in Publication Data
A catalog record for this book has been requested

ISBN10: 0-415-42981-1 (hbk)
ISBN10: 0-203-93741-4 (ebk)

ISBN13: 978-0-415-42981-8 (hbk)
ISBN13: 978-0-203-93741-9 (ebk)

Contents

List of illustrations vi
Acknowledgements vii
List of abbreviations viii

Introduction 1

1 The information age and cyber-threats: shifting meanings and interpretations 12

2 Politics and threat construction: theoretical underpinnings 24

3 The hostile intelligence threat, data security, and encryption set the stage 41

4 Asymmetric vulnerabilities and the double-edged sword of information warfare: developments in the military domain 66

5 Critical infrastructures and homeland security 91

6 Securing the information age: failed securitisation or a new logic of security? 122

7 Cyber-threats and security in the information age: issues and implications 138

Bibliography 145
Index 174

Illustrations

Figures

2.1	Securitisation theory basic diagram	28
2.2	Securitisation theory: including internal/external criticism	29
2.3	Securitisation theory expanded I: adding framing theory	32
2.4	Securitisation theory expanded II: adding agenda-setting theory	35
2.5	Schematic final framework for phases I and II	36

Tables

1.1	Infrastructure threat matrix	23
2.1	Threat-framing keywords	38

Acknowledgements

This book would not have been possible without the support, help, and encouragement of my family, friends, and colleagues. Special thanks go to my husband Gion Mathias Cavelty for his unconditional love and support and for sharing me with my computer, to Victor Mauer for exceptional colleagueship and sharp-mindedness, and to Andy Wenger for his invaluable guidance and support. Thanks also to Christopher Findlay for proof-reading the manuscript with so much enthusiasm and to my team at the Center for Security Studies at ETH Zurich, for making work such an enjoyable experience. And I want to express my deep gratitude to my parents, Thomas and Nicole, who have always supported me and have given me repeated refuge in the Val Müstair.

I also want to give Naruto Uzumaki and Masashi Kishimoto credit for showing me what true determination is and At the Gates, Blind Guardian, Coldeve, Covenant, Dark Tranquility, Dimmu Borgir, Emperor, In Flames, Judas Priest, Manowar, Metallica, My Chemical Romance, Nevermore, and Two Gallants (among others) credit for the stimulation needed to finish this project.

Abbreviations

ACF	Advocacy Coalition Framework
ARPA	Advanced Research Projects Agency
ATA	Anti-Terrorism Act
C2	Command and Control
C2W	Command-and-Control Warfare
C3I	Command, Control, Communications, and Intelligence
C4I	Command, Control, Communications, Computer, and Intelligence
CERT	Computer Emergency Response Team
CIA	Central Intelligence Agency
CIAO	Critical Infrastructure Assurance Office
CICG	Critical Infrastructure Coordination Group
CIP	Critical Infrastructure Protection
CITAC	Computer Investigations and Infrastructure Threat Assessment Center
CIWG	Critical Infrastructure Working Group
CRS	Congressional Research Service
CSTB	Computer Science and Telecommunications Board
DARPA	Defense Advanced Research Projects Agency
DES	Data Encryption Standard
DHS	Department of Homeland Security
DIA	Defense Intelligence Agency
DISA	Defense Information Systems Agency
DoD	Department of Defense
DSB	Defense Science Board
DSBTF	Defense Science Board Task Force
EMP	Electromagnetic Pulse
EO	Executive Order
FBI	Federal Bureau of Investigation
FedCIRC	Federal Computer Incident Response Capability
FEMA	Federal Emergency Management Agency
GAO	General Accounting Office
IAIP	Information Analysis and Infrastructure Protection

ICT	Information and Communication Technologies
IO	Information Operations
IPTF	Infrastructure Protection Task Force
IR	International Relations
IW	Information Warfare
IW-D	Information Warfare Defense
JSC	Joint Security Commission
JTF-CND	Joint Task Force on Computer Network Defense
MoU	Memorandum of Understanding
NAS	National Academy of Sciences
NASA	National Aeronautics and Space Administration
NATO	North Atlantic Treaty Organisation
NBS	National Bureau of Standards
NIAC	National Infrastructure Advisory Council
NIPC	National Infrastructure Protection Center
NIST	National Institute of Standards and Technology
NSA	National Security Agency
NSC	National Security Council
NSD	National Security Directive
NSDD	National Security Decision Directive
NSIRC	National Security Incident Response Center
NSPD	National Security Presidential Decision
NSS	National Security Strategy
OCIIP	Office of Computer Investigations and Infrastructure Protection
PCC	Policy Coordination Committees
PCCIP	President's Commission on Critical Infrastructure Protection
PDD	Presidential Decision Directive
PSYOPS	Psychological Operations
RMA	Revolution in Military Affairs
SCADA	Supervisory Control and Data Acquisition
SPB	Security Policy Board
USA PATRIOT Act	Uniting and Strengthening America by Providing Appropriate Tools Required to Intercept and Obstruct Terrorism (Act)
WMD	Weapons of Mass Destruction

Introduction

> We are at risk. Increasingly, America depends on computers. [...] Tomorrow's terrorist may be able to do more damage with a keyboard than with a bomb.
> (National Academy of Sciences 1991: 7)

> We did find widespread capability to exploit infrastructure vulnerabilities. The capability to do harm – particularly through information networks – is real; it is growing at an alarming rate; and we have little defense against it.
> (President's Commission on Critical Infrastructure Protection 1997: i)

> Our nation is at grave risk of a cyberattack that could devastate the national psyche and economy more broadly than did the 9/11 attacks.
> (Statement in a letter sent to President Bush by former White House adviser Richard Clarke and more than 50 top computer scientists, quoted in Fitzpatrick 2003)

The above quotes are exemplary for the tone and timbre of forewarnings concerned with a 'new' kind of threat to the national security and to the very foundations of developed societies. The most frequent label bestowed upon this phenomenon is that of *cyber-threats*, a rather vague notion signifying the malicious use of information and communication technologies (ICT) either as a target or as a tool by a wide range of malevolent actors. This book is about what I would like to call the 'cyber-threat story'; the story of how and why cyber-threats came to be considered one of the quintessential security threats of modern times in the United States. I focus on the political process that moves threats onto the political agenda, removes threats from the agenda, or alters the face of threats on the political agenda – a political process that I label 'threat politics'. In particular, this study analyses the use of *threat frames*: specific interpretive schemata about what counts as threat or risk, how to respond to this threat, and who is responsible for dealing with it. Cyber-threat frames reveal a great deal about the character of the actors involved in the construction of the threat and also about how security is defined and ultimately practiced in relation to the threat.

Of course, cyber-threats were not a new phenomenon in the 1990s. Viruses and worms have been part of the background noise of cyberspace since its earliest days. For example, in the 1986 movie War Games, a teenager hacks his way into the computer that handles command and control for the US nuclear arsenal. In 1988, the Morris worm brought the ARPANET, the early internet, to a standstill. The Cuckoo's Egg incident, a computer break-in that involved a German hacker who was attempting to access US computer networks, in particular those involved with national security, in the mid-1980s raised awareness that foreign spies had found new ways to obtain highly classified information (Stoll 1989).

In the 1990s, however, the issue took on a new kind of urgency as information technology evolved from modest use of mainly stand-alone systems in closed networks to the development of the internet and other networks and as access devices multiplied and diversified to include a variety of options for portable and wireless access. In the mid-1990s, a quantitative change concerning the threat became apparent: according to most official statistics, the number of cyber-incidents skyrocketed (see, for example, Computer Emergency Response Team 2005; ICSA Labs 2003, 2004, 2005; Information Technology Promotion Agency 2004, 2005). Whether these numbers should be taken at face value is another question, but even if one is highly sceptical about the usefulness and truthfulness of such statistics, one can identify a qualitative difference as well as a quantitative increase in cyber-incidents. This qualitative difference concerns the perceived gravity of the threat: in the mid-1990s, the issue of cyber-security gained momentum when it was persuasively linked to both terrorism and critical infrastructure protection. At times, cyber-threats were even placed at the top of the list of modern threats in the United States. Speaking at the InfoWar conference in Washington in 1999, Congressman Curt Weldon (R-Pennsylvania) reportedly said, 'in my opinion, neither missile proliferation nor weapons of mass destruction are as serious as the threat [of cyberterrorism]' (Poulsen 1999). In May 2001, Senator Robert Bennett (R-Utah) stated that '[attacks against the US banking system] would devastate the United States more than a nuclear device let off over a major city' (Porteus 2001).

Cyber-doom scenarios

To understand these statements, we must be aware of some of the common cyber-threat scenarios. While scenarios should not be mistaken for reality, they are designed to assist in the understanding of possible future developments, and as such, they play a crucial role in the construction of the cyber-threat story. Imagine the following:

- A truck carrying a huge bomb races towards the main entrance of a city centre rail station at rush hour, just as a computer whiz hacks into the emergency response telephone network. There is a huge blast. With the communications system out of action, police and rescue units are paralysed. Emergency teams lose precious minutes attending to the scene, and the number of dead and injured climbs.

- A virus deliberately introduced into the software system of a power station by a terrorist group triggers a complete power loss that plunges a large part of three European countries into darkness. About 168 million people are affected. Power cannot be restored for up to four days in some parts of the affected region. The outage of traffic lights leads to chaos. Millions of car drivers are left without fuel, because petrol station pumps run on electricity. The water supply is seriously compromised; the interruption lasts for days. Both the telephone network and mobile phones are operating, although services are in a critical state. Most Internet providers have to shut down their servers because they are not able to switch to their diesel-driven backup generators. The estimated financial loss is about €970 million. A great number of people die as a result of the power cuts.
- A 12-year-old hacks the system that runs the Roosevelt Dam, near Phoenix, Arizona, which contains nearly 500 trillion gallons of water. The cities Mesa and Tempe are downstream, with a combined population of one million – the child accidentally opens the floodgates: 100,000 people die in the torrents of the rampant Salt River.

The first story is completely fictitious. The second one is only partly made up and is inspired by the major blackouts in the United States and Europe in 2003, which, however, were not caused by a hacker attack (Masera *et al.* 2006: 99–102). The third story, finally, is partly true. The Washington Post reported on 27 June 2002 that a 12-year-old hacker had broken into the computer system that controlled the floodgates of the Theodore Roosevelt Dam in Arizona in 1998 (Gellman 2002). True, a hacker did break into the computers of an Arizona water facility, the Salt River Project, in the Phoenix area. But he was 27, not 12, and the incident occurred in 1994, not 1998. What actually happened was that a 27-year-old hacker dialled into a server that monitored the water levels of canals in the Phoenix area. And while clearly trespassing in critical areas, the hacker never could have had control of any dams, leading investigators to conclude that no lives or property were ever at risk (Green 2002).

Stories like the semi-fictional dam incident can serve as a metaphor for the contemporary debate about the vulnerability of networked societies to cyber-threats. While governments and the media repeatedly distribute information about cyber-threats, real cyber-attacks resulting in deaths and injuries remain largely the stuff of Hollywood movies or conspiracy theory. Statements such as given by Curt Weldon or Robert Bennett do not take into consideration one of the defining features of cyber-threats: their unsubstantiated nature. In fact, menacing scenarios of major disruptive occurrences in the cyber-domain such as the ones above, triggered by malicious actors, have remained just that – scenarios. Certainly, it cannot be disputed that cyber-attacks and cyber-incidents are a costly (and real) problem for the business community and cause minor and occasionally major inconvenience. In the last couple of years, they have likely cost billions of US dollars in terms of lost intellectual property, maintenance and repair, lost revenue, and increased security costs (Cashell *et al.* 2004). Beyond

4   *Introduction*

their direct impact, cyber-attacks may also reduce public confidence in the security of internet transactions and e-commerce, damaging corporate reputations and reducing the efficiency of the economy (Westrin 2001), even though there is no solid proof for this either.

Fact or fiction?

The point is that all we have seen in the last couple of years suggests that computer network vulnerabilities are an increasingly serious business problem, but that the threat that they represent to *national security* has been overstated: despite the persuasiveness of the threat scenarios, cyber-threats have clearly not materialised as a 'real' national security threat. Moreover, it appears that on the whole, and measured in terms of the amount of total internet traffic, our modern, technology-based societies function exceptionally well, and the technological environment has been surprisingly stable, even though many disruptions with various strengths, be they accidental or intentional results of human agency, occur every day (Westrin 2001: 67–8). Thus, one might be inclined to ask whether we are really headed towards a point where a major, society-threatening chain reaction of IT-related events become highly likely or even unavoidable, as some claim (cf. Perrow 1984; Turner and Pidgeon 1997; Tainter 1988; Prothero 2001) – or whether technology rather helps us to evolve towards an increasingly robust society because complex societies are able to overcome crises more easily precisely as a result of their complexity and inbuilt redundancies (Homer-Dixon 2000: 203; LaPorte 1975).

Regardless of the viewpoint taken, there seems to be no straight answer to the question of how vulnerable our modern societies really are. In fact, experts widely disagree how likely cyber-doom scenarios are and how serious a threat they constitute. The majority of official publications are not only very vague about the actual level of threat but also more generally have to leave cyber-threats shrouded in a cloud of speculation (Dunn 2007a, 2007b). This is not helped by poor definitions and careless use of terminology by many government officials, which has created a tendency to 'hype' the issue with rhetorical dramatisation and alarmist warnings. In an unhealthy symbiosis with the mass media – which repeatedly features sensationalist headlines on the topic – this has led to many writings that are full of words like 'could', 'would', and 'maybe' when describing the threat (Bendrath 2001: 83).

At the same time, the considerable hype has created a growing counter-movement of more cautious voices that try to be more specific in their estimates of the threat (cf. Lewis 2002; Wilson 2003). Many of the more technically educated political advisors and journalists have written about the practical difficulties of a serious cyber-attack or the inability of bureaucracies like militaries or intelligence agencies as well as many terrorist groups to really acquire the skills needed to become successful hackers (Ingles-le Nobel 1999; Center for the Study of Terrorism and Irregular Warfare 1999; Green 2002; Shea 2003). Others even consider the debate to be almost entirely dominated by hidden agendas and 'fear-mongering' and point to the fact that combating cyber-threats has not only become a highly politicised issue but also a lucrative one: an entire industry has emerged to grapple with the threat (Smith 1998, 2000; see also Weimann 2004a, 2004b; Bendrath 2001).

Nevertheless, even most sceptics are unwilling to dismiss the threat completely: the consensus among a large part of this community is that even though the danger may be exaggerated as the result of manipulation, neither can it be denied nor can it be ignored (Denning 2000, 2001a), mainly due to the unpredictability and speed of future technological development as well as the dynamic change of the capabilities of potential adversaries (Technical Analysis Group 2003). Therefore, even though everybody agrees that there have been no truly threatening incidents so far, experts seem unable to conclude whether cyber-doom scenarios are fact or fiction, or, if they agree that the threat has not yet materialised, how long it is likely to remain fiction. This is linked to inherent characteristics of cyber-threats – characteristics that they share with a whole set of 'new' threats to security. In this reading, cyber-threats are emblematic of new threats in general, and an analysis of associated threat politics can, within reason, help to understand the political processes associated with other modern threats as well.

The construction of 'new' threats

During the era of the Cold War, threats were directly linked to military capabilities and arose for the biggest part, from the aggressive intentions of other actors in the international system to achieve domination over other states. Underlying this theory is a particular understanding of power as the sum of military, economic, technological, diplomatic, and other capabilities at the disposal of the state (Organski 1968; Singer *et al.* 1972). This distribution of capabilities, which is unequal and shifting, defines the relative power of states and predicts variations in states' balance of power behaviour. Even though this is a simplistic world view, the seemingly clear and straightforward parameters of the threat implied a sense of certainty through calculability.

Following the disintegration of the Soviet Union, a variety of 'new' and often non-military threats were moved onto the security political agendas of many countries (Buzan *et al.* 1998). Even though the label 'new' is not justified in most cases – social and economic inequalities, terrorism or ethnic conflicts, to name just a few, are certainly not creations of the post-Cold War world even though they might have increased in quantity and scale – many of these threats are distinctly different from Cold War security threats. The main difference is a quality of uncertainty about them – uncertainty as to 'when, who, how, why, and where', which is unprecedented (Huysmans 1998a). The reason for this uncertainty is that chief among the new threats on the agenda are those emanating from non-state actors using non-military means. Any combination of threat involving either non-military – or asymmetric – means and/or non-state actors poses significant difficulties for traditional approaches to intelligence collection:

linking capability to intent works well when malefactors are clearly discernible, and intelligence agencies can focus collection efforts to determine what capabilities they possess or are trying to acquire (PCCIP 1997: 14; Davis 2002).

But despite the fact that cyber-threats have not (yet) actually materialised, the ongoing debate creates considerable pressure for decision-makers. Many governments have decided to consider the threat to national security to be serious and consequently, to draft oreven implement a number of steps to counter it (Wenger et al. 2002; Dunn and Wigert 2004; Abele-Wigert and Dunn 2006). The debate on cyber-threats is therefore not only about predicting the future, but also about how to prepare for possible contingencies in the present. As there have been no major destructive attacks on the cyber-level, decisions have to be made based on scenarios and assumptions. The various actors involved – ranging from various government agencies to the technology community – with their at times highly divergent interests compete with each other 'by means of constructed versions of the future' (Bendrath 2003: 51).

That the concept of national security is shaped by perceptions combining both real and imagined threats is of course nothing new – but, this realisation has become more pronounced with the advent of (new) threats that exhibit the characteristics of risks (Daase et al. 2002; Rasmussen 2001). According to the tenets of risk sociology, risks are indirect, unintended, uncertain, and are by definition situated in the future, since they only materialise as real when they 'happen' (van Loon 2002: 2). In the case of cyber-threats, we can observe how such a risk is firmly established, proliferated globally, and maintains a persistent presence on the national security agenda. Furthermore, not only is the issue on the security agenda, but governments actually incur considerable expenditures for countermeasures based on a great deal of uncertainty. These observations raise fascinating questions for the social scientist and for security studies in particular. Why and how is a threat that has little or no relation to real-world occurrences included on the security political agenda of so many countries? Are there specific characteristics that make it particularly likely to be there? When there is no experience in the real world, on what basis are countermeasures drafted? These questions are not primarily geared towards dismantling the hyperbolical aspects of cyber-threats: that they are hyped is in fact just a side effect of their nature. Rather, the present investigation aims to analyse the political mechanisms of threat construction more generally and more comprehensively.

Cyber-threats in international relations

The topic of cyber-threats is situated at the crossroads between various issues, including computer studies, information technology, and information revolution in general, but also security studies, threat construction, or policy design. At the same time, the discipline of international relations (IR) has been very slow to come to grips with issues of information technology and communications in general, and the challenge of the information revolution specifically, while other disciplines such as media, communication, or cultural studies have long discovered the issue. Also, previous research on the topic has generally been highly specific and policy-oriented (see, for example, Arquilla and Ronfeldt 1996; Alberts and Papp 1997, 2000, 2001), and very few attempts have been made to apply IR theory in analysing this development (Eriksson and Giacomello 2006; Giacomello and Eriksson 2007; partly Latham 2003). Research that has focused particularly on aspects of the construction of information-age security threats is also little influenced by theory or is mostly outdated (Bendrath 2001, 2003; Eriksson 2001b; newer: Bendrath *et al.* 2007).

This book approaches the issue from a security studies angle, understood as a sub-field of international relations, though it heavily borrows from other disciplines at all times. While this approach, and the fact that the analysis of threat politics is only slowly developing as a field of research in its own right, primarily among scholars in the UK and in Sweden (Eriksson and Noreen 2002; Eriksson 2001a, 2001b) makes it difficult to explicitly contribute to an identifiable scholarly body of literature, my approach increases the scientific ability to explain aspects of the world: first, there are a lot of unquestioned assumptions in both expert and official writings about the topic, which will be illuminated and evaluated; second, although the topic is of such urgency to security policy, it has received only little scholarly attention so far; and third, there is a possibility to apply theories designed for some purpose in one literature to solve an existing problem of a different kind (King *et al.* 1994: 17).

I take a semi-constructivist stance in this book. Full-fledged constructivists contend that since the very language we use to describe the world is socially constructed, there is no 'objective' basis for identifying material reality at all. Subject and object are mutually constitutive, and no description can exist independently of the social circumstances under which that description is made (Berger and Luckmann 1967; Searle 1995; Haas 1992: 3). When conceived in this way, IR is the mere reflection of discourse and habits, where the word is power, and the only power is the word (Der Derian and Shapiro 1989; Campbell 1992; Walker 1993). More moderate views with a lingering touch of positivism – in which tradition the current undertaking is situated – hold that objects of inquiries can exist independently of the analyst and that although the categories in which they are identified are socially constructed, consensus about the nature of the world is possible in the long run (for example Wendt 1992, 1999; Ruggie 1998; Adler and Barnett 1998; Katzenstein 1996).

Even so, I try to incorporate the notion that the manner in which people and institutions interpret and represent phenomena and structures makes a difference for the outcomes. Intentions and purposes are understood to be embodied within the objectified or institutionalised structures of thought and practice (Adler and Haas 1992: 370; Cox 1992: 135). In other words, the way stakeholders perceive their environment, including the technological substructure and the consequences that arise from it, influences their actions and reactions. As an observer of the cyber-threats story, I am forced to examine a historical process from a high perch. From this meta-theoretical viewpoint, the question of

8 *Introduction*

whether security in the information age is any different from the security in other ages cannot really be answered. However, the peculiarities of information age security are an underlying theme of some significance in the debate, so that I will venture to leave the high observation point behind at times to speculate about what distinguishes this epoch from other times.

Analytical framework

In order to analyse the mechanisms behind (information-age) threat politics, I develop my own analytical framework in the pages that follow. The elusive and unsubstantiated nature of cyber-threats (and other modern threats for that matter) means that only an approach rooted in the constructivist mindset with a subjective ontology is suitable for the analysis of this issue. While traditional security policy research views threat images as given and measurable and assumes that security policies are responses to an objective increase of threats and risks (Walt 1991), post-positivist approaches focus on how, when, and with what consequences political actors 'frame' something – anything – as a security issue, with a strong emphasis on 'speech acts', i.e. political language, and the implications this has for political agenda-setting and political relations (Wæver 1995; Buzan *et al.* 1998; Williams 2003; Reus-Smit 1996).

The basis for the framework used in this book is the 'Copenhagen School's' securitisation approach that focuses on the process of bringing an issue from a politicised or even non-politicised stage into the security domain and takes into consideration various factors surrounding the formation of security policy agendas (Wæver 1995; Buzan *et al.* 1998). The process of securitisation is seen as a socially constructed, contextual *speech act* (Austin 1962; Searle 1969), meaning that if claims for a special right to use whatever means are necessary to remedy a particular issue are accepted in the political arena, an issue is successfully securitised. This in turn signifies that issues are turned into security matters not necessarily because a real existential threat exists, but because an issue is successfully presented and established by key actors in the political arena as constituting such a threat (Buzan *et al.* 1998).

In order to study the broader political process of threat politics, I closely follow the suggestions of a Swedish group of scholars (Eriksson 2001a, 2001b; Eriksson and Noreen 2002) but at the same time expand their framework. The fundamentals of the securitisation approach are expanded by adding insights from framing theory and from agenda-setting theory. Threat framing refers to the process whereby particular agents develop specific interpretive schemas about what should be regarded as a threat or risk, how to respond to this threat, and who is responsible for it. In specific, I analyse why and how cyber-threat frames change over time. Keeping in mind the virtuality of the threat, I particularly look at how, under what conditions, by whom, for what reasons, and with what impact cyber-threats are constructed as a threat to national security and moved onto the security political agenda. Thus, by including the nature of security measures drafted in response to an identified threat into the framework, the efforts are expanded beyond the mere phase of securitisation. In addition, we can gain insights into the nature of countermeasures in place to counter cyber-threats.

Content and structure

In order to be able to recount the story of cyber-threats, some contextualisation is necessary. Therefore, I look at aspects of the information revolution in Chapter 1, always taking into account that we are dealing with a concept that is in constant flux. I then discuss theoretical approaches that deal with security issues in connection with threat politics in the information age and develop the explanatory model and framework for analysis in Chapter 2. This framework is then used to analyse the construction of cyber-threat frames in the United States in Chapters 3 to 5. The reason for the focus on the United States is mainly twofold: for one thing, the United States has been the dominant actor in identifying 'new' threats in general. Furthermore, the United States is the dominant actor in IT issues and 'has been a "sender" of ideas to other states about how to comprehend IT problems and their solutions' (Holmgren and Softa 2003: 15). The United States is also the country with the most activity in this domain, which allows me to study the threat politics process and countermeasures in a very detailed manner.

In the analysis of the development of the cyber-threat discourse, the beginnings of the cyber-threats debate are located with the Reagan administration, among whose major concerns was the prevention of what it viewed as damaging disclosures of classified information as well as the acquisition of 'sensitive but unclassified' information. Subsequent policy efforts can be found in two domains: the first one is linked to the protection of federal agencies' computer data from espionage. This debate was interlinked with the debate on encryption technology and led to the Computer Security Act of 1987. The second area is linked to the growing problem of computer crime, which led to the Computer Abuse Act of 1984/86. In the 1980s and also at the beginning of the 1990s under the presidency of George H. W. Bush, the main issues were the 'foreign intelligence threat' and espionage using computer networks and cyber-crime.

In contrast to the 1980s, the military was a driving force behind the shaping of the threat perception after 1991: on the one hand, the US military began to develop the still loosely articulated concept known as information warfare and moved forward with the integration of advanced intelligence, surveillance, and reconnaissance systems with stealthy, long-range, precision weapons systems (Rattray 2001; Mahnken 1995; Molander *et al.* 1996; Campen *et al.* 1996). On the other hand, the advantages of using and disseminating ICT were seen to imply a disproportional vulnerability. Borders, already porous in many ways in the real world, seemed non-existent in cyberspace. For the United States, this meant that the country and its security forces had to oppose a 'new' threat that had had low priority before, and which, so it seemed, made old security political strategies and architectures obsolete.

Therefore, while cyber-threats or infrastructure protection had played a minor role in the overall security strategies of the administrations of both Ronald Reagan and Bush, they were anchored firmly onto the broader security political agenda as a 'new' threat and gained a prominent role in the national security strategy during the administration of Bill Clinton. The Oklahoma City bombing was an important juncture, after which five very powerful ideas were linked together to form a potent threat frame: asymmetric vulnerability, cyber-threats, terrorism, infrastructures, and ultimately, during the Bush administration, homeland security. By interlinking these security issues that were floating around in the mid-1990s, a very powerful security concept under the collective term 'critical infrastructure protection' was created, a policy issue that subsequently spread around the world and found its way into the security-policy agendas of numerous countries (Dunn and Wigert 2004). Following the Oklahoma City bombing, Clinton set up the President's Commission on Critical Infrastructure Protection (PCCIP), led by retired Air Force General Robert Marsh, to safeguard vital systems such as gas, oil, transportation, water, telecommunications, etc. In 1997, the PCCIP concluded that the security, the economy, the way of life, and perhaps even the survival of the industrialised world were dependent on the triad of electric power, communications, and computers. Furthermore, it stressed that advanced societies rely heavily upon critical infrastructures, which are susceptible to physical disruptions of the classical type as well as new virtual threats (PCCIP 1997).

The issue of CIP remained a high priority on the political agenda; the events of 11 September 2001 merely served to further increase the awareness of vulnerabilities and the sense of urgency in protecting critical infrastructures (Bush 2001a, 2001b). The attacks of 11 September 2001 did not bring many changes for the overall strategy. However, while the Clinton administration had viewed cyber-threats as one of the key dangers of the twenty-first century, the focus under the Bush administration shifted from cyber-tools and methods back towards the more physical aspects of terrorism. During the second Bush administration, the CIP package was integrated with the broader concept of homeland security, making critical infrastructures, defined as assets whose destruction or disruption would have a crippling impact on the heart of US society, the prime object of security. However, while the threat frame as promoted by the PCCIP remained the same, the attention given to the cyber-threat aspect diminished in this period.

Even if it is too early to proclaim a new age of security, the security practices that I analyse point to a change in the nature and especially the logic of security with considerable consequences. Traditionally, national security has been recognised as the responsibility of the government, relying on the collective efforts of the military, the foreign-policy establishment, and the intelligence community. Critical infrastructure protection, however, is imagined as a shared responsibility that cannot be accomplished by the government alone. The maintenance of 'business continuity' for an individual, corporate, or local actor is often regarded as equally important as national or even international security efforts in the realm of cyber-threats. This seems to be a new trend rather than an exception. By looking at the foundations and formation of these practices, this book contributes to the constructivist research agenda by exploring a new security issue in terms of threat perception of key actors and the dynamic interaction between actor constellation, systemic conditions, and institutional settings, and to the more general debate about changing practices of national security and their implications for the international community.

1 The information age and cyber-threats

Shifting meanings and interpretations

To be able to tell the cyber-threats story means to understand the context in which this story takes place. In other words, in order to comprehend cyber-threats, we need to understand many aspects of the phenomenon called 'information revolution'. Some observers regard the information revolution as one major driver of change in the fundamental conditions of international relations in the last decade (Zacher 1992: 58–9; Castells 1996). Although the excitement about the information age was bigger in the 1990s than nowadays – mainly because to some degree, the novelty has worn off as the technology has become more ingrained into our way of living – the seeming dominance and prevalence of information in many aspects of modern life has caused this age to be labelled the 'information age' (Kushnick 1999).

Indeed, who has not often felt that technology is fundamentally changing our way of life? Who can escape the 'suggestive power of virtual technologies' (Virilio 1995)? We are reminded almost constantly that we live in the information age – we communicate through the Internet, we use mobile phones, we get instant world wide news, we download music and movies, we buy merchandise online, and we reserve plane tickets and book hotel rooms on the web. Entire segments of public life, including such diverse sectors as culture, business, entertainment, and research, seem to have been revolutionised by the new technology. It is, in fact, very easy to become excited about the transformative power of new information and communication technologies.

It is common knowledge, however, that the significance of information is not a unique characteristic of our time, but that it has always been vital to humankind. It is also commonly understood that throughout history, advances in scientific–technical fields have repeatedly played a major role in changing human affairs and that there have been other information and communication revolutions, all of which significantly shaped history, human activities, and their institutions (Papp *et al.* 1997; Deibert 1997; Waldrop 1998; Borgmann 1999; Hobart and Schiffman 2000; Freeman and Louca 2002). Far too often, however, technology is seen as an abstract, exogenous variable rather than something that is inherently endogenous to politics (Herrera 2003, 2007). Indeed, technological determinism is and has been an alluring temptation, as a look at the past shows: the conviction that the world is about to enter into a new phase of history is a near-permanent feature of modern life, mirroring a belief in an unbroken line of constant progress closely linked to technological development. Europeans began the twentieth century optimistically, thinking that the railroad and telegraph had made advanced nations too interdependent to be able to afford armed conflict. By the middle of the century, it seemed clear that radio, cinema, and mass media were transforming society as profoundly as steam power and factories had transformed industry in the 1700s (Deutsch 1957). Today, it seems beyond dispute that humankind has progressed from the agricultural age through the industrial age to the information age (Toffler 1981; Naisbitt 1982; Rosecrance 1999).

Besides this feeling of novelty and uniqueness, issues connected to the increasing complexity and rapid rate of change in modern society are often cited to underscore that the information revolution is fundamentally changing modern life. However, complexity and change are not at all new to our times but were already widely discussed in the 1960s and 1970s (LaPorte 1975; Galbraith 1968; Toffler 1970; Ellul 1964). Then as now, developments in the technical sphere seemed constantly to outpace the capacity of individuals and social systems to adapt. And as the rate of technological innovation quickens, it becomes increasingly difficult to predict the range of effects that these innovations will have. Thus, the notion of technology that is 'out of control' and fears of vulnerabilities due to dependency on technology are recurring themes in political and philosophical thought (Winner 1977, 2004; Feenberg 1991; Kelly 1995; Garreau 2005). Indeed, human mastery of technology seems increasingly incapacitated by velocity and speed as the increasing dependence on information and communication technologies (ICT) systems results in a decreasing capacity to understand, represent, and control risk (van Loon 2000: 173). Of course, the issue of cyber-threats is also linked to technophobia more generally, which is not a new development either.

What this shows us is that in our analysis, we must be careful not to fall into the trap of over-interpretation and technological determinism (Smith and Marx 1994) when exploring the characteristics of technology and the implications of the current information revolution (e.g. Toffler 1980, 1981; Drucker 1989; Negroponte 1995). Rather, we must strive to see the issue in the appropriate historical and cultural context, so that prevalent feelings and assumptions may turn into informed understanding of causes and effects of the latest technological and policy developments. In order to achieve this, drivers and underlying assumptions related to the 'information revolution' must be scrutinised, while it is important at the same time to keep in mind that we are looking at concepts that are constantly changing and evolving. The developments are recent and ongoing, and difficulties in grasping their true proportions are inevitable, because we are in the midst of the process ourselves. Furthermore, the implications are far from straightforward: many observers have pointed out that complexity and change are the two defining characteristics of the information age, since the present epoch is marked by persistent opposites and derives its order

14 *The information age and cyber-threats*

from episodic patterns with very contradictory outcomes (Rosenau 1990; CSIS 1996).

The information age: underlying concepts and meanings

The undertaking is complicated by the fact that the 'information revolution' is a very fuzzy concept: the expressions 'information revolution' and 'information age', along with the concepts of 'information society', 'information warfare', 'cyber-terrorism', 'cyberspace', 'e-business', and so on, only entered our vocabulary a few decades ago (Machlup 1962; Solomon 1997; Kushnick 1999; Fisher 2001), but they are now commonplace in the press, political speeches, popular books, and scholarly journals. There are three essential elements in the semantics of the information age: 'information', 'cyber', and 'digital', all three of which are so important that they have become shorthand expressions for the age we live in. The information-age vocabulary is created by simply placing these prefixes before familiar words, thus creating a whole arsenal of new expressions, of which the term 'cyber-threats' is of course also an example. The nature of these terms is such that their meaning has never been precise – nowadays, however, they have been used so extensively that they can basically mean everything and nothing.

But even though the terms have become mere catchphrases, they are so ingrained in everyday language that there is no alternative to their use. This situation confronts scholars dealing with these issues with the need for critical assessment of both the concepts and the phenomena they describe. But why is this important, one might ask? This book is about the structuralist idea that language creates the reality we perceive (Beedham 2005): to look at concepts and their use is therefore more than just an intellectual exercise. Though it may appear far-fetched to some, the imprecision of the vocabulary, which is simultaneously expressive and constitutive of the cyber-threats debate, has a significant impact on the political process. Below, I look at the terms 'information', 'revolution', and 'cyber-'. Further, I address 'complexity' as an issue of key importance in the information age.

Information

If we take the key concept of 'information', for example, we can show that this part of information-age terminology is imprecise, ambiguous, and elusive, often used to express something greatly intangible, which leaves a lot of room for interpretation and makes speakers' use and understanding of these terms greatly dependent on their viewpoint and on their audience. The term 'information' has a variety of different meanings for different academic disciplines. For the communication engineer, information is often nothing more than an organised set of data, a quantity measured in bits and defined in terms of the probabilities of occurrence of symbols (Shannon and Weaver 1949); but for social scientists, it has at least minimal semantic content or meaning (Webster 1995, 1997). In the context of the social sciences, information derives from phenomena. 'Phenomena', 'observable facts', 'events', or 'stimuli' are words that describe everything that happens around us in any medium or form. To become information, they must be observed and analysed by a cognizant receiver.

Information thus is the product of two factors: perceived phenomena or data and the instructions or mechanisms required to interpret that data and give it meaning (United States Air Force 1995). However, information by itself usually has no value: it is a raw material that gains value if further processed in specific ways and if meaning and a certain quality are attached to it. The potential of information for transformation into *knowledge*, which is explained and understood information, or even *wisdom*, the effective application of this knowledge, makes it such an immensely precious resource (Waltz 1998). Therefore, information can be understood as an abstraction of phenomena, a result of our perceptions and interpretations, regardless of the means by which it is gathered. Information is defined to a large extent by the minds and by the cultural context of the people who behold it (Borgmann 1999). This makes information a very abstract, elusive, and context-dependent concept, creating both theoretical and practical problems for the issue of information-age security.

For one thing, information is intangible, meaning that it exists independently of any physical object that carries it. Therefore, information cannot be 'imprisoned' and is easily copied, modified, destroyed, or stolen, usually without leaving any traces (Näf 2001). If information is recorded electronically and is available on networked computers, it is more vulnerable than if the same information is printed on paper and locked in a file cabinet (Dekker 1997). One key to this development is digitalisation: a digital system is one that uses discrete values that represent on/off states, like the binary code used in modern electronics and computing, rather than a continuous spectrum of values. Digitalisation means the transition from the storage of information on fixed material objects dedicated to specific purposes, such as books, phonograph, or film, to the storage of all information in a binary digital format, which can be readily stored on a variety of media. Digital technology is the key to the development of advanced information infrastructures and services, because it facilitates easy movement of the digital information between media and therefore also makes it easier to access or distribute it remotely.

Revolution

The use of the term 'revolution' is also indicative of the debate. A revolution is usually understood as a sudden, radical, or complete change. It is a common perception that indeed the changes and developments all around us are rapid enough to be called sudden, radical, or fundamental. A closer look reveals that these transformations are less sudden, violent, and fast, however, being more of a gradual process with neither clear beginning nor foreseeable end, which makes the application of the term 'revolution' in its restricted sense somewhat questionable. The word 'evolution' would seem much more appropriate for the gradual adjustment and the non-linear nature of the development. Nevertheless, in the context of scientific–technical transformation, the term 'revolution' has been used less strictly (Henry and Peartree 1998a: 1–9): it is also defined to include concepts that can be applied to our case, for example, a 'fundamental change in the way of thinking about or visualizing something: a change of theorems' or, even more aptly, as a 'changeover in use or preference especially in technology' (Merriam-Webster Dictionary). Even so, the term 'revolution' is mostly used in the first sense, giving expression to the common cyber-enthusiasm to which it is so easy to succumb, and a manifestation of the tendency to call everything that is related to the 'information revolution' 'new' and to see it as radically different from what came before.

The cyber-prefix

This brings us to another important issue, linked to the term that I have also freely used to construct a particular terminology: the prefix 'cyber-', which is derived from the word 'cybernetics' and has acquired the general meaning of 'through the use of a computer'. Cybernetics is a theory of the communication and the control of regulatory feedback that studies communication and control in living beings and in the machines built by humans (established by Wiener 1948; Ashby 1956) and is the precursor of complexity thinking in the investigation of dynamic systems, using feedback and control concepts. The morpheme 'cyber-', even though it nowadays seems to have lost the direct link to its origins, is still inextricably linked to systemic thinking. The notion of 'systems' is absolutely central in the context of cyber-threats and has several practical and theoretical ramifications for how the issue is approached.

The rise of cybernetics in the 1940s was the culminating fusion of several conceptual themes and threads of work, some of which reached back for centuries. However, a short excursion into the history of ideas shows us that the rediscovery of 'systems' as an analytical concept is a rather recent development (Smith *et al.* 1996). One explanation for the reappearance of the system paradigm is that the mechanistic scheme of isolable causal chains proved insufficient to deal with theoretical problems in science and practical problems posed by modern technology. The onset of the technological society and the complexity of modern technology forced scientists to deal with complexities in all fields of knowledge, including social sciences (Bertalanffy 1968; Axelrod 1997; LaPorte 1975). The feasibility of the systems approach resulted from various new theoretical, epistemological, and mathematical developments and was furthered by increasing automation, computers, and self-controlling machines (Wiener 1948; Beer 2004).

Since then, systems have been analysed by almost every academic discipline because they seem to materialise everywhere, once we start looking. The notion of system is thus at the same time one of the most pervasive and one of the least well-defined concepts in modern intellectual thought (Casti 1979: 1). In general, 'system' is an abstract concept, the meaning of which is largely context-dependent. It is a model of general nature, a conceptual analogue of certain universal traits of observed entities that usually involves a high degree of generality or abstraction (Bertalanffy 1975: 159). Very simply put, a system is a set of mutually dependent components or variables. More precisely, each component in the system is interrelated with every other component in the set and also interacts with the system environment within the system's boundaries to function as a whole in order to perform a task. The different connotations of a system are created by designating different values or categories for the variables (Bowker 1993). In the engineering disciplines, for example, the term is often applied to an assembly of mechanical or electronic components that function together as a unit. In computing, it describes a set of computer components, an assembly of computer hardware, software, and peripherals, functioning together (Armstrong and Sage 1999). Probably, the most important issue in this connection is that systems are closely associated with notions of complexity.

Complexity

It is an uncontested assumption that complex problems are on the rise in and due to the information age. One possible explanation for complexity in the technical world can be found in the combination of two laws of technical innovation, namely Moore's Law and Metcalfe's Law, which are widely credited as having provided the stimulus that has driven the stunning growth of Internet connectivity (Moore 1965; Metcalfe 1995; Downes *et al.* 1998):

- *Moore's Law* states that the number of transistors per square inch on integrated circuits will double approximately every 18 months, which means that computing power rises exponentially over time.
- *Metcalfe's Law* states that the value of a communication system grows as the square of the number of users of the system, which implies an increasing number of networks, nodes, and links.

At least since the development of Shannon and Weaver's (1949) information theory, formal, semi-formal, or informal notions of 'complexity' have been used to express properties of objects and processes in a variety of fields (Biggiero 2001). Despite or maybe because of the diversity of scientific efforts involved in this work, little agreement has been reached on what, precisely, complexity entails, or how a general notion of complexity may be systematically applied to various fields of research (Çambel 1992; Butts 2001: xi).

According to one simple but straightforward definition, complexity is the sum of interdependencies plus change (cf. Gomez 2001: 151). This means that complexity in information infrastructure systems is increasing, as an exponential technological development leads to change and brings forth an increasing number of networks, nodes, and links to growing interdependencies. In addition, the complexity of these systems grows with the extension of the geographical reach and the expansion of the services provided, the introduction of new components with richer functionality using diverse technologies, and the layering of systems over systems (Kyriakopoulos and Wilikens 2000; Masera and Wilikens 2001).

Mainly as a consequence of their interactions with the information infrastructure, the critical infrastructures are being composed into networks-of-networks of varying sizes. Three main, interrelated trends affect these infrastructures: 1) their increasing complexity, with an acceleration that reflects the general evolution of technology; 2) their interconnectedness, put into practice at different layers: organizational, procedural, informational, and material; and 3) a growing reliance on ICT, both for internal use and for interaction with external systems (Masera and Wilikens 2001). Therefore, infrastructures are complex and interdependent systems, and their interaction with the surrounding, pre-existing technical and social environments is not fully controllable.

System complexity has two immediate consequences for our topic. First, a well-known theory claims that technological systems that are interactively complex and tightly coupled will be struck by accidents that cannot be prevented. Because of the inherent complexity, independent failures will interact in ways that can neither be foreseen by designers nor comprehended by operators. If the system is also tightly coupled, the failures will rapidly escalate beyond control before anyone understands what is happening and is able to intervene (Perrow 1984; Turner and Pidgeon 1997). This overall pessimistic perspective on accidents and the limited possibilities of preventing them and coping with them resonates in much of the cyber-threats debate. Second, the dynamic interactions of complex, decentralized, open, unbounded (technical) systems means that our abilities to articulate and evaluate the problem will be overtaxed, thus creating a practical challenge for those involved in drafting security measures. As Forrester (1961) showed in the early 1960s, complex systems behave counter-intuitively due to parallel occurrences happening at different speeds, irregularities, and non-linear cause/effect relationships, meaning that the human brain is unable to 'read' these systems correctly.

Moreover, the uncertainty resulting from complexity and the overtaxing of our abilities is seen as a decisive factor. Ambiguity about the nature of threats leads to 'national-security uncertainty' and incoherence in the shaping of policy issues (Goldman 2001). Specifically, if the cues provided by the international environment are uncertain, ambiguous, and too complex, they render traditional planning assumptions and standard procedures obsolete. In the face of uncertainty and complexity, decision-makers increasingly rely on the know-how of specific expert groups.

However, as previously mentioned, I contend in this book that individuals do not respond directly to objective reality, if such a thing exists, but through socially constructed frameworks of thought. In theoretical terms, this means that perceptions of complexity on the part of decision-makers will influence the threat perception of key actors. But I also argue that there are some hard facts grounded in real-life experiences when it comes to the information infrastructure and what we can do with it. In fact, all actions in cyberspace are predetermined by the way systems function have been programmed to behave. If you hack into a computer, you can only do this because the system has been programmed (albeit unintentionally) to allow you to access it, to enter a password, or to exploit a buffer overflow.

Cyber-threats: the networked global information infrastructure as weapon or as target

As outlined above, information is an abstraction of phenomena and is therefore distinct from technology. In contrast, however, what one can do with information, and especially how fast one can do it, is greatly dependent on technology. This means that technologies are lending this current revolution its defining characteristics and singularities. And because cyber-threats are the result of malicious use of the (global) information infrastructure, the (current and future) characteristics of the technological environment have a considerable impact on the perception of the threat. The features of the tools of the information revolution, often subsumed under the heading of ICT, are an important part of the cyber-threats story. In addition to the future aspects, there is also a historical dimension to be considered: the technological substructure has constantly been changing, and its characteristics have influenced the perception of the threat, as we will show below.

What is it, then, that distinctly characterises the phenomenon? This question is best answered by pointing out the increased speed, greater capacity, and enhanced flexibility with which data can be gathered, processed, and transmitted today. This significantly enhances humankind's ability to communicate, utilize information, and overcome earlier obstacles to communication in terms of distance, time, and location. Eight of the most important technologies of the current scientific–technical revolution are as follows: advanced computing, networking, and semiconductors; cellular/wireless technology; digital transmission/compression; fibre optics; improved human–computer interaction; and satellite technology (Alberts *et al.* 1997; Hundley *et al.* 2000).

The marriage, especially of computers and telecommunications, the integration of these technologies into a multimedia system of communication that has global reach, and their availability world wide and at low cost has brought about a fundamental transformation in the way humans communicate and thus interact. A secondary impact of the revolution is the heightened interest in, and exploding demand of, these technologies, resulting from, but also leading to, factors such as falling costs, increased availability, greater utility, and ease of use of these tools. This has led to an immense proliferation of ICT, occurring unevenly but steadily throughout organizations, societies, and between international actors. A return to the ways of before is all but impossible: societies in developed countries already rely heavily on these technologies, not only for storage of information but also for processing, with the aim of letting these technologies perform more and more demanding tasks.

The nature of incidents

Even though the historical dimension has to be taken into account and even though the tools have changed, the nature of incidents has remained more or less constant. Events that could potentially damage the information infrastructure can be categorised as 'failures', 'accidents', and 'attacks', even though these categories of events are not necessarily mutually exclusive or even easily distinguishable (Ellison et al. 1997; Avizienis et al. 2000; OCIPEP 2003). Failures are caused by deficiencies in the system or in an external element on which the system depends; they may be due to software design errors, hardware degradation, human error, or corrupted data. Accidents, on the other hand, include the entire range of randomly occurring and potentially damaging events, such as natural disasters. Usually, accidents are externally generated events (i.e. from outside the system), whereas failures are internally generated events. Finally, attacks are orchestrated by an adversary. This category, even though not necessarily the most prominent one, is of prime importance in the cyber-threats debate.

In practice, it is often difficult to determine whether a particular detrimental event is the result of a malicious attack, a failure of a component, or an accident (Ellison et al. 1997: 3), which means that from the practitioner's point of view, the distinction between a failure, an accident, or an attack is often considered less important than the impact of the event, at least in a short-term perspective. Technically speaking, information is a string of bits and bytes travelling from a sender to a receiver. If this string arrives in the intended order, the transfer has been successful. If the information is altered, intercepted, or deviated, however, problems are likely to arise. In practice, this means that the first and most important question is not what exactly caused the loss of information integrity, but rather what the possible result and complications of an incident may be. A power grid might fail because of a simple operating error without any kind of external influences or because of a sophisticated hacker attack. In both cases, the possible result is the same: a blackout and the accompanying domino effect of successive failures in systems that are linked through interdependencies. Analysing whether a failure was caused by a terrorist, a criminal, a simple human error, or a spontaneous collapse will not help stop or reduce the domino effect.

In the context of national security and threat politics, however, the possibility of a human attack is of special interest. Even though the immediate response has to be tailored to the actual event on the technical level, mid- or long-term strategies work on a different level, and the identity of the attacker is crucial for calibrating the right response: if the attack was perpetrated by a state actor, military responses can be activated; when the threat originates from sub-state actors, the primary response should consist of law-enforcement measures. We will see that the question of who or what is threatening is an important aspect of the cyber-threat story, in particular because it often remains unclear who is behind an attack, due to the nature of the global information infrastructure.

The actors and tools

From the beginnings of the information age, it has been understood that there are more and more state actors as well as non-state actors who are willing to contravene national legal frameworks and hide in the relative anonymity of cyberspace (PCCIP 1997; National Academy of Sciences 1991). If these actors carry out their attack using 'cyber-' weapons and strategies, one label often bestowed upon them is that of 'hacker', another catchphrase in the information-age vocabulary that has a variety of meanings and a long record of misuse. It is used in two main ways, one positive and one pejorative: in the computing community, it describes a member of a distinct social group, a particularly skilled programmer or technical expert who knows a set of programming interfaces well enough to write novel and useful software. In popular usage and in the media, however, it generally describes computer intruders or criminals. In fact, different types of hackers must be distinguished (Levy 1984; Erickson 2003; OCIPEP 2003), mainly in terms of their motivation and skill level.

The first example consists of the so-called script kiddies. Script kiddies are considered to be on the lowest level of the hacker hierarchy. They download readily available code from the Internet rather than writing their own. The driving force of script kiddies has been shown to be boredom, curiosity, or teenage bravado. We will see in the case studies that many incidents that have been attributed to state actors were really perpetrated by script kiddies. Hacktivists belong to a similar category. Hacktivism is generally considered to involve the use of computer attacks for political, social, or religious purposes. Hacktivists are motivated by a wide range of social and political causes and use hacking techniques against a target's Internet site with the intent of disrupting normal operations but not causing serious damage (Denning 2001b). Examples of such activities include web 'sit-ins' and virtual blockades, automated e-mail bombs, web hacks and defacements of websites, computer break-ins, and computer viruses and worms. This activity gained a lot of attention during the Kosovo conflict (Dunn 2002), an aspect of the debate that we will look at in more detail below. Finally, there are various sorts of 'true' hackers. Hackers themselves like to distinguish between 'crackers' or 'Black Hat Hackers', someone who (usually illegally) attempts to break into or otherwise subvert the security of a program, system or network, often with malicious intent; and 'sneakers', or 'White Hat Hackers', who attempt to break into systems or networks in order to help the owners of the system by making them aware of its security flaws. Some use the term 'grey hat' or, less frequently, 'brown hat' to describe hackers whose activities alternate between 'black' and 'white' areas (McClure *et al. 1999).*

There are various tools and modes of attack, used with different intents, such as *Trojan horses*, destructive programs that masquerade as benign applications but set up a back door so that the hacker can later return and enter the system; *viruses and worms*, computer programs that replicate functional copies of themselves with varying effects ranging from mere annoyance and inconvenience to compromise of the confidentiality or integrity of information; *logic bomb*, programs designed to execute (or 'explode') under specific circumstances, to delete or corrupt data, or to cause other undesirable effects; and *buffer overflow attacks*, which involve sending overly long input streams to the attacked server, causing parts of the server's memory to overflow in order to either crash the system or execute the attacker's arbitrary code as if it was part of the server's code. The result is full server compromise or 'denial of service'.

Often, *system intrusion* is the main goal of attacks; this is one of the prime dangers if executed successfully. If the intruder gains full system control, or 'root' access, he/she has unrestricted access to the inner workings of the system, so that the intruder can tamper with any files; authorise new users; change the system to conceal the intruder's presence; install a 'back door' to allow regular future access without going through log-in procedures; add a 'sniffer', an application that can capture passwords and other data while it is in transit either within the computer or over the network to capture the user IDs and passwords of everyone who accesses the system (Anonymous 2003; Hack FAQ 2004). Due to the characteristics of digitally stored information, an intruder can delay, disrupt, corrupt, exploit, destroy, steal, and modify information (Waltz 1998). Depending on the value of the information or the importance of whatever application for which this information is required, such actions will have different impacts with varying degrees of gravity for various stakeholders.

It would, however, be misguiding to restrict cyber-threats to virtual means of attack or incidents: the means of attack against the information infrastructure can be both physical (hammer, backhoe, and bomb) and cyber-based (hacking tools) (Krutskikh 1999; Sibilia 1997; Devost *et al.* 1997: 78). The same is true for the target: it is not that easy to understand what exactly the information infrastructure is. This is due to the fact that it has not only a *physical* component that is fairly easily grasped – such as high-speed, interactive, narrowband and broadband networks; satellite, terrestrial and wireless communications systems; and the computers, televisions, telephones, radios, and other products that people employ to access the infrastructure – but also an equally important *immaterial*, sometimes very elusive (cyber-) component, namely the information and the content that flows through the infrastructure, the knowledge that is created from this, and the services that are provided (Dunn 2005: 263).

The so-called 'infrastructure threat matrix' (see Table 1.1) distinguishes four types of attacks, all four of which involve the malicious use of the information infrastructure either as a target or as a tool. However, it is becoming increasingly difficult to distinguish between purely physical and virtual components of the information infrastructure, as we will also see in the case studies.

In the cyber-threats debate, hacking is considered a modus operandi that can be used not only by technologically skilled individuals but also by malicious actors with truly bad intent, such as terrorists or foreign states or simply by actors *both* technologically skilled *and* malicious. Hackers that fall in one of the last two categories, in particular, have the knowledge, skills, and tools to attack the information infrastructure. Even though they generally lack the motivation to

Table 1.1 Infrastructure threat matrix

Mean/tool	Target	
	Physical	*Cyber*
Physical	Severing a telecommunications cable with a backhoe Smashing a server with a hammer Bombing the electric grid	Use of electromagnetic pulse and radio-frequency weapons to destabilise electronic components
Cyber	Hacking into a SCADA system that controls municipal sewage 'Spoofing' an air traffic control system to bring down a plane	Hacking into a critical government network Trojan horse in public switched network

Source: Devost *et al.* 1997: 78; see also OCIPEP 2003.

cause violence or severe economic or social harm (Denning 2001a), it is feared that individuals who have the capability to cause serious damage, but little motivation, could be swayed to employ their knowledge by sufficiently large sums of money provided by a group of malicious actors.

All of these aspects play a role in the cyber-threat story. In the next chapter, I will show how the issue can be approached theoretically. We will focus on approaches that show a special interest in how threats are politicised: instead of conceiving threats as something given and objectively measurable, they focus on the process by which a shared understanding of what is to be considered and collectively responded to as a threat to security is inter-subjectively constructed among key actors (cf. Connolly 1983; Fuchs and Kratochwil 2002).

2 Politics and threat construction
Theoretical underpinnings

In order to explore the political process that moved cyber-threats onto the political agenda, I will assemble a theoretical framework in this chapter. This will provide the reader with the necessary vocabulary and background to understand some of the thoughts developed in later chapters. The approach most closely associated with issues of threat construction in political science is the so-called Copenhagen school's securitisation theory (Wæver 1995; Buzan *et al.* 1998). It serves as a starting point for the framework of analysis that is developed in this chapter. However, despite its key role in this study and in security studies more generally, securitisation theory has a number of shortcomings. These are discussed in the following, and amendments from additional strands of theory that add analytical depth to certain problem areas of the Copenhagen school will be introduced. In pulling these various theoretical strands together, I create a dynamical framework based on securitisation theory that mainly focuses on threat frames presented by key actors at various stages in time.

The framework goes beyond securitisation and focuses on the more comprehensive topic of threat politics. Absent any established definition, we understand threat politics to be the political process by which threats are moved onto and removed from the political agenda or which alters the face of threats on the political agenda. In particular, I want to develop a better understanding of the mechanisms that come into play when 'new' threats are put onto the security-policy agenda or when they are removed or altered; and, more specifically, the relationship between these mechanisms and the actual measures that are composed to counter the threat. Furthermore, a two-phase approach is needed in order to truly capture the mechanisms of threat politics. The first phase is about the initial framing and securitisation move, until the issue has made its way 'successfully' onto the agenda and elicits its first policy response; the second phase starts when the issue of cyber-threats is on the agenda and subsequently begins to undergo change. Apart from being only partially satisfactory, the few approaches that address threat politics more or less directly (see Eriksson and Noreen 2002; Buzan *et al.* 1998; Eriksson 2001a, 2001b; Bendrath *et al.* 2007) focus almost exclusively on the *agenda setting* or securitisation stage and therefore offer very few explanations for the second phase.

Securitisation theory and beyond

The securitisation approach takes into consideration various factors surrounding the formation of security policy agendas and is often associated with a constructivist meta-theory, even though it is the product of two different meta-theoretical positions: the (neorealist) positivism of Buzan and the (post-structuralist) post-positivism of Wæver (Buzan *et al.* 1998: 35; Wæver 2003). According to the Copenhagen school of security, problems become a security issue not necessarily because a real existential threat exists, but because the issue is successfully *presented* and *established* by key agents such as a threat (Buzan *et al.* 1998), which, as a side-note, basically absolves the researcher from the task of judging whether a threat is real or not. The process of bringing an issue from a politicised or even non-politicised stage into the security domain is called *securitisation* (Wæver 1995).

The notion of securitisation is based on speech act theory as developed by Austin (1962) and Searle (1969), which says that the use of language not only can but even normally does have the character of performative acts, in the sense that expression is a social act involving a sender and a receiver who operate under arbitrary conventions or 'constitutive rules' that affect their behaviour. In speech act theory, the question is how language can function as a social force in different kinds of situations. Security speech acts are significant utterances in a security framework by actors that are in a position to 'define' security and shape responses to envisaged threats. In accordance with this theory, the study of securitisation aims to gain an understanding of who securitises (the actor) which issues (the threat subject), for whom or what (the referent object), why (the intentions and purposes), with what results (the outcome), and under what conditions (the structure) (Buzan *et al.* 1998: 32). By naming these variables, the approach delivers the basic components to work with when studying threat politics.

Buzan *et al.* are rather unspecific concerning some variables, mainly pertaining to the characteristics of the threat subject, the reasons for securitisation, and the outcome/impact. More details are given for *securitising actors*, understood to be actors, mainly state representatives in a position of power who make the argument about a threat to the referent object. Frequent players in this group include political leaders, bureaucracies, governments, and pressure groups (Buzan *et al.* 1998: 36, 40). In addition to securitisation actors, the theory looks at a category called 'functional actors' – actors that play a central role in a sector by influencing its dynamics but are not involved in securitisation themselves (Buzan *et al.* 1998: 36). Furthermore, the object whose survival is assumed to be both necessary and currently threatened, the *referent object*, is explored in length. The Copenhagen school distinguishes five sectors of security (military, political, economic, societal, and environmental), each with distinct referent objects, such as nation, state, firm, society, and nature (Buzan *et al.* 1998: 36–40).

Wæver (2003: 26) himself addresses two main conceptual weaknesses when taking stock of the Copenhagen school's research program: the concepts of 'audience' and 'extraordinary measures', both of which lie at the very heart of the theory. The trouble with operationalising these two concepts leads to some difficulty in establishing whether observed processes are in fact processes of securitisation or not. The vague criterion given by the theory is that issues become securitised when they are taken out of the 'normal bounds of political procedure', which in turn amounts to a call for exceptional measures (Buzan et al. 1998: 24). In addition, securitisation moves are only successful if an audience 'accepts' the security argument (Buzan et al. 1998: 25). However, it remains largely unclear which audience has to accept what argument, to what degree, and for how long. In practice, a clear distinction between 'extraordinary' and 'normal' measures is sometimes very difficult and depends very much on the viewpoint of the analyst. In fact, actors employ definitions, concepts, and practices of security contextually at all times. Exceptional measures are therefore also highly contextual and subjective: they might not always be 'security measures' in a restricted sense, and security measures might not always be exceptional to everyone. Additionally, we can also identify different kind of exceptional measures: those that are regulated by existing norms and institutions and those that are radical exceptions or violations of regulations (Werner 1998). One way of avoiding this empirical problem is to ignore the designation of labels such as 'normal' and 'extraordinary' and to focus instead on the rhetorical structure of statements made about the measures to be applied (Wæver 2003: 26).

In this book, however, I will not focus primarily on the question whether securitisation has been successful. Instead, I am interested in the nature of security measures drafted in response to a securitisation move, be this move successful or not. The securitisation process, or, rather, the particulars of threat politics, is interesting to me if the issue under consideration not only makes it onto the (security political) agenda, thus being included in a list of subjects or problems that government officials pay some attention to, but also has some kind of implications by leading to actual policy decisions on countermeasures. By focusing on security as a practice with an outcome, I will gain additional insights into the variety of countermeasures in place to counter modern threats. The threat politics approach allows a more open approach to these political processes, because it does not 'freeze' the meaning and notion of security in the same way as the specific speech act form of security does, which is particular to the post-Cold War period and does not leave room for possible future changes in the concept (Huysman 1998a, 1998b; also Wæver 2002; McSweeney 1996: 85, 1998).

Another critique to consider is levelled at the approach from the so-called 'Paris school' (Wæver 2003, 2004). Scholars from the Institut d'Etudes Politiques de Paris have held against the Copenhagen school that by focusing exclusively on discursive practices, its approach has tended to overlook some of the important *non-discursive practices* of security formation by agencies in the security domain (Bigo 1998). The Paris school's approach focuses mainly on the action of those actors who are endowed with both the 'symbolic capital' and the capacity to inter-link heterogeneous discourses by establishing 'the truth' about certain threats. These actors are called the 'professionals of security' (Aradau 2001a). Certain voices are inherently endowed with more weight than others due to the symbolic capital at their disposal, which corresponds to their positions of authority. Within the state, there are in fact various positions of authority from which security issues can be voiced; this multiplicity of positions leads to struggles between competing discourses, the goal being to gain legitimacy and to become the dominant discourse.

According to the Paris school, the securitisation process cannot be reduced to simple rhetoric but implies extensive mobilisation of resources to support the discourse. The institutions that bring forth professionals of security are bureaucratic extensions of the state; deprived of their Cold War exterior enemy, these bureaucracies need to legitimise their existence by constantly redefining their role as the protector of society, and they do so by securitising practices. The will to fight, however, is no longer sufficient; new practices and institutions need to be created to deal with the quasi-ubiquitous danger that the 'new' threats constitute (Huysmans 1998c; Aradau 2001a; Bigo 1994). From the subsequent 'turf battles', one professional or group of professionals of security will emerge as the 'winning' actor at a given time. The crucial question in this context is as follows: who wins the discursive struggle, when, and for what reasons; or, in short, who wins why when?

The idea is that within a discourse, various groups seek to assert themselves and their pattern of argumentation and thus attempt to establish a dominant discourse pattern (Townson 1992). In order to convince any kind of audience that they are acting appropriately, the participants of the discourse seek to be argumentatively persuasive. Discourse participants have better prospects of convincing when they refer to an already existing discourse formation (Nadoll 2000). According to Townson, three fundamental aspects are central to the struggle for discursive dominance (Townson 1992: 25–33):

1 *Naming*: the establishment of new terms in a discourse, e.g. the term 'cyber-terrorism';
2 *Referencing*: seeking to establish linkages with existing terms, which have positive connotations but are not ideologically contingent (e.g. morality, responsibility). In the instance of threat frames, the connotations are negative, not positive, because the 'grammar of security' stresses urgency and evokes an existential threat to security;
3 *Signifying*: being able to dominate a particular discourse and being the only one who knows the 'true' meaning of certain terms.

The actor who is able to dominate these three aspects within a discourse controls the attachment of meaning to specific terms (linguistic dominance) and therefore controls the discourse (discursive dominance or discourse hegemony). The resulting dominant discourse concurs most closely with common experiences and other indicators of 'truth' (Boekle *et al.* 2000, 2001).

The securitisation approach does not offer any direct explanations for the

28 *Politics and threat construction*

question of 'who wins why when'. However, it assumes that certain features of the securitisation speech act are decisive for determining whether issues are included in the security agenda or take on societal salience, since the former can act as 'facilitating conditions' of the security speech act (Buzan *et al.* 1998: 32). They help to explain when securitisation is likely to be successful. There are two main facilitating conditions for securitisation: first, the speech act follows the grammar of security, meaning that it constructs a plot containing an existential threat and a point of no return and offers a 'securitised' way out; second, the securitising actor holds a position from which an authoritative claim about security can be made (Buzan *et al.* 1998: 31–3). In the upcoming chapter on framing theory, I will specifically address this issue and look at how specific features of the speech act can be related to winning the discursive battle.

Figure 2.1 depicts the securitisation theory as proposed by the Copenhagen school. Shaded in grey are those variables for which conceptual or theoretical clarification is needed. Apart from 'extraordinary measures' and 'audience', which were treated in detail above, two variables are hardly mentioned in the theory: the characteristics of the threat subject and the 'why' question. Question marks indicate processes, causal relationships, or mechanisms that remain unclear. Primarily, this is a representation of the 'who wins why when' question, but it also describes the role of the facilitating conditions and the 'audience' in connection with successful securitisation.

Figure 2.2 shows an expanded and amended version of the basic securitisation theory that takes into account the criticism from inside and outside the Copenhagen school. For one thing, we no longer look at securitisation processes within five predefined sectors. The role of functional actors remains unclear: their particular importance for threat politics will need to be explored in more detail in the case studies. It is assumed, however, that functional actors influence the dynamics of a certain issue area but are not themselves, by definition, part of the securitisation/framing act, so that this variable is best introduced as an external influencing factor. Furthermore, by adding professionals of security who,

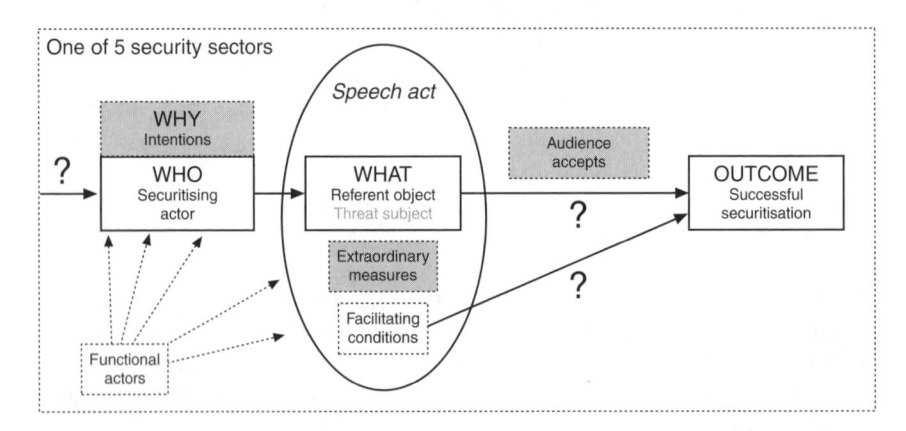

Figure 2.1 Securitisation theory basic diagram.

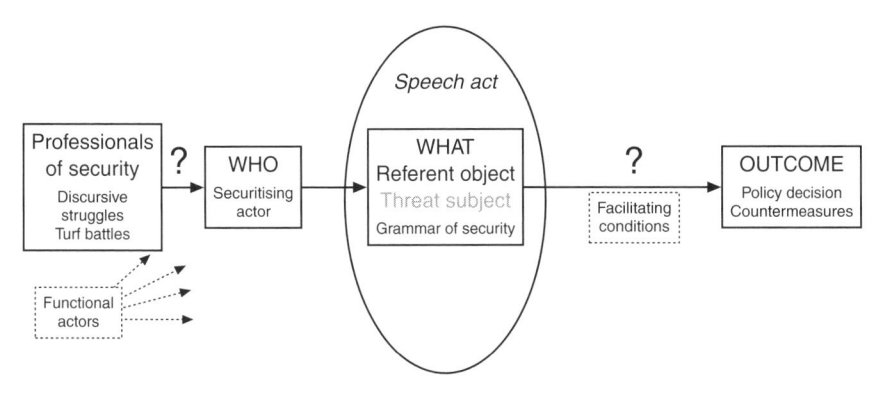

Figure 2.2 Securitisation theory: including internal/external criticism.

according to the Paris school, need to legitimise their own existence, we answer part of the 'why' question. Extraordinary measures are integrated into the speech act. Again, question marks and grey shading are used to highlight the issues that we want to expand.

In the subsequent chapters, I will focus on three main issues: first, the connection between the speech act and facilitating conditions. I will look more closely at how threats are presented and what that means for a particular threat and examine how the 'grammar of security' can be analysed (Expansion I: frame analysis); Second, I will seek additional clarification of the mechanisms and processes that put issues onto the agenda and, in addition, elicit a response (Expansion II: agenda setting); and third, the question 'who wins why when' will be addressed (Expansion I and II).

Expansion I: frame analysis

In order to explain why certain issues or threats make it onto the agenda and others do not, some scholars in the security studies domain have established a stronger link to (cognitive) framing research that explains the success of certain issues by special traits of 'frames' employed by key actors (Eriksson and Noreen 2002; Eriksson 2001a). Framing theory is rooted in linguistic studies of interaction and points to the way in which shared assumptions and meanings shape the interpretation of any particular event (Oliver and Johnston 2000).

The main problem with framing theory is that the term 'frame' has become a very vague and often misused concept through extensive and imprecise use by a variety of scholars from different disciplines (Fisher 1997). This makes it necessary to offer some explanation as to how I employ the concept in this study. Put simply, framing is understood to refer to the subtle selection of certain aspects of an issue in order to cue a specific response; the way an issue is framed explains who is responsible and suggests potential solutions conveyed by images, stereotypes, messengers, and metaphors (Ryan 1991: 59). Threat framing, in particular, refers to the process whereby particular agents develop specific interpretive schemata about what counts as threat or risk, how to respond to this threat, and who is responsible for it.

Frame analysis can be seen as a special strand of discourse analysis that mainly focuses on relevant content and argumentation (Gamson 1992). Framing is an empirically observable activity: frames are rooted in and constituted by group-based social interaction, which is available for first-hand observation, examination, and analysis of texts (Snow and Benford 1992). The high relevance of frames as social patterns is an outcome of the fact that frames define meaning and determine actions. Specifically, socially accepted frames influence the actions of actors and define meaning in the public mind (Gamson 1992: 110; Snow *et al.* 1986: 464), so that the establishment of specific threat frames is ultimately an instrument of social development and change. Social contests for the legitimate definition of reality – in other words, the struggle for discursive hegemony – are held by ways of different categories as expressed in frames. Frames are therefore the basic instruments used in the struggle for discursive hegemony. In the case of threat framing, the process of categorising something as a particular threat has practical consequences when key actors begin seeing the world according to these categories.

Framing theory addresses three main questions, the second of which will be our main focus: 1) how frames influence social action; 2) which frames are particularly successful for what reasons; and 3) how frames can be changed (Snow and Benford 1988). From the many disjointed and many incompatible strands of frame theory, we focus on the approach of Snow and Benford. They outline three types of framing (Snow and Benford 1988: 199–202) that help to specify the Copenhagen school's speech act idea:

1 *diagnostic framing*, which is about clearly defining a problem and assigning blame for the problem to an agent or agencies. In the terminology used in this book, this equals designating the threat subject and referent object of security;
2 *prognostic framing*, which is about offering solutions and proposing specific strategies, tactics, and objectives by which these solutions may be achieved;
3 *motivational framing*, to rally the troops behind the cause or a 'call for action'.

To this list, they add a fourth key element, *frame resonance*, meaning that the frame content must appeal to the existing values and beliefs of the target audience to become effective. Frame resonance is therefore in part similar to the concept of the 'facilitating condition' of the speech act.

Frames have been studied either as dependent or as independent variables (Scheufele 1999). Studies of frames as dependent variables have examined the role of various factors in influencing the creation or modification of frames, while studies in which frames serve as independent variables typically look at the effects of framing. In our analysis, we are interested in both questions: in our two-phase framework, phase I treats frames more like a dependent variable, while phase II sees them more like independent variables. In a more dynamic perspective that integrates both phases, we observe continuous processes where threat frame building serves as input for subsequent frame effects.

When looking at frames as dependent variables, one mainly asks what factors influence the way key actors frame security issues. In the literature on framing theory, scholars focus on social–structural or organisational variables on various levels (Swidler 1986, 1995; Donati 1992; Fisher 1997). I want to look at institutions and on the larger context in which key actors act, two factors that constrain the process of reality construction and, subsequently, framing. Institutions can be seen as organisations, but also as accepted patterns or rules that structure how actors interact and what choices they have as they attempt to pursue their particular goals. In addition, they can be conceived as normative orders or collections of values that shape behaviour through their capacity to socialise their members with corresponding norms and routines (Rittberger 1993; Guzzini 2002; Jepperson *et al.* 1996). The institutional context reveals that the actors in question are dependent on norms and bureaucratic subcultures within their organisations. Furthermore, systems of representation and systems of power are considered to be part of this variable. Though they may not set solid boundaries to the way in which people think, they do define individuals' knowledge of how others will interpret their actions (Swidler 1995: 39).

Second, I have already argued that individuals do not respond directly to (objective) reality but through socially constructed thought frameworks. In theoretical terms, this means that the environment perceived by decision-makers will influence the threat perception of key actors. In this analysis, specific traits of the information age as explored in the previous chapter, such as complexity, have a direct influence on the dynamics of threat politics.

It is clear that different kinds of actors will develop different kinds of threat frames – so that it matters for threat politics which group of actors, with which particular threat frame, 'wins' the discursive struggle. This also means that we need to be more specific about the link between actors, their characteristics, and the frames they construct. In public policy literature, two attributes of actors are sometimes distinguished: beliefs and resources (Rothmayr *et al.* 2003). I assume that both of these directly influence the framing process but will not analyse them specifically in the case studies. *A belief* is an idea about or mental image of how the world is structured, how it works, and how it should work (Putnam 1976; Young 1977). Beliefs are a cultural resource for framing, and constructed threat frames originate in actors' belief systems. At the same time, various characteristics of belief systems constrain the production of meaning and thus can affect the mobilising potential of framings. *Resources*, on the other hand, include power, status, money, information, and prestige. Resources are conceptualised as a tool that, to varying degrees, gives actors the ability to effectively pursue their goals in the policy arena, formally or informally. Specific positions of authority and 'symbolic capital' are also resources.

32 Politics and threat construction

When looking at frames as independent variables, we are more interested in what kind of effects threat frames have. Specifically, we look at what mobilising potential they generate. This question is closely connected to the facilitating conditions of the speech act, or, more specifically, to the mobilising potential of threat subject, referent object, and the solutions proposed. Regrettably, there is a considerable grey zone in the literature concerning the issue: the Copenhagen school, whose investigation focuses almost exclusively on the referent object, largely ignores the threat question. However, Buzan and his colleagues speculate whether actor-based threats are a precondition for a security problem. By pointing briefly to insights from 'attribution theory', they come to the conclusion that 'probably, they usually are' (Buzan *et al.* 1998: 44).

Attribution theory is concerned with how individuals interpret events and how this relates to their thinking and behaviour (Heider 1944, 1958; Weiner 1974, 1986; Jones *et al.* 1972). Attribution theory assumes that people try to determine why people do what they do, i.e. they attribute causes to behaviour. Evidence suggests that securitising actors have the tendency to 'actorise' threats so that most threats will be linked to actors, even though threats might originate in structural conditions. For example, nuclear power accidents, power outages, floods, epidemics, and similar phenomena are obvious examples of events that result from structural problems rather than agency (Sundelius 1983; Eriksson 2001b: 11–2); however, the blame for them is mostly attributed to actors. Apart from linking threats to antagonistic states, threats can also be blamed on non-state actors. In fact, we assume that frames that link threats to non-state actors might be even more effective than those that link them to hostile foreign states, as this particular attribution plays effectively on the blurring of the distinction between internal and external threats as well as on the difficulty of assigning responsibility to either private or public spheres of action, which creates confusion and fear and is likely to have a high mobilisation power (Sundelius 1983; Eriksson 2001b: 11–P12; Bendrath *et al.* 2007).

Figure 2.3 shows the framework after adding the insights from framing

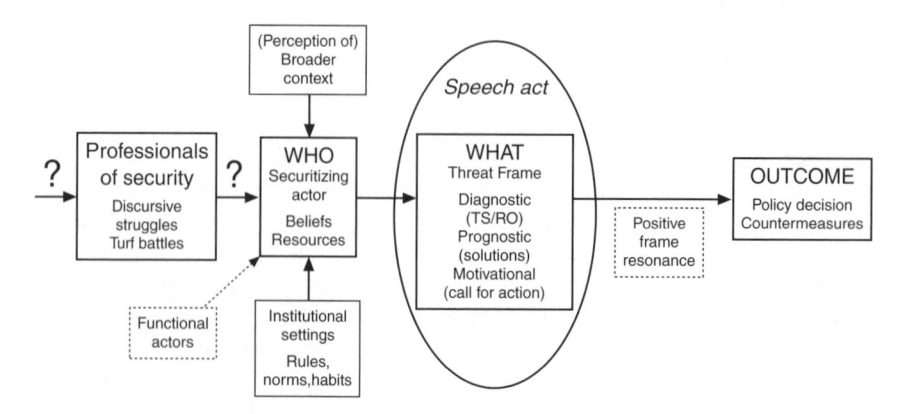

Figure 2.3 Securitisation theory expanded I: adding framing theory.

theory. We have specified the attributes of the speech act by introducing the concept of threat frames with three distinct parts. The variable 'facilitating conditions' can be substituted by the concept of 'positive frame resonance'. The framing process is influenced by the beliefs and resources of the framing actors, which are, in turn, influenced by institutional restraints and perception of the broader environment.

At this stage, we have established that the struggle for discursive hegemony is won by those actors who a) are in the position to shape the security discourse (professionals of security) and b) construct a threat frame that appeals to some kind of still undefined 'audience'. In order to gain additional knowledge on the mechanisms behind threat politics, we will look at agenda-setting theory in the next section.

Expansion II: agenda-setting theory

The question why certain problems and not others have political salience is addressed indirectly by agenda-setting theory, as developed by Kingdon (2003). In addition, agenda setting answers 'how' and 'when' issues are propelled onto the agenda and provides a more detailed account of the process by which this is done and the conditions that are necessary. Specifically, Kingdon (2003: 166–8) identifies *problems*, *policies*, and *politics* as three relatively independent 'streams' through which various participants interact to ultimately place items on the agenda:

- *Problems*: There is usually a long list of problems that people in and around government could attend to – some are given attention, some are ignored (Kingdon 2003: 90–115). Below, we will look more closely at why certain of them come to the attention of decision-makers.
- *Policies*: There is a 'policy primeval soup' in which ideas float around. From time to time, policies in the form of proposals are selected or float to the top (Kingdon 2003: 116–44); The policy stream is dependent on a group of 'hidden' participants consisting primarily of specialists in government, academics, and special interest groups (Kingdon 2003: 117, 199–200; see also Adler and Haas 1992). Solutions to various societal conditions are constantly being proposed and debated in these specialist circles, but these ideas need a problem and a proponent before they can be elevated to the status of agenda items. This means that in this elitist view of agenda setting, top politicians, often called 'visible' participants, tend to be more important than bureaucrats and non-governmental actors at the end of the agenda-setting process.
- *Politics*: Other elements of the political stream include the public mood, pressure group campaigns, election results, parliamentary majorities, changes in the political administration, etc.

In our context, a particularly important aspect is how *conditions* become identified as *problems* (Kingdon 2003: 109–13; Eriksson 1999a). Conditions that are less than ideal are pervasive throughout society and are seldom acted upon by government until they are perceived as (serious) problems. In fact, without problem recognition, securitisation or the framing of a threat would be unlikely. This underscores the importance of adding another variable to our framework that more concretely addresses various reasons for securitisation moves. According to agenda-setting theory, officials become aware that conditions have reached this stage as a result of indicators, focusing events, or formal and informal feedback (Kingdon 2003: 90–115):

- *Indicator*: a more or less systemic indicator in the form of statistics, particular studies, or budgetary impacts that shows clearly that there is a problem;
- *Focusing events*: a crisis, a disaster, or the personal experience of a policy maker;
- *Formal and informal feedback*: feedback messages as part of the normal course of events, in the form of systematic monitoring and evaluation studies, or in the form of complaints or routine casework.

Kingdon (2003: 166) distinguishes between the governmental agenda – a set of policies being actively considered by the government – and the decision agenda, those issues which command the attention of individuals at the highest levels of government. From time to time, predictably or unpredictably, an opportunity arises for supporters of a certain proposal to gain attention for their problems, or, in other words, a *policy window* opens, which allows them to move an issue onto the decision-making agenda. A window opens because of change in the political stream or when a new problem comes to the attention of officials. In accordance, there are *political* and *problem windows*. When such a window opens, the three streams (problems, policies, and politics) are usually coupled together by *policy entrepreneurs*, defined as advocates who are willing to invest their resources – time, energy, reputation, or money – to promote a position in return for anticipated future gain in the form of material, purposive, or solidarity benefits (Kingdon 2003: 122–4; 179–83).

Even though the security agenda is a part of the political agenda with particular features implying a higher grade of urgency than other public issues, many of Kingdon's insights are applicable to the context of threat politics. The framework can be expanded in a final step by adding a 'why' variable, representing a policy window as described by Kingdon. There are two possible occasions for policy windows and thus two reasons for the securitisation move: it opens either due to a change in the political stream (political window) or due to a new problem (problem window). New problems are identified through indicators, focusing events, or formal and informal feedback. I further add top decision-makers as a kind of 'audience' who must approve of an idea in order to elevate it onto the decision-making agenda and the notion of a 'policy entrepreneur' who has to like an idea and to invest in it. However, it is unclear whether the policy entrepreneur and the securitisation/framing actors are separate entities or how the three actor variables (professionals of security, securitising actors, and policy

Politics and threat construction 35

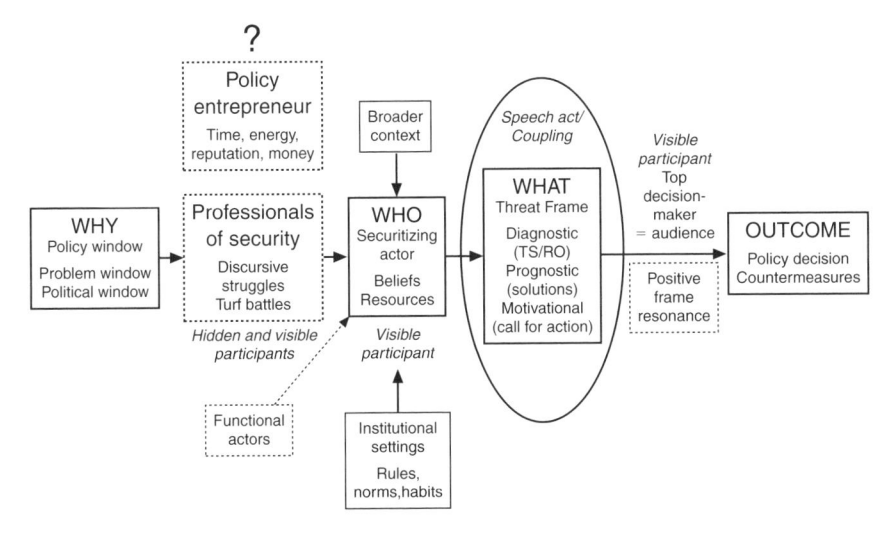

Figure 2.4 Securitisation theory expanded II: adding agenda-setting theory.

entrepreneurs) interact. Finally, I adopt the idea of coupling as proposed by Kingdon. I assume that coupling and framing by speech act are one and the same. According to what was said concerning the establishment of discursive dominance, the coupling of existing terms with negative connotations to create a sense of urgency ('referencing') is expected to be an observable practice in threat politics (see Figure 2.4).

A two-phase dynamic framework for the study of threat politics

As mentioned before, a two-phase approach is required in order to truly capture the mechanisms of threat politics: the first phase covers the initial framing, until the issue has made its way 'successfully' onto the agenda and elicits its first policy response; the second phase starts when the threat is on the agenda and subsequently begins to undergo change. Even though both work with the same variables, they each demand different key questions and emphases.

The Securitisation Phase (Phase I). This looks at how threats first appear on the agenda, i.e. what kind of threat frame was employed by whom, and with what result. In my understanding, a threat framing is 'successful' when it elicits its first security policy response.

The Re-Framing Phase (Phase II). This starts when the specific threat is on the agenda and its features begin to undergo change. This second stage will help us understand why threat frames change over time and will produce more evidence for how the mechanisms of threat politics work. It is, in theory, also possible for a threat frame to disappear from the agenda completely. A process set

Figure 2.5

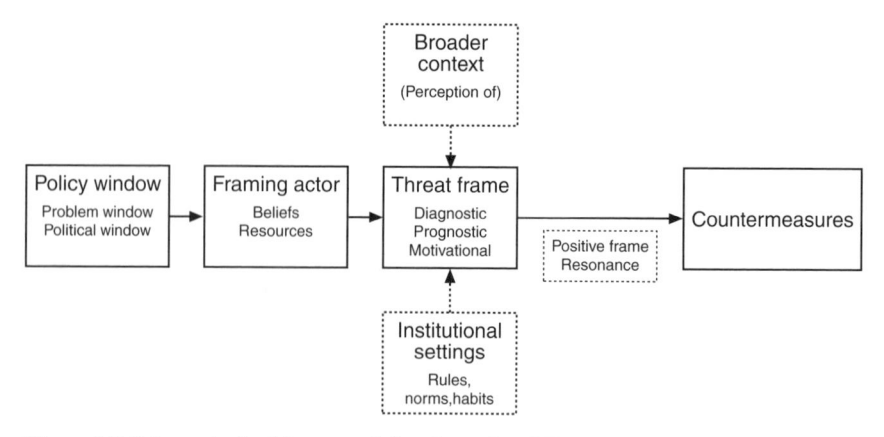

```
                    ┌─────────────┐
                    │  Broader    │
                    │  context    │
                    │(Perception of)│
                    └──────┬──────┘
                           ▼
┌──────────────┐  ┌──────────────┐  ┌──────────────┐                      ┌────────────────┐
│Policy window │  │Framing actor │  │ Threat frame │                      │                │
│Problem window│─▶│   Beliefs    │─▶│  Diagnostic  │─────────────────────▶│ Countermeasures│
│Political     │  │  Resources   │  │  Prognostic  │   Positive frame     │                │
│window        │  │              │  │ Motivational │     Resonance        │                │
└──────────────┘  └──────────────┘  └──────┬───────┘                      └────────────────┘
                                           ▲
                                    ┌──────┴───────┐
                                    │ Institutional│
                                    │   settings   │
                                    │    Rules,    │
                                    │ norms,habits │
                                    └──────────────┘
```

Figure 2.5 Schematic final framework for phases I and II.

in motion by a policy window is one possible explanation for such a change in the threat frames. Change in one of the two actor attributes as defined in the previous chapter may also be a likely reason. Beliefs are fixed, or at least relatively stable in the short run; however, they may also change, for example, as a result of policy learning (Sabatier 1988; Sabatier and Jenkins-Smith 1993), due to turnover of participants, or, alternatively, as the result of a change in the external environment. Figure 2.5 shows a schematic version of the framework with four key variables and three 'influencing' ones.

I expect that a 'policy window' will trigger the process of securitisation/framing or re-framing. Professionals of security, who are influenced by the perception of the larger environment, and their institutional settings develop specific threat frames to talk about a specific threat. Actors and threat frames are closely interconnected – no threat frames exist without actors, and it is possible that especially superior threat frames help certain actors to gain discursive hegemony and dominate the debate. The formation of threat frames is thus influenced by institutions and by the broader context in which the threat framing occurs. When these threat frames appeal to the audience (top decision-makers), countermeasures will result. Below, the key variables are introduced in more detail.

Policy windows

I want to identify policy windows in the case studies, either as a result of change in the political stream – such as swings in the public mood (see also Rose and Davies 1993), pressure group campaigns, elections, etc. – or as a result of a new problem that comes to the attention of decision-makers – either due to focusing events, indicators, or due to feedback. In accordance, I will distinguish between a) problem windows and b) political windows. Each of these represents a change from the status quo that may affect the beliefs and resources of actors and, through these actors, initiate the re-framing of cyber-threats.

Policy windows are prior in time to the securitisation move and re-framing. We should be able to identify them by focusing on the sequence and structure of events and/or the testimony of actors explaining why they acted as they did (Adler 1997: 329–30). It will be regarded as proof of a link between policy windows (problem definition) and action taken by actors in the policy when people state that they did something because of something else, or when there is reference to an incident, a report, etc. in another report. In particular, I aim to explore to what extent policy windows were responsible for triggering the first framing of the issue as a threat process. The following assumptions are made: when a condition turns into a problem that threatens national security in the eyes of professionals of security, the first threat frame emerges. Then, if an event changes the beliefs or resources of professionals of security – either directly or indirectly by first influencing their perception of the broader environment – a re-framing of the threat frame is initiated. At the same time, if an event changes beliefs or resources of relevant professionals of security, then new discourse strands are interlinked or decoupled by referencing.

Securitisation/framing actors

There are many groups of actors involved in the 'threat politics' process at various stages in time. Based on what we already know, I make the following assumptions about actors:

- Actors can be either individuals or groups of individuals who share a set of basic beliefs and have resources.
- Specific actors or actor constellations develop a specific threat frame. This threat frame can be deduced from their statements and can be identified from official documents.
- One actor or actor constellation wins the discursive struggle at a given time.
- There are hidden and visible participants. Visible participants, most notably top-level politicians, are pivotal in setting the decision-making agenda, while hidden participants, such as experts and analysts, have a greater role to play in formulating the specific policy alternatives.
- Functional actors influence the dynamics of a specific issue area.
- The securitising/framing actor will most likely emerge from the so-called professionals of security, actors endowed with both symbolic capital and the capacity to inter-link heterogeneous discourses in the security domain.
- A top-level politician needs to be in place to put the issue onto the decision agenda.

I also suppose that a different group of actors shapes the issue once it is on the agenda and once an issue undergoes re-framing. It is still largely unclear, however, how and why this group differs from the group of securitising actors, what this means for the threat politics mechanisms, and what this observation actually explains. It is also uncertain what exact role functional actors play. In addition, is the act of securitisation always a conscious, wilful act, or, are there also 'accidental' securitising actors? And, if an issue is already on the agenda, is it necessary for a top-level politician to be in position each time the issue is reframed?

We assume that only professionals of security are actively involved in threat framing, and if professionals of security develop threat frames, they develop them according to their beliefs, resources, and bureaucratic ties. If beliefs or resources of professionals of security change, then the perception of the broader context or the institutional settings has changed. Interpretations and solutions to threats are constantly being proposed and debated in circles of specialist (hidden participants), but these ideas need a (disturbing) event before they can be turned into threat frames in the public spheres of action.

It is likely that we will only be able to identify framing actors indirectly, by asking who performs the security speech act with its specific rhetorical structure concerned with survival and the priority of action – or rather, who attempts to do so, as the number of securitisation, or rather, threat framing moves, is much larger than instances of successful framing. In some occurrences, we might have to identify framing actors in retrospect, by analysing from whom the winning threat frame originated. In order to identify security speech acts and instances of threat framing, we will develop a list of keywords that are indicators for a securitisation move (see Table 2.1).

Threat frames

Threat frames emerge as the result of the values, resources, and beliefs of key actors. A frame has three main parts: 1) a diagnostic frame, expressed in the threat subject and the referent object; 2) a prognostic frame, which includes pro-

Table 2.1 Threat-framing keywords

Threat framing keywords (for cyber-threats)
• Computer (-based) attack
• Computer intrusion
• Critical information infrastructures
• Critical infrastructures
• Cyber-attack
• Cyber-security
• Cyber-terrorism
• Cyber-threat
• Cyber-vulnerability
• Cyber-war(fare)
• Electronic Pearl Harbor
• Information operations
• Information warfare
• National security (in connection with information security, etc.)
• Vulnerabilities of information infrastructure

posals of solutions, strategies, tactics, and objectives by which these solutions may be achieved; and 3) a motivational frame, to mobilise supporters. Furthermore, it must appeal to certain key actors (top-level decision-makers). If the frame resonance is positive, the issue is put on the agenda.

Winning threat frames can be found in official policy documents, other threat frames in reports, in hearings transcripts, or in any other document. Once we have identified these threat frames, we analyse why a particular one has prevailed, by focusing on the variables derived from our framework. It is proof of a link between two instances when people state that they did something because of something else or if these actors see something as the cause of something else.

Data for the case studies is collected from official policy papers, hearings, and other statements of key actors as well as from a secondary analysis of existing literature. This material includes books, articles, and Internet resources. Top-level documents reflect actual presidential intentions, as opposed to public statements of purpose, which frequently leave out sensitive details and, on occasion, directly conflict with the stated goals of the administration. There is a variety of document types that we will encounter. An Executive Order, for example, is a legally binding edict issued by a member of the executive branch of a government, usually the head of that branch. Executive Orders are usually based on existing statutory authority and require no action by Congress or the state legislature to become effective, but they have the same legal weight as laws passed by Congress (Olson and Woll 1999). Orders concerned with national security or defence issues, on the other hand, constitute a specific subset of Executive Orders. These have generally been known as National Security Directives but have been given different names by various presidential administrations.[1] Security Directives are intended to be internal documents for use only by the federal agencies and officials to whom they were addressed and not for dissemination to the public or even the Congress. Presidents have utilized the classified directives, many of which are top secret, as a primary means of defining and executing national security policy – and have sometimes rejected Congressional demands to review them. The threat frames that they imply are therefore of prime importance for our study. An Act of Congress, finally, is a bill or resolution adopted by both houses of the US Congress.

Relevant documents were identified a) by a key-word search in the Congressional Hearings database; b) through allusion to securitisation key words in other documents; and c) by browsing through official reports and policy papers with promising titles. I do not specifically focus on media coverage, though it is often considered a key factor in the construction of new threats (Bendrath 2003; Conway 2008; Debrix 2001). But, though the media might have a catalysing influence in some instances, threat frames are not created in the media. In fact, studies that focus on the representation in the media often represent a skewed image of the debate and threat pictures (for example, Bendrath *et al.* 2007) and fail to show any connection between media coverage and the perceptions and especially actions of decision-makers. In my framework, the media influences the process of threat politics through Kingdon's (2003: 90–115) indicators, focusing events, or formal and informal feedback. The media thus plays a role, mainly by riding the wave of the topic and bringing the issue to the attention of the wider public, but it does not play a role in shaping the issue in the political process.

In order to localise threat frames in the texts, I have developed an initial list of keywords that make the speech act an act of 'securitisation' or more generally, an act of cyber-threat framing (Table 2.1).

Discourse strands are coupled together in accordance to a change in beliefs or resources as initiated by a disturbing event. In addition, several assumptions can be made concerning attributes of winning threat frames: The broader the range of threat subjects in a threat frame, the more likely it is that the threat frame will be successful; and the more the referent object is about domestic and social well-being, the more likely it is that the threat frame will be successful. In addition, the more urgent the motivational call, the more likely it is that the threat frame will be successful.

Countermeasures

The nature of countermeasures is an integral part of threat politics and of the study of new threats. However, the last variable is not truly a dependent variable in the sense that causality can be easily established between the previous variables and countermeasures. As stated, we rather see countermeasures as a variable to define whether a framing process has been successful. We assume that the diagnostic part of the winning threat frame is incorporated into countermeasures or at least can be found in its major parts.

Note

1 'National Security Decision Directives' under Reagan, 'National Security Directives' under Bush Sr, 'Presidential Decision Directives' under Clinton, 'National Security Presidential Directives' or 'Homeland Security Presidential Directives' (after 11 September 2001) under Bush Jr.

3 The hostile intelligence threat, data security, and encryption set the stage

Historically, the link between the (modern) information infrastructure and national security was first forged in the military domain. More than 60 years ago, the precursors of computers played a considerable role in the race to break military code systems during the Second World War (Kahn 1996; Hinsely and Stripp 2001). The invention of the radio has also had a big impact on military affairs (Berkowitz 2003). The biggest difference to the contemporary cyber-threats debate is, however, that information technology (IT) was predominantly treated as a *force enabler* rather than a source of vulnerability, so that no effort at threat framing is discernible until the 1980s. In the context of this book, it is nonetheless important to note that the link between information infrastructures and national security was firmly established in military writings after the Second World War (see, for example, Rona 1976; Bellin and Champan 1987; Hables Gray 1997), so that the connection between the two topics became an accepted part of military thinking. On these grounds, the issue met with little resistance in the early 1990s, when it rose to prominence as one of the prime issues in US strategic thinking. These early developments in the military domain are the focus of the first sub-chapter.

But, even though the military saw IT mainly as a force enabler, the awareness of how vital reliable and interoperable telecommunications are for the federal government can be traced back at least to the Cuban Missile Crisis, when difficulties in terms of communication between the United States, the Soviet Union, NATO, and other national leaders threatened to complicate the crisis even more (Fursenko and Naftali 1997). After an investigation of communication systems serving national security needs was conducted in 1963, an interdepartmental committee recommended the formation of a single unified communications system to support the president, the Department of Defense (DoD), diplomatic and intelligence activities, and civilian leaders. Consequently, in order to provide better communications support to critical government functions during emergencies, President John F. Kennedy issued a Presidential Memorandum on 21 August 1963 establishing the 'National Communications System' (Kennedy 1963). The mandate of the National Communications System, which still exists today, includes linking, improving, and extending the communications facilities and components of various federal agencies in order to further the interconnectivity and survivability of vital information infrastructures.

In accordance with these developments, the link that was established between telecommunications and national security in the 1960s was that communication was necessary to ensure the operability of government and especially, its ability to act in a timely and effective manner at all times. Therefore, the functioning of communication systems was seen as vital for the ability to ensure the security and well-being of the nation. This reasoning still resonates in a specific 'twist' of the cyber-threats debate: emergency management and response. But, although these issues are of importance even today, the particular cyber-threat image that we are interested in, and which began to emerge in the 1980s, extends to other dimensions. In order for the issue to evolve from a relatively marginal issue into a mass phenomenon, rapid development of technology in the civil sector and the emergence of the global information infrastructure were necessary. Before the advent of personal computers and their networking capabilities elevated the problem to yet another level, it was the telephone system that was exploited by the so-called 'phreaking' techniques. As the 1970s gave way to the 1980s, the merger of telecommunications with computers – the basis of the current information revolution – meant that everybody with a computer at home was theoretically able to exploit emerging networks. The revolutionary introduction of the personal computer created a rise in tech-savvy users, many of whom would dial into bulletin board systems with a modem and download or disseminate information on how to tinker with technology.

During this time, the first *cyber-threat* frames emerged. By our definition, cyber-threats emerge from the malicious use of information and communication technologies (ICT) either as a target or as a tool by a wide range of malevolent actors. Taking the emergence of these kind of topics into account, we can trace the beginnings of the cyber-threats debate back to the Reagan presidency, where we find policy efforts in connection with IT in two domains: the first one linked to the growing problem of computer crime, which led to the Computer Abuse Act in 1984, a piece of legislation that set the stage for computer crime prosecution in the years to come, and the second one linked to the protection of federal agencies' computer data from espionage, which was interlinked with the debate on encryption technology and led to the Computer Security Act of 1987. These developments, continued under President H. W. George Bush, are the focus of our second sub-chapter. Finally, we look more closely at cyber-threat frames in the years between 1981 and 1992 in the remaining sub-chapters.

Information technology, the revolution in military affairs, and the birth of information warfare

IT was linked to national security in the wake of the more general debate in the Cold War about technological innovation and warfare. As early as the 1950s, a series of thinkers recognised that the Cold War was linking vast military machines, nations, and globe-spanning alliances into new information networks

(Berkowitz 2003). One function of those networks was the systematic, in-depth assessment of the other side's capabilities, in comparison with one's own, combining intelligence operations abroad and analysis at home. More generally, in the early days of the Computer age, the debate was about how IT could be employed to win wars. The goal of substituting firepower for manpower, or what General James Van Fleet (quoted in Brodie 1973: 91) during the Korean War described as the desire 'to expend fire and steel, not men', ultimately led to an effort to develop a new way of waging war that depended less and less on quantitative material superiority and attrition to ensure victory.

This approach was part of what the then Secretary of Defense Harold Brown called the 'offset strategy' in the 1970s, which was based on the need to counter the (perceived) overwhelming quantitative superiority of Soviet and Warsaw Pact forces in Europe (David 1997). The idea was that superior numbers of Soviet troops and tanks would have to be offset 'not by American manpower, but by our unique strength; not raw numbers and not nuclear weapons, but technology' (Brown cited in David 1997: 84). The aim was not simply to field better weapons than the Soviet Union; rather, the offset strategy was intended to give US weapons a systematic advantage by supporting them on the battlefield in a manner that greatly multiplied their combat effectiveness. This was the point at which the development of precision-guided munitions and off-board sensors and the fusion of high-tech systems with conventional weapons set off the current revolution in military affairs (RMA) (Cohen 1996: 39; David 1997; Cooper 1997; Libicki 1999).

Despite this focus on positive and force-enhancing aspects of technology, it would be wrong to argue that the United States was not aware of its own vulnerability. Concepts like electronic warfare, understood as denoting military action involving the use of electromagnetic and directed energy to control the electromagnetic spectrum or to attack the enemy (Price 1989a, 1989b, 1989c), command-and-control warfare, or psychological operations – all concepts that would become part of the umbrella concept of information warfare later – had already played a role in war-fighting since at least the end of the Second World War. And because the need to defend one's own vulnerable points was an integral part of these concepts, even if often implicitly, we can argue that IT, as a potential source of threats, was naturally securitised by the military very early on.

A specific aspect of early conceptions of the threat is the electromagnetic pulse (EMP) debate. This topic is closely linked to the nuclear age, but the target was the early information infrastructure. The discussion started following a US high-altitude test in the Pacific in the early 1960s that disrupted radio stations and electric equipment throughout nearby Hawaii (Weldon 1997; Wood 1999). After this experience, large amounts of money were expended to defend especially vital military equipment against the destructive effects of EMPs (Weldon 1997). If we refer back to the table in the introduction, this has a distinct physical-on-physical component, though the target was the early information infrastructure. But until the 1980s, the threat was perceived differently than in the 1990s: IT was seen only as a target and not yet as a weapon; thus, one important part of the contemporary cyber-threats debate was still lacking.

The term 'information warfare' was finally coined in 1976 when the Boeing corporation published engineer Thomas Rona's (1976) study 'Weapons Systems and Information War'. In this publication, he argued that communications and information support networks were sufficiently linked and cross-dependent to be inviting targets. He speculated that, in the emerging computer age, the most effective means to attack adversaries would be to focus on their information systems (Berkowitz and Hahn 2003). He noted that '[c]ountermeasures aimed at the external flow of information will be further improved to the point that they may well become crucial in influencing the outcome of future engagements' (Rona 1996; Rona, quoted in Berkowitz 2003: 30). Rona's work was an outgrowth of electronic warfare in the Second World War and the introduction of practical computers and networks. Most importantly, the RAND Corporation had begun research in 1962 into robust, distributed communication networks for military command and control, and Defense Advanced Research Projects Agency (DARPA) sponsored research into a 'cooperative network of time-sharing computers' in 1965: the beginnings of the Internet. Strictly speaking, this piece of work contained the ideas that would later turn into discussions concerning the double-edged sword of information warfare. However, it took a while until the DoD really began to shift its thinking towards identifying dependence on IT as carrying the potential for a severe threat to the United States. In fact, it was not until the emergence of vast open networks and the end of the Cold War that this threat perception began to prevail. The first major test combining concepts linked to IT for offensive purposes came during the Persian Gulf War at the beginnings of the 1990s, with the desert flanking move that checkmated Iraqi forces in Kuwait, an issue that I will turn to below.

Computer security becomes a national security issue

Though President John F. Kennedy had been concerned with national telecommunications systems and President Jimmy Carter had signed the Top Secret (directive) PD/NSC 58 entitled 'Continuity of Government' in June 1980, which covered data processing and communications systems (Ball 1981), Ronald Reagan was the first US president to address the problem of cyber-threats as we understand it. One of the Reagan administration's major concerns was to prevent what it viewed as damaging disclosures of classified information as well as the acquisition of 'sensitive but unclassified' information (Richelson 2005). Consequently, the major focus of the early cyber-threats debate is the security of classified or sensitive data.

We can identify two main developments, which we will discuss in two separate sub-chapters. The first track has a strong link to the early days of the popularisation of the information revolution, characterised by the Internet's transformation from a government experiment into a mass phenomenon and by the proliferation of home computers. During the 1980s, 'hackers' like Kevin

Mitnick and Captain Crunch gained notoriety, first through phone manipulation, so-called 'phreaking', and later through hacking or computer intrusion. Computer crime, or crime committed with the help of or against a computer, became a major issue. At the time, numerous books appeared that addressed computer insecurity (cf. Norman 1983; Parker 1983; Bequai 1986; Mungo and Clough 1993). But, even though it was called computer *crime*, there was a distinct national-security dimension to the problem from the beginning: computer intrusion was successfully interlinked with the foreign intelligence threat, mainly due to a couple of well-publicised incidents that involved data theft by foreign individuals.

The second track, the issue of encryption, is interrelated but different. It is less concerned with external intrusion than with means of protecting digital classified information on the one hand, and with being able to eavesdrop on, and ultimately apprehend, perpetrators on the other. One major issue in this field is the disagreement between the government and the private sector and academia, concerning encryption technology and the role of the intelligence community, namely the National Security Agency (NSA), in securing the information infrastructure. In fact, this debate represents a clash between two fundamentally different concepts of security, one held by the national security community and the other by the private sector.

Phreaks, hackers, and foreign spies – confronting computer crime in the name of national security

It was during the 1960s and mid-1970s that computer crime started to take off. According to some statistics, by the mid- to late-1970s, scores of such crimes were turning up every year, and losses were estimated to be as high as US$300 million, though there are actually no valid statistics on the losses incurred from this type of crime, because no one knows how many cases go unreported (Kabay 1998; Parker 1976, 1980a, 1980b, 1983). From early on, the discussion about computer misuse was determined by notions of computer-related economic crimes, which until today are regarded as the central area of computer crime. In this field, the central offences are those of computer manipulation, computer sabotage, computer extortion, hacking, and computer espionage, as well as software piracy and other forms of product piracy (Sieber 1986, 1998).

Again, the development of the debate is closely linked to change in the technological substructure. First, there was widespread digitalisation. As shown above, digital technology brings with it the possibility to move the digital information easily between media, and therefore, also to access or distribute it remotely. There are various reasons why digitally stored information is superior to information in any other form for almost every possible use, but the same reasons are also responsible for the ease with which information can be tampered with today: digital information can be computed. It can be sorted, combined, searched, rearranged, and presented in an endless variety of ways; it can be endlessly reproduced; it can be amplified, transmitted, stored, retrieved, and reconverted without any of the information being lost (Negroponte 1995).

Between 1950 and approximately 1975, computer programs and data were generally stored on cardboard cards with holes punched in them. If a vandal or thief were to break into an office and either damage or steal the punch cards, the delinquent could be adequately punished under traditional laws relating to breaking and entering, vandalism, or theft. There were several such incidents: in 1967, for example, a New York bank employee shaved fractions of cents from interest on long-term accounts by writing a program to deposit these fractions to his account. After a few years, he had amassed over US$200,000 (Sieber 1998; Goodman and Brenner 2002). Even though a computer and a program were involved, this was still a problem concerning theft by an employee working at the bank in question.

After about 1975, when it became more common to enter programs and data from remote terminals using a modem and a telephone line, the nature of the issue began to change. Change in technology meant that a criminal could alter data and programs from home, without physical entry into the victim's building. An example of a more sophisticated computer crime is the Rifkin case of 1978, where consultant Stanley M. Rifkin stole approximately US$10.2 million from a California bank. While working as a consultant for the Security Pacific National Bank in Los Angeles, he had learned the secret computer code that the bank used to transfer funds to other banks telegraphically at the end of each business day. With this information and his mastery of the bank's computer, he devised a plan for siphoning this money out of the bank (Rawitch 1979; Mitnick and Simon 2003: 4–6). He used the funds to buy Russian diamonds in Switzerland, which he smuggled back into the United States and attempted to sell, but he was captured.

When the 1980s came along, hackers were no longer just regarded as minor nuisance. In one of the first arrests of hackers in 1983, the Federal Bureau of Investigation (FBI) apprehended the Milwaukee-based '414s', which were named after the local area code. The members of the group, young people ranging from ages 16 to 22, were accused of 60 computer break-ins in various venues ranging from the Memorial Sloan-Kettering Cancer Center to Los Alamos National Laboratory (Elmer-Dewitt 1983; Bailey 1984). The group gained a lot of attention, and one member, Neil Patrick, even appeared on the cover of the 5 September 1983 edition of *Newsweek*. Despite the fact that the incident had no real consequences, the ease with which the 414s entered scores of computers seemed to reveal a high level of negligence among operators of multi-million-dollar computer systems. In effect, a journalist noted, 'they left the front door open and put out the welcome mat' (Covert 1983; Ross 1990). The members of the 414s were not prosecuted, due to their agreement to stop their activities and pay restitutions. Neil Patrick even testified about the dangers of computer hacking before the US House of Representatives in September 1983.

As a result of the extensive news coverage and as a reaction to the growing wave of intrusions, Representative Dan Glickman (D-Kansas) called for an investigation and new laws regarding computer hacking. Thereafter, the Congress enacted the first federal computer crime statute, the 'Counterfeit Access

Device and Computer Fraud and Abuse Act' in 1984. In its first paragraph, the act unmistakably links the topic of computer fraud/crime to national security: it makes it a crime to access a computer without authorisation in order to obtain classified information about the defence or foreign relations of the United States. The act also aimed to protect financial data by outlawing attempts to access and to obtain information from financial records of a financial institution or in a consumer file of a credit-reporting agency. Access for the purpose of using, destroying, modifying, or disclosing information found in a computer system used for government business was also made illegal (Burke 2001). It further gave the Secret Service the jurisdiction to conduct investigations into computer crime in addition to the FBI. This outcome reflects the result of a computer-crime 'turf-battle' between the Secret Service and the FBI (Sterling 1993: Chapter 3). As the Treasury's police, the Secret Service aimed to move from fighting the counterfeiting of paper currency and the forging of cheques to the protection of funds transferred by wire as money became less physical. This goal was reached in part, but the role of the Secret Service subsequently remained marginal in comparison to that of the FBI.

At its inception, the act aimed at the protection of federal government computers, as well as the protection of financial records and credit information on computers belonging to the government and financial institutions. The Congress broadened its scope in 1986, when certain amendments extended protection to 'federal interest computers', defined as referring to computers that the government itself owns or is using, and added three additional types of computer crimes (Dodd 1990; Nemerofsky 2000). In 1996, the act was further amended by the 'National Information Infrastructure Protection Act'. Its definition of a 'protected computer' was expanded enough to effectively cover any computer connected to the Internet (Drummond and McClendon 2001).

In 1988, the ARPANET, the precursor of the Internet, had its first automated network security incident, caused by what is usually referred to as 'the Morris Worm', developed by Robert Morris, a student at Cornell University. This self-replicating automated network attack tool set off an exponential explosion of copies at computers all around the ARPANET. The worm used so many system resources that the attacked computers could no longer function. As a result, 10 per cent of the US computers connected to the ARPANET effectively stopped at about the same time. The General Accounting Office (GAO) assessed the financial damage at between US$10 and US$100 million (GAO 1989), but as with all guesses or statistics concerning the economic damage caused by computer incidents, the basis for these figures is unclear. However, it is safe to say that the worm had a devastating effect upon the Internet at that time, both in terms of overall system downtime and in terms of its psychological impact on the perception of security and reliability of the Internet. The Morris Worm prompted the Defense Advanced Research Projects Agency (DARPA, the new name for ARPA) to charge the Software Engineering Institute, a federally funded research and development centre at Carnegie Mellon University in Pittsburgh, Pennsylvania, with setting up a centre to coordinate communication among experts during security emergencies and to help prevent future incidents (CERT 1988). This centre, now called the Computer Emergency Response Team (CERT) Coordination Center, still plays a considerable role in computer security today – and is the example of a countermeasure on the IT security/technical side (Scherlis *et al.* 1990). Morris was the first case prosecuted under the Computer Act (GAO 1989). After appeals, he was sentenced to three years probation, 400 hours of community service, and a fine of more than US$10,000.

Shortly after the Morris Worm, another incident might have had an even bigger impact: Clifford Stoll, a computer specialist of Lawrence Berkeley National Laboratory in northern California, published a book entitled 'The Cuckoo's Egg', in which he described an international security incident involving the Internet (Stoll 1989). This volume raised awareness that the ARPANET could be used for destructive purposes that went beyond mere pranks or breakdowns. The incident Stoll described was the story of a simple accounting error in the computer records of systems connected to the ARPANET that led him to uncover an international effort, using the network, to connect to computers in the United States and copy information from them. These US computers were not only located at universities but at military and government sites all over the country. He spent a year stalking an elusive, methodical hacker, code named 'Hunter', who was using numerous techniques from simply guessing passwords to exploiting software bugs to setting up bogus 'Cuckoo's Egg' programs to break into US computer systems and steal sensitive military and security information. As was later revealed, Hunter, paid in cash and cocaine, was apparently part of a spy ring that reported to the Committee for State Security (KGB). After their initial discovery in 1988, the process of identification and apprehension of the Hanover hackers by the US and German intelligence and law enforcement agencies took over 18 months, in part because the government agencies Stoll went to at first did not take the issue seriously enough. After this incident, virulent cyber-crime plus the involvement of a foreign intelligence service formed the first type of cyber-threat frame with implications for national security.

The encryption debate and the role of the NSA

Apart from the crime/foreign intelligence cyber-threat package, there was a second theme of importance for the cyber-threat debate at the time: the battle over influence in matters of cryptology. The science of cryptology is the practice of converting information to an obscured form to prevent others from understanding it, often applied to ensure secrecy of important communications. Extensive academic research into modern cryptography began in the open community during the 1970s. Before that time, cryptography had been the sole province of a few groups with exceptional needs for secrecy. When it began to change into a mainstream discipline with a far larger group of stakeholders, the former groups put up considerable resistance.

The Reagan administration's concerns about damaging disclosures of classified information were closely interlinked with questions of cryptology. That concern presented itself in documents such as Executive Order (EO) 12356 of 1982, named 'National Security Information', which prescribed a uniform system for classifying, declassifying, and safeguarding national security information (Reagan 1982a, 1982b; Schroeder 1982), as well as in a number of national security decision directives (NSDD), such as NSDD 19 on the 'Protection of Classified National Security Council and Intelligence Information', NSDD 196 on 'Counterintelligence/Countermeasure Implementations Task Force', and NSDD 197 on 'Reporting Hostile Contacts and Security Awareness'. The most controversial of these security directives were NSDD 84 of 11 March 1983 on 'Safeguarding National Security Information' and NSDD 145 of 17 September 1984 on 'National Policy on Telecommunications and Automated Information Systems Security'. Controversial parts of NSDD 84 – polygraph tests and prepublication review of writing for public consumption – were abandoned after massive opposition from Congress and other interest groups, so that this particular NSDD did not cause much further upheaval. NSDD 145, however, became the first culmination point in the ongoing conflict between the academic and government cryptography communities and ultimately led to the Computer Security Act of 1987, a congressional effort to curb the influence of the NSA when it came to information security.

The NSA is an agency responsible for both collection and analysis of message communications and for safeguarding the security of US government communications against similar agencies elsewhere. Because of its listening task, the NSA had been heavily involved in cryptanalytic research for a number of years, continuing the work of its predecessor agencies that had been responsible for breaking many codes and ciphers during the Second World War. By the 1970s, however, interest in cryptography was growing not only in commercial but also in academic circles, and academic research in cryptography had achieved several major breakthroughs (Diffie and Hellman 1976; Dam and Lin 1996). This led to direct confrontation with the NSA, which insisted on prepublication review clauses in contracts and grants for government-sponsored university research, wanted contact between cryptographers and foreign visitors to remain restricted, and demanded that the NSA be allowed to review material to be presented at open meetings (Saco 1999). One reason for this was that cryptology was on the Commerce Control List (Export Administration Act of 1969, 50USC.App. 2401–20) as well as on the Munitions List (until 1996), along with other items that are 'inherently military in character' and was thus treated as a dangerous good whose export needed to be closely monitored by the national security apparatus (Committee on Science, Engineering, and Public Policy 1982; Office of Technology Assessment 1987: 142).

Furthermore, responsibility for computer security standards within the civilian government resided with the National Bureau of Standards (NBS), part of the Department of Commerce, until 1984. During the 1970s, National Bureau of Standards (NBS) became a pivotal player in the development of computer security standards, particularly of the then widely accepted Data Encryption Standard

(DES), the federal standard for encrypting unclassified, sensitive information since 1976. The result of these developments was that NSA faced unprecedented competition from a civilian agency within the Department of Commerce and from academia in the area of encryption technology, which it viewed as a key national security prerogative (Electronic Privacy Information Center 1998b). At around the same time, the suspicion arose that the algorithm used for DES had been covertly weakened by the intelligence agency so that they – but no one else – could easily read encrypted messages (Beth *et al.* 1992). Such was the situation when NSDD 145 was released.

With NSDD 145, the DoD (as 'Executive Agent') and the NSA (as 'National Manager') were authorised to undertake a 'comprehensive and coordinated' approach to 'protect the government's telecommunications and automated information systems' that 'process and communicate classified national security information and other sensitive information concerning the vital interests of the United States' (Reagan 1984c). In addition, NSDD 145 authorised the NSA to protect communications and computer systems in the private sector. As a result, the NSA was assigned responsibilities that fell outside of the scope of its traditional foreign eavesdropping and military and diplomatic communications security roles. NSDD 145 also permitted the NSA to control the dissemination of government, government-derived, and even non-government information that might adversely affect national security. Some even argued that such a broad definition included *all* kinds of information (Berman 1987; Electronic Privacy Information Center 1998a, 1998b).

On 29 October 1986, National Security Adviser John Poindexter even further expanded the NSA's information security role when he signed the National Telecommunications and Information Systems Security Policy (NTISSP) No. 2, officially titled 'Protection of Sensitive, but Unclassified Information in Federal Government Telecommunications and Automated Information Systems' (Text in Office of Technology Assessment 1987: Appendix B). Poindexter's directive extended the NSA's mandate to include the protection of unclassified sensitive information residing in the commercial databases of private corporations. This would have meant classifying information that had previously been designated 'sensitive but unclassified'. Under the revised definition, 'sensitive' information included not just unclassified information that would 'adversely affect national security' if acquired by hostile nations but any unclassified information that might affect any 'other Federal Government interests' (Poindexter 1986; Richelson 2005), a definition so broad that it could have been applied to almost anything.

This development gave rise to considerable concern within the private sector and in Congress, as well as academic circles, especially since the NSA quickly began to exercise its newfound authority. The last straw was the NSA's announcement that it would stop endorsing the DES after 1988 and would instead focus on a set of classified, hardware-based standards for modular products that were incompatible with the DES (Landau 1994). In the face of such concerns, Congressmen Jack Books and Dan Glickman introduced the Computer

Security Act of 1987. The bill was intended to reverse the executive policy that permitted the intelligence community broad say over the development of technical security standards for unclassified government and non-government computer systems and networks and sought to restore non-national security control over computer security for non-defence-related government agencies and the private sector (Electronic Privacy Information Center 1998b).

The Computer Security Act of 1987 established a federal government computer-security program that would protect sensitive information in federal government computer systems and would develop standards and guidelines for unclassified federal computer systems to facilitate such protection. Specifically, the Computer Security Act once more assigned responsibility for developing government-wide security standards and guidelines for computer systems as well as security-training programs to the NBS (now the National Institute of Standards and Technology, or NIST). Under the law, the role of the NSA was limited to providing technical assistance in the civilian security realm. To further clarify the relationship between the NIST and the NSA, a Memorandum of Understanding (MoU) was formalised in 1989 that established mechanisms for implementing the Computer Security Act of 1987. This MoU, again, was very controversial because of concerns in Congress and elsewhere that it ceded much more authority to the NSA than had been intended under the Act (Rotenberg 1992; Office of Technology Assessment 1994: 143).

The issue was largely unresolved when US President George Bush Sr came into office in 1989. Ever since 1987, there had been a seamless opposition concerning the role of the NSA and its violation of the Computer Security Act. For example, a group called Computer Professionals for Social Responsibility revealed that the NSA had been the driving force behind the selection and development of a standard for digital signatures and that the NIST had attempted to shield the NSA's role in the development of these signatures from public scrutiny (Rotenberg 1992). The digital signature was used by individuals for the authentication of computer messages that travel across the public computer network and for the encryption of private messages. Subsequently, a new twist in the discourse began to emerge more forcefully: the issue of privacy (Electronic Privacy Information Center 1999). Privacy is generally understood as the ability of an individual or group to prevent information about themselves from becoming known to people other than those they choose to give the information to. There are various sorts of privacy; but in our context, the issue is that of privacy from government interference (Schneier and Bansiar 1997).

In continuation of his predecessor's policy, President Bush issued National Security Directive (NSD) 42, entitled 'National Policy for the Security of National Security Telecommunications and Information Systems', on 5 July 1990, which superseded the controversial NSDD 145 (Bush 1990b). After a grass-roots organisation had requested a copy of the revised and (classified) NSD from several agencies in vain, it filed a suit and won, so that the directive was disclosed to the public. The text of the directive, in many points identical to NSDD 145, immediately raised several questions concerning the administration's compliance with the Computer Security Act (Electronic Privacy Information Center 1998a). By its own terms, NSD 42 'expands' the DoD's authority to include 'information systems'. The new NSD 42 granted the NSA broad authority over 'national security systems', a term that had not been defined in the Computer Security Act and thus, it was feared, could be interpreted as required.

The term 'national security systems' gave the director of the NSA broad new authority to set technical standards. Specifically, this term once more eviscerated the distinction between civilian and military computer systems. This was all the more true because the military and intelligence agencies tended to argue that national security included international economic activity. The logical question that followed from this was whether NSD 42 also granted the NSA authority over computer security in the economic sphere. In the end, questions about the extent of military involvement in civilian and private sector computer security remained unresolved (Rotenberg 1992). This situation raised the practical question of whether safeguards designed for use by defence and intelligence agencies could meet the needs of commercial users without jeopardizing US intelligence objectives. It also raised the broader issues of the appropriate role of defence and intelligence agencies in civilian matters and of how openness and free-market forces can coexist with secret operations and restrictions on sensitive information. The debate basically centred on the question of whether 'security' meant the security of US society as a whole, i.e. 'national security' – or whether it only referred to the security of individual users or technical systems and should therefore be handled by authorities other than national security bodies (Berman 1987).

We can see that the period between 1982 and 1992 is dominated by patchy approaches and especially the 'failure' to strengthen the NSA's role in computer security, a situation partially resolved with the Computer Security Act of 1987. This countermeasure was not truly geared towards any external threat but tried to cement the roles and responsibilities of the players within government: the secrecy imperative that had historically dominated the field of communications security was beginning to waver. At that time, cryptology was still one of two sciences (the other being nuclear energy) that was given special status under federal statute (Kahn 1967), but that prerogative was already being weakened by constant opposition from the private sector and academia. The encryption debate, which remains partly unresolved to this day, pitted the US government, particularly its law enforcement, intelligence, and national security interests, against the private sector as the place where the main innovations in information technology were being made.

The national security institutions were concerned about their inability to access electronic communications protected by strong encryption. On the one hand, encryption protects individual and corporate privacy and is a fundamental building block of electronic commerce. On the other hand, police and intelligence agencies oppose denying the government access to electronic information because terrorists and other criminals can use encryption technology to conduct illegal activities while avoiding government monitoring. Though a very specific twist in the cyber-threat debate, the issue remains important and is exemplary for the difficulties inherent in the national security community's relationship to the private sector. In 1993, the Clinton administration proposed a government-designed encryption chip called the 'Clipper chip' as the industry standard, which became a public relations fiasco (Landau 1994; Froomkin 1995, 1996). Until 1996, the US government considered any applications offering more than 40-bit encryption to be 'munitions', and it was therefore illegal to export such technology. The government started to allow the export of 56-bit encryption in 1996, with some restrictions: corporations willing to commit to the development of key escrow encryption products – systems that would accommodate the needs of law enforcement for court-authorised access to electronic communications – were permitted to export 56-bit encryption technologies for up to two years. The law enforcement community in particular wanted to eventually outlaw all forms of encryption that did not contain keys that the government could use to unlock the encrypted communications (Freeh 1997). However, on 14 January 2000, the US government published new encryption export regulations, allowing any encryption commodity or software of any key length to be exported, after a technical review, to commercial firms and other non-government end users in any country except for Cuba, Iran, Iraq, Libya, North Korea, Sudan, and Syria, the alleged 'seven state supporters of terrorism' (White House 1999).

In this struggle, the argument that national security and economic security had become one and the same clearly backfired. Many of the fundamental advances in personal computing and networking during the 1970s and 1980s were made by people influenced by the technological optimism of the new left and the counter-culture, best expressed in Marshall McLuhan's (1964; see also McLuhan and Fiore 1967) predictions that new technology would have an intrinsically empowering effect on individuals. A contradictory mix of technological determinism and libertarian individualism became 'the hybrid orthodoxy of the information age' (Barbrook and Cameron 1995). Many West Coast ex-hippies became involved in developing new information technologies. By the 1990s, some of them had even become owners and managers of high-tech corporations in their own right. The emergence of the so-called 'Californian Ideology', promoted through magazines, books, TV programmes, websites, newsgroups, and net conferences, mirrored their passionate belief in electronic direct democracy, in which everyone would be able to express their opinions without fear of censorship (cf. Barlow 1994, 1996). This was so fundamentally different from what the US government wanted to establish as 'truth' that various exponents of this counter-culture began to forcefully react by promoting their own ideas of reality.

When a condition turns into a problem: the Cuckoo's Egg and the Morris Worm as policy windows

In the following sub-chapters, I will explore how the first threat frames appeared, how they changed over time, and what the main reasons for these changes were. During this first period, the amount of attention given to computer and communications security issues grew incrementally in response to highly publicised incidents such as computer viruses and penetrations of networked computer systems. This development was catalysed by a pivotal change in the technological environment: the proliferation of home computers and the beginnings of widespread networking changed the nature of the threat.

In our discussion of theoretical concepts, we assumed that we should be able to identify a 'securitisation' phase or at least a period during which the issue was first successfully framed as a threat. It is obvious that it is not so simple to identify the exact point in time when the first such framing occurred. It is clear, however, that a closed circle of security professionals from the military was the first group to link information technology to national security due to their monopoly in defining national security matters at the time. We have also argued that a securitisation move in the military domain was not needed per se, because information technology was naturally 'securitised' as part of a bigger development involving the use of technology for military purposes. The fact that technology has always been the major driver for changes in military affairs is widely acknowledged and has been the topic of numerous publications (Krepinevich 1994; Metz and Kievit 1995; Henry and Peartree 1998b; Creveld 1989, 1991). It is also agreed that information has been a key element of warfare since the beginnings of mankind, as asserted by Sun Tzu, the 'darling' of US information warfare pundits. Even though it was first seen mainly as an opportunity or force enhancer, the acceptance of the pre-eminence of information provided a solid basis for the shift towards the vulnerability paradigm in the wake of the major reorientation of security policy after the end of the Cold War.

When the general issue of cyber-crime came to the attention of policymakers, there was a clear link to national security from the start, even though on a different and less urgent level than the one that would be established in the 1990s. The information infrastructure was already being perceived as a weapon as well as a target, but in the years 1981–93, the measures to combat cybercrime focused mainly on digital classified information and the theft thereof by means of computers. Therefore, the main perceived threat was that of the 'foreign intelligence threat'. Cryptology is closely connected to this particular topic, as it plays a key role in the securing of government information. In addition, cryptology is linked to the ability to monitor civilian communications for intelligence reasons and especially the ability to eavesdrop on and to identify criminals. While there was little disagreement when it came to the issue of cyber-crime, cryptology proved a far more difficult topic, as it involved two completely different conceptions of security and went beyond a close-knit security community to include exponents of the private sector and the academia.

According to theory, officials become aware that conditions have turned into problems they need to address as a result of indicators, focusing events, or formal and informal feedback (Kingdon 2003: 90–115). As stated, one of the aims of the case study is to identify policy windows, which can either be problem windows – the result of a new problem that comes to the attention of decision-makers, or political windows – the result of change in the political arena. From the study of official documents, we learn that the condition that was identified as the core of the problem in the 1980s was the spread of information technologies into many aspects of life and especially their link to automated systems. In the period between 1983 and 1992, the link to national security was mainly made via the threat of espionage, which, it was reasoned, had become easier due to the interlinking of information infrastructures. Specifically, the driving forces for threat politics in this period seem to have included the apparent insecurity in the early days of the networked computer environment, the appearance of the first viruses and worms, plus the increasing activity of 'hackers' of all sorts.

All examples from our case study belong to the category of focusing events that made officials become aware that conditions had reached a problematic stage:

- The case of the *414s Gang* is cited by the US Congress in the legislative history of the federal computer crime statute [S.Rep. No. 99–432, 99th Cong. 2d Sess. 5 (1986)]. Though it was just one of many such break-ins, the case was a media event and likely served to make clear that there was need for action: if teenagers were able to penetrate computer networks that easily, it was more than likely that better organised entities such as states would be even better equipped to do so.
- *The Cuckoo's Egg incident* made clear that the threat was not just one of criminals or kids playing games, but that classified or sensitive information could be acquired relatively easily by foreign nationals, or by hackers employed by foreign states for that matter. This incident helped to consolidate the link between the information infrastructure and national security by establishing a link to the more traditional and well-established espionage discourse, in a case of referencing, according to Townson. The impact of this incident was such that it also led to a couple of directives on how to handle data, thus triggering concrete countermeasures on a technical level.
- Another case with considerable impact was the launch of the *Morris Worm*, the first major automated attack, which brought the emerging Internet to a standstill and led to the establishment of the CERT. This case was the first one prosecuted under the new Computer Crime and Abuse Act and generally had a compelling impact on the awareness of the Internet's insecurity. It also led to a number of official reports that scrutinised the emerging issue of information security.

If we turn to indicators and other forms of feedback, we note that their influence is less palpable than that of focusing events. Statistics were not very widespread in the period under discussion, so that there is no apparent link between statistics and the perception of the threat. Some reports, however, seemed to have acted as feedback by bringing the topic to the attention of decision-makers, even though such reports were scarce compared to the 1990s. One early example of a topical report is the GAO (1989) report on computer viruses, written after the Morris Worm incident by request of the Subcommittee on Telecommunications and Finance of June 1989, 'Computer Security Virus Highlights Need for Improved Internet Management'. At that time, the Internet was already well advanced in a development that would turn it 'from a prototype network to a large-scale multi-network' (GAO 1989). The report mainly highlighted the lack of a focal point of responsibility for Internet security, security weaknesses at some sites, and problems in developing, distributing, and installing software fixes for known flaws.

In the same year, another report by the National Academy of Sciences, Computer Science and Telecommunications Board (CSTB) on the 'Growing Vulnerability of the Public Switched Network', sponsored by the National Communications System, argued on a different level when it cautioned that 'Virtually every segment of the nation depends on reliable communications' (Computer Science and Telecommunications Board 1989: 9). The committee concluded that a serious threat to communications infrastructure was developing because public communications networks were becoming increasingly vulnerable to widespread damage from natural, accidental, capricious, or hostile agents (Computer Science and Telecommunications Board 1989: 11–14). This enlargement of the threat from the local, confined space of the early Internet to the larger society is an early instance of later threat frames with a great deal of persuasiveness. This larger threat frame can also be found in a report published by the CSTB in 1990. The report, entitled 'Computers at Risk: Safe Computing in the Information Age', began with the following, now famous, observation:

> We are at risk. Increasingly, America depends on computers. They control power delivery, communications, aviation, and financial services. They are used to store vital information, from medical records to business plans to criminal records. [...] The modern thief can steal more with a computer than with a gun. Tomorrow's terrorist may be able to do more damage with a keyboard than with a bomb.
> (National Academy of Sciences 1991: 7)

The National Research Council's report thus provides early notice of new challenges confronting the protection of US information infrastructures. It looked beyond the protective efforts of individuals and separate organisations to address the broader problems of securing the US national information infrastructure for the first time. As this report was highly influential and the specific threat frame it proposed turned into the dominant one in later years, we will look at the document and its threat frame in more detail in the next sub-chapter. It is difficult to establish with any certainty whether these reports actively shaped decision-makers' perception of the threat or whether they are the expression of an already changed perception, but what we will see below is that these reports are frequently alluded to in later years, in order to stress certain points.

Furthermore, we believe that it was of great importance for the development of countermeasures that the topic gained a lot of attention in popular culture during this period. One particular movie that spurred the imagination was the film *War Games*, released in 1983. In this film, a young hacker sees an advert for online war games and starts trying to hack into the company's server. When he finally gets access, he starts to play a simulated game called 'global thermonuclear war' – unfortunately, he has hacked into the military simulation computer at the Pentagon, which starts to act out a response to an attack from Russia. In the end, the Third World War can barely be averted. Even though rooted in a Cold War mindset, the popular conception of a hacker as a teenage boy hunched over his computer and able to pose a severe threat to national security was both reflected in and popularised by the movie. In addition, the 1980s saw the emergence of the so-called 'cyberpunk culture', spearheaded by the first cyber-thriller novel *Neuromancer* by William Gibson, which gave 'cyberspace' its name. Cyberpunk is a sub-genre of science fiction and dystopian fiction, focusing on advanced technology such as computers or information technology coupled with some degree of breakdown in the social order. The exact impact of these products on the behaviour of policy-makers remains unclear in the absence of any more in-depth research, but it certainly brought the issue to the attention of a broad audience and captured the imagination of the media.

It thus seems as if policy windows had played a role in setting the relevant policy processes into motion. All the identified policy windows are problem windows rather than political windows. Generally speaking, events popularised through the media and government reports have the biggest influence on the political process. The nature of the incidents is connected to the state of the technological *substructure*, which, though already accessible from the outside with a modem, is just turning into a mass phenomenon. We can also see that one particular countermeasure, in our case the NSDD 145, acted as a policy window of some sort – it evoked strong reactions that led to the correction of the proposed NSDD. In this sense, one 'countermeasure' proves to be the triggering event for another countermeasure and clearly reveals struggles between conflicting interests and discourses.

Struggles over the meaning of 'national security'

The key question to be addressed in Phase I or the 'Securitisation phase' concerns the characteristics of the actors that first frame cyber-threats as a national security threat and how they do it. As stated above, actors can be either individuals or groups of individuals who share a set of basic beliefs and have specific resources in a specific institutional setting. We try to find out what different frames exist in which community, at what stage in time, and which particular threat frame wins for what reason. In addition, we want to identify the actors that are active in reframing the issue and see what particular threat frame they promote.

We can identify a variety of actors that played a part in the game of framing the threat in terms of national security in the mid-1980s. As stated, the military was the first to link information technology to security, but it did not perceive information technology as a source of threats until later. As we have shown by alluding to the EMP discussion, the information infrastructure was sometimes seen as a possible target for attacks; in our understanding of the issue, however, the cyber-threat image only truly emerged when the information infrastructure was also considered a likely weapon.

Furthermore, the ideas concerning the vulnerability of information infrastructure ideas seemed to have come from the 'outside': experts who were external to the actual policy process, such as Rona and Stoll, shaped certain ideas and formulated possible countermeasures. It is not surprising that 'experts' shape ideas. The rise of the modern administrative state has led to the expansion and professionalisation of bureaucracies (cf. Blondell 1982). The increasingly technical nature of problems has fostered an increase in the respect paid to technical expertise and, in particular, to that of scientists (Beck 1986, 2001; Haas 1992: 7–11, 1993), an idea that is also an integral part of Bigo's theory. Second, the current systemic environment of world politics, which is characterised by a high degree of complexity and a multitude of relevant actors (Czempiel and Rosenau 1989; Rosenau 1990), has considerably complicated the decision-making processes. This creates conditions of uncertainty where actors must make choices without adequate information about the situation at hand. Complexity and uncertainty in a given issue-area enhances the necessity and thus the role and the influence of expert groups (Haas 1992: 12; Antoniades 2003: 34). Experts also have an intrinsic interest in establishing fields of expertise in which they have the discursive dominance.

It can also be observed that functional actors, who influence decisions in the field and are important in affecting the dynamics of the issue while not themselves participating in the framing process (Buzan *et al.* 1998: 36), play a decisive role. The actors from whom the threat emanates, in our case 'hackers' or 'spies', take on a pivotal role by creating incidents that act as policy windows but do not generate threat frames of their own. Other actors, such as the NSB (later NIST), were also not visibly active themselves in the threat-framing process but were influential in fuelling the encryption debate by their action. In distinguishing between the two, we can identify two kinds of functional actors: actors who are part of the policy-making circles (internal actors) and actors who are situated outside of this process (external actors).

The actors who were visibly involved in the framing process are the typical professionals of security in the US national security and intelligence community: the NSA, the FBI, specialised bodies of Congress, and the president and his staff. No policy entrepreneur seems to have been necessary to fuel the process of threat politics. As we have shown, tension between commercial and military interests dominated public policy-making, as it related to computer security during the 1980s. The most distinctive turf battle with aspects of a discursive struggle took place between the NSA and the private sector/academia. The struggle was mainly about the meaning of 'national security' and about the continued securitisation of cryptology. At the time, the NSA was losing control over this technology and tried to retain it by claiming the need for more security. Furthermore, there was another area in which the agency wanted to stake a claim and push for more influence – computer intelligence-gathering, the most critical element of which is the knowledge of how to exploit computer systems for intelligence reasons.

The Cuckoo's Egg case, where spies were exploiting computer networks on behalf of the Soviet KGB, gave the NSA and other intelligence agencies the opportunity to try to expand their charters in this direction. Later, when GAO official Jack L. Brock testified before the Senate Subcommittee on Government Information and Regulation on the case of a Dutch hacker attack on DoD sites in 1991, claiming that 'at many of the sites, the hackers had access to unclassified, sensitive information', his use of the term 'unclassified, sensitive information' was a boon for the NSA. It could confidently try to resurrect the tenets of NSDD-145 by arguing that it was necessary to protect such information, even though it was available via the publicly accessible Internet (Electronic Privacy Information Center 1998b). However, the Computer Security Act of 1987 and the activity after the revision of NSDD 145 (resulting in NSD 42) progressively restricted the main focus of the NSA's activities to the protection of defence systems, leaving civilian, notably security concerns related to the civil government system, to the NIST. Partly as a result of the changing policy context, the NSA was forced to scale back its interaction with commercial organisations; because of its defence-oriented charter, the NSA could not actively foster the development or widespread dissemination of technology for use in the non-classified or commercial world (National Academy of Sciences 1991: 20–1).

The foreign intelligence threat frame

In the period 1982–93, there are six policy-relevant documents to consider: two EOs, two NSDs, and two Acts of Congress. Both EOs (EO 12382, 13 September 1982, 'President's National Security Telecommunications Advisory Committee' and EO 12472, 3 April 1984, 'Assignment of national security and emergency preparedness telecommunications functions') serve mainly to establish new bodies and advisory boards, indicating that old structures no longer sufficed to tackle the problem and that the issue was seen as 'new' in the sense that knowledge of its causes and consequences first needed to be generated. These two documents do not truly enhance our understanding of cyber-threat frames, as both only implicitly assume a threat focus. EO 12382 does so in the context of implementing specific measures to improve the telecommunications aspects of the US national security posture (Reagan 1982b), and EO 12472 does so in the context of emergency management. It amends Kennedy's memorandum on the National Security Council (NSC), which views telecommunications as a necessary auxiliary tool for emergency management but not as a source of threats (Reagan 1984b).

The two security directives (NSDD 145, 17 September 1984, 'National Policy on Telecommunications and Automated Information Systems Security', and the NSD 42, 5 July 1990, 'National Policy for the Security of National Security Telecommunications and Information Systems') also mainly created new committees and steering groups but had far more serious consequences, as they tried to interfere with fragile power structures.

National Security Decision Directive Number 145 (NSDD 145)

The first official threat frame can be found in the controversial NSDD 145 on 'National Policy on Telecommunications and Automated Information Systems Security', issued on 17 September 1984. The problem as described in this document is that the technological development has led to an increased supply in IT technology, which is therefore proliferating.

> Recent advances in microelectronics technology have stimulated an unprecedented growth in the supply of telecommunications and information processing services within the government and throughout the private sector. As new technologies have been applied, traditional distinctions between telecommunications and automated information systems have begun to disappear. Although this trend promises greatly improved efficiency and effectiveness, it also poses significant security challenges.
>
> (Reagan 1984c)

The document describes the fusion between telecommunications und computers, a development that is seen to bring opportunities as well as dangers. Therefore, this development is depicted as a double-edged sword. Furthermore, it is seen as an issue that concerns both the government and the private sector. The document then specifically addresses the problem as it relates to the US government. The focus is on 'classified national security information', mirroring the concern about data security as described above. The integrity of classified information is seen as a national security issue:

> Within the government these systems process and communicate classified national security information concerning the vital interests of the United States. Such information, even if unclassified in isolation, often can reveal highly classified and other sensitive information when taken in aggregate. The compromise of this [sic] serious damage to the United States and its national security interests.
>
> (Reagan 1984c)

In this document, it is clearly established that the security threat consists of the vulnerability of information networks to external intrusion. It is also stated that 'security', understood in this context as information security, is a vital element of the operational effectiveness of the national security activities of the government and of military combat-readiness, thus making the national-security connotation even more explicit. In particular, the 'hostile intelligence threat' is singled

Intelligence threat, data security, and encryption 61

out: 'Telecommunications and automated information processing systems are highly susceptible to interception, unauthorized electronic access, and related forms of technical exploitation, as well as other dimensions of the hostile intelligence threat' (Reagan 1984c). Overall, there is an emphasis on *foreign* exploitation. The likely reason for this focus is that the national security community conducts extensive background checks on individuals before it grants access to systems or information. Its countermeasures, therefore, tended to emphasise attacks by outsiders (National Academy of Sciences 1991: 20). However, it is striking that we already find allusion to other threat subjects than nation-states, namely terrorist groups and criminals:

> The technology to exploit these electronic systems is widespread and is used extensively by foreign nations and can be employed, as well, by terrorist groups and criminal elements. Government systems as well as those which process the private or proprietary information of US persons and businesses can become targets for foreign exploitation.
> (Reagan 1984c)

As we will see, this threat frame already contains many of the ingredients of later threat frames, even though in a slight variation. The threat subject ranges from foreign nations to terrorists to criminals. The referent object at this stage is limited to government systems and business systems that carry critical information. Further, we can see that it is a fairly narrow threat frame that is concerned mainly with classified material and does not yet encompass the society-threatening aspects of cyber-threats. This can be attributed to the technological substructure, which still lacked the quality of a mass phenomenon that it would acquire once computer networks turned into a pivotal element of modern society (Ellison *et al.* 1997) and once networks in a more abstract sense had become a metaphor for many aspects of modern life in the 1990s (Castells 1996; Arquilla and Ronfeldt 1996, 2001).

As stated by theory, a threat frame also has a prognostic frame, which describes solutions, strategies, tactics, and objectives by which these may be achieved. The prognostic frame is the envisaged countermeasure or policy against the threat. In NSDD 145, it is vaguely stated that a comprehensive and coordinated approach must be taken to protect the government's telecommunications and automated information systems against current and projected threats. The document calls for mechanisms for formulating policy, for overseeing systems security resource programs, and for coordinating and executing technical activities. This is to be achieved through 'telecommunications and automated information systems security', which is defined as 'protection resulting from the application of security measures (including cryptosecurity, transmission security, emission security, and computer security)' and also includes the physical protection of sensitive technical security material and sensitive technical security information. The systems that need to be protected are loosely defined as 'systems which generate, store, process, transfer, or communicate information of use to an adversary' (Reagan 1984c: 1). Naming, and especially signifying, is done more or less involuntarily by labelling various aspects of information-age security.

The measures that NSDD 145 proposes are mainly technical remedies for a technical problem. The goal of these countermeasures is not only to prevent the theft of information through interception, unauthorised electronic access, or related technical intelligence threats but also to prevent tampering with information in order to prevent its exploitation. The enhanced role envisaged for the NSA should also be read as part of the prognostic frame. As we have elaborated above, this point met with great opposition. This shows that it was not the diagnosis as such that was refuted but the means to counter the threat, and therefore the prognostic part of the threat frame. As we will see, this is a pattern that proves true for the entire cyber-threats debate. This is not very surprising because the prognostic threat frame has particular relevance for 'real-world' consequences such as influence, resources, etc. Finally, the motivational framing or the call for action is not elaborate (GAO 1995). It is mainly stressed that compromising classified national security information could pose serious damage to the United States and its national-security interests, and that 'assuring the security of telecommunications and automated information systems which process and communicate classified national security information, and other sensitive government national security information, and offering assistance in the protection of certain private sector information are key national responsibilities' (Reagan 1984c).

All in all, the terminology that is employed is imprecise, and a considerable controversy arose especially over the meaning and use of the term 'sensitive but unclassified' that first appeared in Presidential Directive/National Security Council-24 (PD/NSC-24), signed by President Jimmy Carter in 1977 but was not defined further. The term took centre stage in NSDD 145, but again it was not defined. The absence of a precise definition for such a pivotal concept was widely criticised, especially by the General Accounting Office (GAO): in congressional testimony in 1985, the GAO complained that this directive could conceivably give national security agencies control of the management systems of civilian agencies and private commercial interests 'because it established a new category of "sensitive, unclassified government or government-derived information, the loss of which could adversely affect the national security interest..." without clearly defining the types of information in this category' (GAO 1985: 15; Knezo 2003: 11). This shows that what matters in the discursive struggle is not only naming and signifying but also naming and then *non*-signifying, by keeping established terms as vague as possible. In any discursive struggle, this can be very helpful because ambiguity guarantees a lot of room for manoeuvre.

Apart from this elaborate threat frame, we find a more restricted one in the Computer Crime and Abuse Act in 1984 and 1986. All in all, this is a sub-frame of the main frame. Even though its title includes the word 'crime', the document is also concerned with national security and foreign relations. This signifies a blurring of boundaries of internal and external threats, turning computer crime into more than just crime by linking it to the possible exploitation of classified information, which by definition makes it a national security threat. The text of the act reads as follows:

> Whoever knowingly accesses a computer without authorization or exceeds authorized access, and by means of such conduct obtains information that has been determined by the United States Government [...] to require protection against unauthorized disclosure for reasons of national defense or foreign relations, or any restricted data [...] with the intent or reason to believe that such information so obtained is to be used to the injury of the United States, or to the advantage of any foreign nation [...] shall be punished.
> [Computer Fraud and Abuse Act 1986 (US) 18 USC 1030(a)]

According to this text, what needs to be protected is information to which a specific value, specifically a value linked to national security, is attached. The threat subject is an individual, a 'hacker', who either acts in his own interests or in the interest of a foreign nation. This act seems to be tailored to occurrences such as the Hanover spy case (Cuckoo's Egg), but the first individual actually prosecuted in court under this act was the creator of the Morris Worm. The prognostic part of this threat frame is the level of punishment. As we will show below, this legal instrument became the foundation stone of the countermeasures envisaged to address the cyber-threat. This is in strange contrast to the threat frame, which mainly focuses on foreign exploitation and espionage.

While the Computer Abuse Act and its 1986 update continue until today to serve as the basis for prosecution, the Computer Security Act was mainly a reaction to the perceived encroachment of the NSA after NSDD 145. The importance of words and their meanings was clearly revealed during the Morris Worm case. The awkward wording of the initial versions of the Computer Abuse Act (1984 and 1986) meant that it was unclear whether the prosecutors had to prove that Robert Morris had the specific intent to cause damage. Morris argued that the damage he had caused had been unintentional and, thus, that his action had not been illegal (Eichin and Rochlis 1989; Denning 1990; Froehlich *et al.* 1997). Morris was found guilty, following a jury trial, of violating 18 U.S.C. s 1030(a)(5)(A). He was sentenced to three years on probation, 400 hours of community service, a fine of US$10,050, and the costs of his supervision. His lawyers appealed the conviction to the Circuit Court of Appeals, but the conviction was upheld. His lawyers then appealed to the Supreme Court.

The US Supreme Court decided the question in 1991 by refusing without comment to hear Morris' appeal: the case particularly highlighted the difficulty of prosecuting a creator of a virus who does not necessarily intend the disastrous consequences wrought by the infectious spread of his creation. A GAO report released in 1989 noted other flaws in the federal computer statute. While the law made it a felony to access a computer without authorisation, the law did not define what was meant by 'access' or 'authorisation', the GAO (1989) reported.

This was one specific example of how difficult it is to work with fuzzy issues, fuzzy words, and fuzzy meanings. It made some legal experts worry that computer users who entered a computer system without authorisation, either unwittingly or with the intention of merely looking around, could be given penalties that were overly severe and that the Computer Crime and Abuse Act was a 'bone breaker' law that could transform otherwise law-abiding computer users into felons and inhibit creative uses of computer technology. For many, this piece of legislation would therefore have qualified as an 'extraordinary' or 'exceptional' measure.

Subtle reframing of NSDD 145

The first (subtle) reframing of the threat frame described above occurred under the first Bush administration. There are no additional actors in the game, and no additional conflicts between them discernible. President Bush only slightly updated the controversial NSDD 145. This seems to signify that the topic of cyber-threats was of no big importance for the new administration, except that the latter tried to strengthen the role of the NSA once more: after the passing of the Computer Security Act in 1987, the NSA had lost the struggle over how far it could go in the name of national security. Bush's NSD 42 sought to re-establish the NSA's former prerogatives in the name of national security, thus perpetuating the still-unresolved debate on cryptography.

With NSDD 145 and NSD 42, we have two documents that can be directly compared for changes in the threat frame. We find the following (relevant) differences and similarities: both feature the same threat subjects and stress that the technology to exploit these electronic systems is widespread and is used extensively by foreign nations and can be employed by terrorist groups and criminal elements, as well. Of specific interest, however, are passages that were deleted. For example, the explanation for the need to protect electronic systems is shortened, and there is less emphasis on classified national security information, which was not one of particular concerns to the Bush administration. In addition, a considerable part concerning government involvement with the private sector is deleted, a point that merits further attention.

In 1984, the document had stated that the government had a strong role in encouraging, advising, and even assisting the private sector in identifying systems that handle sensitive non-government information, which was a clear statement that the government wanted the private sector to identify information that was of value for national security. In addition, the government wanted to formulate strategies and measures for providing protection, with information and advice on the implementation of this policy being sought from the private sector. In cases where the implementation of security measures across non-governmental systems was in the interest of national security, the private sector was to be encouraged, advised, and assisted in undertaking the application of such measures (Reagan 1984c). This basically meant that the government was ready to force the private sector to comply with its wishes, which, in connection

Intelligence threat, data security, and encryption 65

with the NSA's expanding role more generally, became a major issue. The fact that this particular section was completely deleted in the 1990 document can be regarded as a sign that the pivotal role of the private sector in the protection of information infrastructures was now even more acknowledged. The only passage that remained unchanged from the earlier version stated that initiatives with the private sector were to be sought to maintain, complement, or enhance information systems security (Bush 1990b).

We have already mentioned the vagueness of the terminology in NSDD 145. NSD 42 was far from being clearer, on the contrary. It introduced a new term – the government's 'national security telecommunications and information systems (national security systems)' (Bush 1990b). This phrase, which was not defined in the Computer Security Act, again raised questions given the expansive interpretation of 'national security' historically employed by the military and intelligence agencies and the broad scope that such a term might have when applied to computer systems within the federal government. The prognostic frame remained unchanged. Together with a lot of the introductory text, the call for action was deleted. As NSD 42 clearly takes NSDD 145 as a starting point, such motivational framing might not have seemed necessary any longer.

As we can see, the differences between the threat frames in NSDD 145 and NSD 42 are very slight. The threat subject remains the same. The referent object is also essentially the same, but there is far less emphasis on the link between classified information and national security, heralding a shift that we can observe throughout the 1990s. There is less emphasis on defining the referent object; in fact, this point seems to have been left deliberately vague. There is, on the one hand, a difference in terminology and, on the other, a difference that does not become obvious in the threat frame – namely the increasingly important role that is allotted to cooperation with the private sector.

4 Asymmetric vulnerabilities and the double-edged sword of information warfare

Developments in the military domain

While cyber-threats had played a minor role in the overall security strategy and orientation of the administrations of both Ronald Reagan and George H. W. Bush, during the Clinton administration they were anchored firmly within the broader security political agenda as a 'new' threat and gained a prominent role in the national security strategy. To understand this development, we must first take into account the major reorientation of general security policy after the end of the Cold War. At the core of the debate lie the problem of 'new' threats and the inability of the traditional security apparatus to counter them.

Unlike in the 1980s, the military was initially the driving force behind the shaping of the threat perception in the 1990s. As a result of the military's involvement, the biggest catchphrase in the debate was 'asymmetric vulnerabilities': the advantages offered by the use and dissemination of information and communication technologies (ICT) were seen to entail a disproportional vulnerability, which led experts to fear that those enemies who were likely to fail in conventional conflict with the US war machine might instead plan to bring the United States to its knees by striking against vital points on its territory (Berkowitz 1997) – points that are essential for national security and for the essential functioning of industrialised societies as a whole and not necessarily to the military specifically. This had a significant impact on the drafting of countermeasures.

Furthermore, and as I have previously argued, the rapid development of the information infrastructure played a considerable role in the perception of the threat at the time. Some argue that the beginnings of the current information revolution go back to the invention of the telegraph (Alberts *et al.* 1997), but it was only in the early 1990s that a confluence of events brought about what can be described as a 'techno-crescendo' of information revolution dreams, when computers became popular with the masses and knowledge workers began to outnumber factory workers (Kushnick 1999: 22). One of the most noteworthy features of this more recent technological environment is the tendency towards 'connecting everything to everything' and thus creating vast open networks of different sizes and shapes (Ellison *et al.* 1997). It was this marriage of computers and telecommunications and the worldwide assembly of systems such as advanced computer systems, databases, and telecommunications networks that make electronic information widely available and accessible – sometimes called the global information infrastructure – that helped turn the current revolution into a mass phenomenon of grand proportions with a major impact on national security matters.

The Internet as a key component of the networked global information infrastructure is often used as a showcase for the inherent insecurity of this technological environment. Since every computer that is 'online', or connected to a larger part of the global information infrastructure, becomes part of the Internet, this insecurity weighs particularly heavy, as every such machine becomes, in theory, susceptible to attack and intrusion. Much of this inherent insecurity is due to 'historical' reasons: the Internet began in the 1960s as the ARPANET, a US Department of Defense (DoD) project to create a nationwide computer network that would continue to function even if a large portion of it were destroyed in a nuclear war or natural disaster (Denning 1997). During the next two decades, the network that evolved was used primarily by academic institutions, scientists, and government institutions for research and communications. All of the early network protocols that still form part of the Internet infrastructure were thus designed for openness and flexibility, while security was a secondary consideration. In the early 1990s, finally, the nature of the Internet changed significantly when the US government began pulling out of network management and commercial entities offered Internet access to the general public for the first time, in a development that coincided with the advent of increasingly powerful, yet reasonably priced personal computers with easy-to-use graphical operating systems (Berners-Lee 1999).

The commercialisation of the Internet had a considerable impact on making the network inherently insecure because of significant market-driven obstacles to information technology (IT) security: there is no direct return on investment, time-to-market impedes extensive security measures, and security mechanisms often have a negative impact on usability (Näf 2001), so that security was and is often sacrificed for functionality. Beyond the various governing boards that work to establish policies and standards, the Internet that emerged was bound by few rules and answers to no single organisation. Thus, the Internet was seen as a primary example of an *unbounded system*, a system characterised by distributed administrative control without central authority, limited visibility beyond the boundaries of local administration, and lack of complete information about the network (Ellison *et al.* 1997). While conventions exist that allow the different parts of the Internet to work together, there is no global administrative control to assure that these parts behave in accordance with these conventions (Akdeniz 1999; Cukier 1999; Giacomello 1999; Baird 2002). To a large part, it was the extensive and widespread dependence on the Internet that called attention to the importance of information to national security in the first place (Campen 1992; Campen *et al.* 1996; Hundley and Anderson 1997; Chapman 1998; Campen and Dearth 1998; Halperin 2000).

In this chapter, I will analyse the development of cyber-threat frames in the military domain. First, I will look at the development of the information warfare

(IW) doctrine and its impact on the cyber-threats debate. Second, I will look at how this doctrine was employed during the first conflict waged (not only, but also) in cyberspace: the Kosovo conflict. Third, several incidents that involved defence computers and that seemed to highlight the increasing vulnerability of this infrastructure are scrutinised. Finally, I will look at the threat frames in military documents and show how it became clear that the military could not play a major role in countering cyber-threats.

Asymmetry and the development of the IW doctrine

Throughout the Cold War, asymmetry had already been an important element of US strategic thinking but was seldom called by that name. Matching Soviet quantitative advantages in Europe with qualitative superiority on the side of the United States and North Atlantic Treaty Organisation (NATO) was integral to US strategy, as expressed in the concept of massive retaliation in the 1950s. While concerns about these asymmetric threats prompted a series of US responses to perceived Soviet preponderance in some areas, asymmetry also became applicable to other forces without the size and resources of the USSR, such as the National Front for the Liberation of South Vietnam (Alexander 2004). Asymmetry also took central stage in the analytical method developed by Andrew Marshall and Albert Wohlstetter of the RAND Corporation, which looked for imbalances between two forces (Wohlstetter 1959, 1961; Husain 2003; Berkowitz 2003). But only after the Cold War did the United States truly develop a fear that its huge conventional military dominance would force any kind of adversary – states or sub-state groups – to use asymmetric means, such as weapons of mass destruction, information operations (IO), or terrorism.

The gist of asymmetric tactics is the intention to circumvent an opponent's advantage in capabilities by avoiding his strengths and exploiting his weaknesses (Kolet 2001). The fear of asymmetric forms of warfare can ultimately be seen as part of the DoD's struggle to understand the post–Cold War security environment. Basically, since the global distribution of power was unbalanced, it followed that asymmetric strategies would be a natural evolution (Metz and Johnson 2001: 2; Blank 2003): The United States, as the only remaining superpower, was seen as predestined to become the target of asymmetric warfare. The spread of IT had a substantial influence on this perception and was seen as a factor making it much easier to attack the United States asymmetrically, as such an attack no longer required big, specialised weapons systems or an army: borders, already porous in many ways in the real world, were non-existent in cyberspace. For the United States and its armed forces, this meant preparing to oppose a 'new' threat, which had had low priority before, and which, so it seemed, made old security political strategies and architectures obsolete.

In general, the Second Persian Gulf War of 1991 created a watershed in US military thinking about IW. Alan Campen, one of the first analysts who wrote about this issue, stated that the Gulf War 'differed fundamentally from any previous conflict' in that 'the outcome turned as much on superior management of knowledge as [...] upon performances of people or weapons' (Campen 1992: vii). A small American task force led a pinpoint attack on Iraqi radar and communication systems, preventing the Iraqi forces from gathering information about what was going on in their western desert. At the same time, allied flanking units used geographical positioning systems and a well-defended network to keep observing, while remaining oriented within the larger battle plans (Biddle 1996; Alexander 2004).

As a result of the conflict, the concept of a Revolution in Military Affairs (RMA) began to gain ground. On the one hand, there was an increasing desire to move forward with the integration of advanced intelligence, surveillance, and reconnaissance systems with stealthy, long-range, precision weapons systems that would establish dominance in future battlefield engagements, and on the other, RMA thinkers stressed the importance of developing a concept that, until then, had only been loosely articulated, known as IW, in which the ability to degrade or even paralyse an opponent's command, control, communications, and intelligence (C3I) systems was emphasised (Rattray 2001: 314–15; O'Hanlon 2000). Furthermore, American military thinkers began to establish the implications of the conflict and publish scores of books on the topic. For example, David Ronfeldt and John Arquilla attributed the success of the United States and its international allies to the preservation of their own networks coupled with the disruption of the enemy's. From cases like this, Ronfeldt and Arquilla derived the famous paradigm of network-centric warfare, stating that large armed forces operating in centralised command structures were not suited for such combat and were in fact vulnerable. Instead, small, heterogeneous units operating within a network would be the most effective agents. Digital networks, such as the Internet or a group's intranet, would become important battlefields (Arquilla and Ronfeldt 1997b). In general, a cottage industry in IW concepts, studies, and proposals arose in the 1990s (Mahnken 1995; Molander *et al.* 1996; Campen *et al.* 1996; Alberts and Papp 1997; Arquilla and Ronfeldt 1997a; Alberts *et al.* 1997; Arquilla and Ronfeldt 1999; Copeland 2000). At the same time, books like the Tofflers' *War and Anti-War* heightened the awareness and study of implications of IW at a popular level (Toffler and Toffler 1993).

US experts developed the belief that the RMA would reinforce established tendencies that would make the US's military capabilities far superior to that of any other country or even of any group of countries, according to what they called 'America's Information Edge' (Nye and Owens 1996). These thinkers hold that speed, knowledge, and precision will minimise casualties and lead to the rapid resolution of wars, thus minimizing the problems associated with the challenges to the political utility of force, reducing risks far enough to maintain public support for military operations (Metz 2000a, 2000b). In this reasoning, the central resources of conflicts are no longer physical weapons, but the abstract information processes and contents, which moves the object of warfare from the tangible realm to the abstract (Waltz 1998: 10). There was a gradual move from the physical battlefield towards the 'noosphere' (Arquilla and

70 *Asymmetric vulnerabilities*

Ronfeldt 1999: x), an enlargement of battlefields to include the virtual domain and, ultimately, the human mind.

But the military also slowly began to grasp the implications of IW in terms of its own vulnerability. After the Gulf War, a twofold debate developed that was triggered by the benefits of the 'information differential' provided by command, control, communications, computers and intelligence (C4I) component systems employed in the Gulf, as well as by the experiences with the threat of data intrusion as perpetrated by hacker attacks during the conflict (Devost 1995: 10). Even though military computers that are connected to the Internet generally do not contain confidential information and do not carry out vital tasks, such computers were nevertheless used for logistics, accounting, and personnel management. At the time of the Gulf War, the United States used the Internet to transmit logistics information, sometimes even without encryption (Brandt 1995). In the spring of 1991, during Operation Desert Storm in the Gulf, computer hackers from the Netherlands accessed US military computers connected to the Internet. In all, around 34 DoD sites were penetrated, according to the General Accounting Office (GAO 1991). This incident was one among some of the key incidents that helped bring home the realisation of 'vulnerability'.

On a different level, the reaction to the technological developments after the Gulf War manifested itself in the publication of new doctrinal papers that included an information component. IW as a concept was formally launched in December 1992 with the dissemination of DoD Directive 3600.1, classified Top Secret. As apparent by allusions to it (e.g. in Defense Science Board 1994) and later revealed by an unclassified version, published in 1995 and subsequently revised in October 2001 (DoD 2001a), the concept included both offensive and defensive aspects. Early definitions of IW depict it as 'actions taken to achieve information superiority by affecting adversary information, information-based processes, information systems, and computer-based networks while defending one's own information, information-based processes, information systems, and computer-based networks' (Defense Science Board 1996). In many points, this is synonymous with the 'C4I for the Warrior' vision released by the Joint Chiefs of Staff in 1992 (Joint Staff 1992: 1; Fredericks 1997), showing the closeness of the two concepts and the origin of IW ideas. The ultimate lesson from the Gulf War, so it seems, was that the ability to 'see' the battlespace was the key to victory in the newly emerging environment. The main goal of the armed forces became thus to dominate the information spectrum and to obtain *information superiority*. Information superiority is 'the capability to collect, process, and disseminate an uninterrupted flow of information while exploiting or denying an adversary's ability to do the same' (Joint Chiefs of Staff 1996: 16) or, in other words, superiority in the generation, manipulation, and use of information sufficient to assure military dominance for the side that possesses it, which requires success in both offensive and defensive IW operations (Libicki 1997a, 1997b).

In the summer of 1994, before the doctrinal development started to gain traction, the Defense Science Board (DSB), a Federal Advisory Committee established to provide independent advice to the secretary of defence, published an early and comprehensive discussion of IW concepts. The study, entitled 'Report of the Defense Science Board Summer Study Task Force on Information Architecture for the Battlefield' (Defense Science Board 1994), provided a major impetus to official efforts and concerns surrounding a strategic level of IW (Rattray 2001: 318). According to the authors of the report, 'Information Warfare […] is a national strategic concern. Our economy, national life and military capabilities are very dependent on information – information often vulnerable to exploitation or disruption' (Defense Science Board 1994: B-7). In this 1994 study, IW is already depicted as a double-edged sword. The study group notes an overall dependency of modern life on ICT. This problem, according to the report, equally affects the military not because of its task of defending the nation but because it is heavily reliant on the civilian infrastructure (Defense Science Board 1994: B-8). It follows logically that the protection of these assets cannot be solely a military challenge. The blurring of boundaries between civil and military responsibilities and contexts becomes obvious when the authors stress that the use of the word 'warfare' in the term IW does not limit IW to a military conflict, declared or otherwise, as IW targets the entire information infrastructure of an adversary – political, economic, and military, throughout the continuum of operations from peace to war. Because they can be used in peacetime, in preparation for war, and in war, IW activities blur the concept between peace and war (Defense Science Board 1994: 28).

Similar topics were addressed in a report of the Joint Security Commission called 'Redefining Security'. The Joint Security Commission (1994) was convened on 11 June 1993 and tasked with developing a new approach to security that would assure cost-effective security measures in times of shrinking defence budgets. This general study on security after the end of the Cold War features a very strong focus on information systems. Major issues covered by the report include classification and problems concerning the handling of sensitive information in the information age, pointing to the fact that these issues were far from having been resolved in the 1980s. In accordance with the DSB report, the Joint Security Commission warned that computer networks were likely to be the battlefield of the future and that the risk was not limited to military systems. Also, the report considered the security of information systems to be one of the top priorities, creating a new sense of urgency:

> The Commission considers the security of information systems and networks to be the major security challenge of this decade and possibly the next century and believes that there is insufficient awareness of the grave risks we face in this arena.
>
> (Joint Security Commission 1994: 1)

According to the commission, if an enemy attacked the unprotected civilian infrastructure (for example, the public telephone system), the potential economic and other results could be disastrous. This was one of the reasons why information risks were promoted as a prime threat of the coming century.

At the same time, doctrinal development in the United States continued, including plans for offensive use of IW: after the Air Force (1995) had published a seminal document entitled 'Cornerstones of Information Warfare' and the Army had followed suit with its Field Manual 100–6 (Department of the Army 1996), the concept of information superiority also took centre stage in the Joint Chiefs of Staff's 'Joint Vision 2010' paper, released in July 1996 by the then Chairman General John Shalikashvili (Joint Chiefs of Staff 1996). The trend seemed to limit IW to offensive military measures in times of crisis or war. Early publications had regarded IW as a form of warfare at the strategic/security political level for the entire time scale of peace-crisis-war, command-and-control warfare (C2W) as the military function at the operative level, and IO at the tactical level. This began to change around the mid-1990s when IO began to be understood as actions taken at every level of war. Acknowledging this, the DoD and the Joint Chiefs of Staff moved to adopt the term IO instead of IW in 1997, the main rationale for the change being that the term 'warfare' was more generally perceived as a specific term dealing with actions in a crisis or conflict, whereas the term 'operations' could deal with peacetime military missions as well (Rattray 2001: 328–9; Dunn 2002: 118–19). Dropping the word 'war' in dealing with information activities was an elegant solution not only because the revised term stresses or implies the non-violent nature that such undertaking could have, but also because the activities included such a wide range of actors outside the military realm.

By 1998, the US military had developed a Joint Doctrine for Information Operations (Joint Publication 3–13), which also covers computer network attacks on civilian infrastructures (Joint Chiefs of Staff 1998). The main emphasis of this document is on organizational transformation, on the strategic, operational, and tactical planning aspects of IO, and on training through exercises, modelling, and simulation as key ingredients to successful IO. The threats faced are seen as more ambiguous and regionally focused than during the Cold War period, leading to a wide variety of factors that challenge stability in the areas of responsibility. To ensure effective operations in this new security environment, commanders must achieve and sustain information superiority. To accomplish this, they must integrate offensive and defensive aspects of IO. Information superiority or battlespace illumination is meant to provide commanders with a near-perfect picture of the battlefield so that they can make near-perfect decisions. This means that they have to have access to all of the latest available information, anytime and anywhere. To enable this, the military developed plans to implement a 'System of Systems' (Owens 1995; Mahnken 1995), a highly capable network for information exchange and related services that also holds the bulk of battlespace knowledge (Copeland 2000: 56–61). The different parts of this system are linked by what has been called a 'Global Grid' or 'the Grid', the means by which each part of the system is linked and can be accessed.

IO as defined in Joint Publication 3–13 are applied across all phases of an operation, the whole range of military operations and at the strategic, operational, and tactical level of war; they involve actions taken to affect the adversary's information and information systems while defending one's own information and information systems, taking advantage of the world's growing sophistication, connectivity, and reliance on IT. The commander is told to apply the term 'adversary' broadly to include a wide range of organisations, groups, or decision-makers. IO may be conducted across the range of military operations, hopefully having their greatest impact on adversary decision-makers in peace-time and during the initial states of a crisis. The primary goal is therefore to maintain peace, defuse crises, and deter conflict. If deterrence fails, however, all IO capabilities might be applied to meet the stated objectives (Joint Chiefs of Staff 1998: Chapter II, 7).

The United States thus propagated a doctrine that went far beyond being a mere guideline for technology-supported military operations; it openly considered the use of non-military and asymmetrical alternatives in international conflicts. The candid announcement of the intention to focus activities in conflicts on IO and furthermore to exploit IO as a tool for international politics detached from military battlefield operations – e.g. to conduct computer espionage and sabotage, as well as 'truth projection', a form of 'perception management' defined as 'actions to convey and/or deny selected information and indicators to foreign audiences to influence their emotions, motives, and objective reasoning' (Department of Defense 2001c), over electronic mass media at all times – increased the worldwide proliferation of these ideas.

But, in spite of the growing interest and the great efforts made in this field, the US military had not acquired the capability to successfully wage a large-scale (cyber-) war by 1999. The few cyber-missions during the Kosovo war showed this quite clearly. The US Air Force carried out some cyber-attacks against the Serbian air defence system but afterwards came under heavy criticism for the inefficiency of these measures (Dunn 2002).

Kosovo: the first war fought in cyberspace

In 1999, the NATO's intervention against Yugoslavia (known as Operation Allied Force) marked the first sustained use of the full spectrum of IO components in combat. During Operation Allied Force, both sides used IW aspects to harm the enemy. Much of this involved traditional use of propaganda and disinformation via the media, but there were also extensive efforts to intercept the other side's communications, to jam or deceive sensors, and to conduct other forms of electronic warfare (Cordesman 2000). The increasing use of the Internet during the conflict also gave it the distinction of being the 'first war fought in cyberspace' or the 'first war on the internet' (Denning 2001b).

The most important component of NATO's 'information operations' in this conflict still proved to be the traditional bombing of Serbia's command-and-control (C2) infrastructure. C2W consists of attacks against the leadership to 'decapitate' the enemy's command structure and sever it from the body of its command forces (Libicki 1995). This concept is not new, but efforts to coordinate C2W aspects in a joint, high-tech environment had only been undertaken in the early 1990s, which led to a quasi-substitution of C2W with C4I. Even though NATO changed its justification for its offensive operations against Serbia and its military objectives several times during Operation Allied Force, the core intention remained to weaken the Yugoslav military and security forces in order to impair their ability to wage combat operations. C2W, in the context of IO, seeks to weaken the adversary's ability to direct the disposition and employment of forces. The principal problem with the Serbian C2 infrastructure proved to be its dual-use character: the dual-use nature of targets created rightful questions concerning NATO's selection of targets, particularly since the alliance kept insisting that its aircraft were only targeting militarily significant targets while taking all possible measures to avoid civilian damage (Dunn 2002: 139–42).

Targets included the headquarters of the Serbian Socialist Party and Milosevic's private residence, the Yugoslav and Serbian Interior Ministries, the Yugoslav Army headquarters and the Defence Ministry, but also the Serbian state television building, as well as power transmission facilities at Obrenovac and elsewhere. In terms of the classification presented in the table in the Chapter 1, this measure was categorised as a physical/physical activity. The strikes destroyed the five main electric yards that distributed power to the Serbian armed forces, 'the power which supplies his [Slobodan Milosevic's] airfields, his headquarters, his communication systems, his command-and-control network; and no power means no runway lights, no computers, no secure communications' (Shea 1999b). They were destroyed by 'graphite bombs' that caused the transformer yards to short out, rather than disabling the generators themselves. Later, heavier munitions destroyed the grid completely. NATO stressed that by cutting off electricity, it had forced the Yugoslav army to divert large amounts of fuel to very inefficient generators, 'another way of choking off their military's ability to move and to support itself' (Jertz 1999).

Apart from bombings, the conflict also saw the widespread use of Psychological Operations (PSYOPS), which, according to doctrine, are based on the projection of 'truth' with credible messages. Although nothing new, PSYOPS gained new prominence as part of the general doctrine governing IO. They are basically designed to convey selected information and indicators to foreign leaders and foreign populations to influence their emotions, motives, objective reasoning, and ultimately their behaviour, to get the 'human factor' to favour friendly objectives. Examples of such operations include promises, threats of force or retaliation, and conditions of surrender (Department of the Air Force 1998: 11). In Kosovo, PSYOPS measures were not a great success. The two main activities consisted of dropping leaflets and broadcasting Western information: by the end of May, the alliance had dropped over 50 million leaflets, most of them dumped off aircrafts and carried by the wind. Several different types of leaflets were released, both in English and in Serbo-Croatian (Jertz 2001). However, there was never any indication that any of these had an effect on the morale of the Serbian forces. An official Yugoslav Army spokesman later called the leaflets 'clumsily, almost amateurishly written, lacking the basic knowledge of the people's spirit', as well as featuring poor Serbian wording and syntax (quoted in Arkin 1999).

The other major PSYOPS operation was the employment of EC-130 'Commando Solo' planes – airborne radio stations transmitting one-hour programmes four times daily. They broadcast NATO briefings as well as some news reports from Radio Free Europe and Voice of America, officially written by independent journalists for both television and radio, interspersed with European pop music. The efforts were unable to affect the FRY state media: 'Commando Solo' was hampered by the air defence threat in the area when it tried to broadcast directly to the Yugoslav troops, since it is a slow-moving platform and thus an easy target. Fear of anti-aircraft defences also forced it to fly far away from Belgrade, its signals being far too weak to affect TV coverage at all (Satchell 1999). The upshot of these efforts was that attempts to influence Serbian emotions and motives with credible messages failed. Serbian President Slobodan Milosevic maintained information superiority over his own people at all times.

A thoroughly new development from the total wars of the twentieth century is that all possible channels with the other side remained open throughout the campaign: telephone calls, faxes, and e-mails all continued to cross boundaries (Ignatieff 2000). In Kosovo, the interlinked networked world created conditions of relative transparency that made it easier for both sides to anticipate each other's next move and also personalised and documented the conflict in a unique way. The military was aware of the impact of instantaneous broadcast, the global availability of the same data and information to all the conflict parties, and the effects on the strategic direction and the range of military operations. NATO regarded Milosevic as an 'opponent with a very comprehensive intelligence-gathering organization' (Shea 1999a). Its spokespeople claimed more than once that too much information given at the daily press briefings would jeopardise the safety of NATO troops and endanger its projects and operations, especially because they believed that the Serbs monitored TV very closely and used that information to make various defensive calculations (Bacon 1999). The alliance was also aware of the fact that the Yugoslav army had a network of 'ham radio' operators who monitored communications among aircraft. Because the lack of interoperable secure communications among the NATO member states forced them to rely on non-secure methods of transmission (Cohen and Shelton 1999), they had to assume that some of the aviators' conversations could be heard, which likely gave advance warning of some targets (Bacon 1999).

Besides these impacts on military operations, the Kosovo conflict witnessed the rise of one very important issue: the use of the Internet in conflicts by a wide variety of actors. It was the first armed conflict in which all sides, including a variety of actors not directly involved, had an active presence on the Internet and the first conflict where the Internet was used extensively for the exchange and publication of conflict-relevant information, some of which could only be found online. Organisations and individuals throughout the world used the Internet to publish information on the conflict. Governments and government-related organisations tended to upload material that supported their official policies. NATO used the Internet as a primary distribution channel for material such as spy satellite imagery that showed targets before and after they were hit, cockpit videos, transcripts of press conferences and morning briefings, and slides presented there. In some more clearly politically motivated cases, it was also used to request support for political activities. The London-based Kosova Task Force, for example, relied on the Internet to coordinate its actions: to mobilise support, it distributed action plans to Muslims and supporters of Kosovo (Denning 2001b). Serbs used e-mail distribution lists to reach tens of thousands of users, mostly in the United States. These e-mails, which for the most part were sent to US news organisations, called for an end to the bombing, some of them using heated anti-NATO rhetoric, others containing moving stories describing life during the bombardment (Denning 2001b: 5–8). Some newsgroups were flooded with thousands of postings on Kosovo each day. Most of the contributions just aimed at fighting a war of words, abusing the other side. Others, however, contained interesting information and rumours or questioned the reliability of NATO's press briefings, pointing to inconsistencies in their accounts. On one military string of e-mails, plane spotters noted the take-off times of aircraft from British bases, information that might have been useful for the Serbian military (Taylor 1999; Jertz 2001).

It is indeed likely that the intelligence services of both sides monitored the digital traffic. In anticipation of Serbian censorship measures, Western private parties set up anonymous remailers, so that individuals who feared government reprisals could post their messages to discussion forums without being identified. However, censorship or attempts to change outgoing e-mail messages occurred only sporadically, if at all (Denning 2001b: 6–7): it appears likely that this kind of information flow across battle lines appeared too valuable to be stopped. NATO claimed to have deliberately abstained from bombing Internet service providers or shutting down the satellite links providing Internet services to Yugoslavia because 'full and open access to the internet can only help the Serbian people know the ugly truth about the atrocities and crimes against humanity being perpetrated in Kosovo' (Taylor 1999) Serbs thought that Serbian accounts would evoke sympathy and make the Western public more doubtful of their leader's actions, eventually undermining public support, while NATO thought that allowing the Serbian people to communicate with democratic voices in the West would weaken their morale, and in turn erode their support for the regime. While the first assumption was partly right, the second was not: hopes that communication of the Serbian people with democratic voices in the West would undermine their support of the regime remained fruitless; even though Serbs had access to Western news reports through the Internet and via satellite and cable television, many simply did not believe the Western media: they considered the coverage on Western television stations such as CNN and Sky News to be as biased as the news on the Yugoslav stations (Satchell 1999).

Nonetheless, in this conflict, where public opinion was the main target of political rhetoric, the Internet became a valuable source of additional and especially of alternative information. As the NATO briefings began to evoke an escalating sense of frustration and irritation among journalists – the alliance's aggressive information policy also included the dissemination of false and speculative stories (Goff 1999) – they looked for other ways to get to relevant information. Transcripts of press briefings show that journalists actively used the Internet as an alternative source of information to supplement the official information provided by NATO. This aspect is important for credibility struggles: in the extensive media war, it was not enough to justify actions by trying to claim that Right was on the alliance's side and stressing that the military action was effective: alternative sources of information seriously challenged NATO's credibility more than once, so that the alliance was in danger of losing the propaganda battle not only against the enemy but also on the home front (Dunn 2002).

Apart from the propaganda war, one pattern that seems of significance is the online activity called 'hacktivism'. 'Hacktivism' stands for the merger of hacking and activism, covering operations that use hacking techniques for political-activist reasons, mostly directed against a target's Internet site with the intent to disrupt normal operations but not causing serious damage (Denning 2001b). In hacktivism, the Internet is mainly used to draw attention to a cause, helped by the news media that report readily and regularly on such incidents. This was also the case with attacks on various Internet servers during the Kosovo conflict. Disruption of the NATO server, for example, began on March 27: the attacks included so-called 'ping'-bombardment to cause denial of service, e-mail spamming attacks, and viruses. After the bombing of the Chinese embassy in Belgrade, Chinese hackers joined the online war, targeting US government sites, including the White House site, which was unavailable for three days (Brewin 1999).

Actions that not merely deny information but also cause destruction by replacing content are slightly more aggressive: the Serbian hacker group, for example, substituted two US government sites with anti-NATO sites in the beginning of April, calling NATO the 'National American Terrorist Organization'. On the other side, 'Dutchthreat', a Dutch hacker group, broke into Yugoslav web servers and replaced an anti-NATO site with a pro-NATO 'Help Kosovo' page. Several Russian hacker groups also participated in targeting and changing NATO websites (Dunn 2002: 150). A Serbian newspaper even claimed that a member of the hacker group 'Black Hand' had broken into a US Navy computer and had deleted all data. DoD officials never commented on the incident, but nevertheless, US Navy servers did remain temporarily unavailable at the end of March 1999 (Bendrath 1999). The Hacker News Network later announced that around 14 military or other governmental websites had been hacked in connection with Operation Allied Force. Despite the high degree of attention that these denial-of-service and defacement attacks garner, they are only directed against an organisation's public face and are relatively harmless, even though they are considered to be an inconvenience as well as an embarrassment. But the success of such attacks is generally limited, especially since most of the attackers involved are only teenagers. Apart from the economic impact, which is very hard to measure, the political impact of hacktivism attacks is also highly questionable.

The question remains whether any of these attacks were state-sponsored and therefore fall under the definition of strategic IW. A report by the Center for Strategic and International Studies (CSIS) on homeland defence makes it sound that way when it says: 'Serbia launched a computer attack on the NATO web page – perhaps the first attack of its kind.' (Cordesman 2000: 45). Other sources maintain that it is rather doubtful whether the Yugoslav government orchestrated these attacks: an after-action review of the alleged Serbian attacks on DoD websites and computer systems asserts that it is not clear whether any of these were sponsored by the Yugoslav government (cf. Wolfe 1999). Successful attacks against internal NATO military C2 networks are unlikely anyway, because the latter are administered through separate channels that are not directly accessible over public networks and are protected by highly efficient security measures as well as by operating systems and other software that is not commercially available and therefore cannot be exploited for 'bugs'. Other reports claim that NATO was able to penetrate some Yugoslav air defence systems in order to manipulate and alter data to protect NATO's attacking aircraft (Cordesman 2000: 47; Hoffmann 1999). It is uncertain how much, if any, of the false target information actually appeared on Serbian radars and data read-outs. The primary method of attack seems to have been the projection of false radar images supported by false communications and emissions designed to deceive Serbian electronic intelligence (Fulghum 1999: 33–6).

There is also rather substantive evidence against the rumours that during Operation Allied Force, the United State launched the first offensive 'cyber-war' in history. The numerous publications and press releases on this topic as well as military rhetoric before and even during the conflict raised expectations that this new warfare tool would be employed in conflict. The rumours reached their first apex at the end of May 1999, when a Newsweek article reported on the launch of computer attacks on Yugoslav systems by the United States (Vistica 1999). The article quoted defence analysts as saying that US computer hackers had burrowed into Serbian government e-mail systems to read Belgrade's mind on a daily basis, while others had used the Internet to infiltrate the global banking systems in search of accounts held by Milosevic and other Serbian leaders. Later in the year, the *Washington Times* took the story up again and wrote that while details still remained classified, top US military officials had confirmed that the United States had launched a computer attack on Yugoslav systems during NATO's bombing campaign, in the first such broad use of offensive cyber-warfare during a conflict, and had thus 'triggered a superweapon that catapulted the country into a military era that could forever alter the ways of war and the march of history' (Hoffmann 1999; Burns 1999).

There are at least two strong points that argue against most of these claims: first, cyber-warfare against a relatively low-tech enemy cannot be expected to be overly effective. At the very beginning of Operation Allied Force, an article explained that according to military experts, NATO's IW efforts were more likely to target radar transmissions than web-connected computers, mainly because Yugoslavia had little in the way of an Internet infrastructure and because its military was not likely to be using the web to communicate (Seminerio 1999). The second point that weighs even stronger is that because cyber-war ideas were still in their infancy, the United States found that there was neither a clear basis in law for punishing computer attacks nor any legislation that would allow retaliation against possible Serbian attacks. Other reports state that while the US Air Force had planned such cyber-attacks in depth, their execution was blocked by some exponents of the US intelligence community, which felt that such measures would do more to corrupt the quality of intelligence collection than to damage Serbs operations (Cordesman 2000: v and 47). The uncertainty surrounding international law, especially because of the continuing unpredictability of the effects of information attacks, evoked fears that their use might make US military commanders liable to war crimes charges (Metz 2000b).

The same laws of armed conflict that are applied to bombs and missiles must also apply to a military cyber-attack: for example, assaults aimed at civilian targets such as financial systems or power and water facilities could constitute a war crime. A 50-page booklet with guidelines for waging cyber-war, entitled 'Assessment of International Legal Issues in Information Operations', issued in May 1999 by the Pentagon's Office of the General Counsel warns commanders foremost to be cautious of targeting institutions that are essentially civilian in nature (Department of Defense 1999). Another constraint for the use of 'cyber-weapons' was the fear of giving away an alleged strategic advantage. Some experts believe that the Pentagon did actually hack into Serbian computers to spy, but refrained from causing chaos, principally for strategic reasons: widespread use of these new weapons and tools probably would accelerate and focus foreign military research on them and threaten to deprive the United States of its IW edge in a field where foes could catch up quickly and cheaply. This argument is similar to the one made in connection with nuclear weapons in the 1950s (Borger 1999; Minkwitz and Schöfbänker 2000).

The example of Operation Allied Force showed that NATO was far from being able to win the multifaceted information battle as defined by the United States. In fact, the experience indicated how cautiously parties to a conflict must handle the control and release of information to the public in order to remain credible in extensive and aggressive media wars, not only to win sympathy for the views of one's own side but also to sustain the public support of democratic electorates, a point in which NATO clearly failed. Moreover, the operation indicated that the refusal of high-tech forces to risk lives would likely reinforce the shift of hostilities away from the traditional battlefield and closer to the struggle for civilian opinion and morale at home. This resonated well with the general perception of a heightened vulnerability due to the information revolution. Apart from the experiences made during the conflict, various incidents involving defence computers, to which we will turn

80 *Asymmetric vulnerabilities*

next, helped to highlight the increasing vulnerability of the defence infrastructure.

Computer-attacks against DoD sites shape the threat perception

Ever since Cliff Stoll tracked down the German hacker who had attacked his lab back in 1986, the problem of intrusions into protected government network had been a high-priority issue. The Dutch hacker incident during the Gulf War was an early example of an occurrence that succinctly shaped the perception of vulnerability of the armed forces (Brock 1991). Pursuant to a congressional request, the GAO (1996) published a report with the title 'Information Security: Computer Attacks at Department of Defense Pose Increasing Risks' in May 1996. In this report, the GAO reviewed the extent to which DoD computer systems had been attacked, focusing specifically on the potential for further damage to DoD computer systems and on challenges the DoD faced in securing sensitive information on its computer systems.

Of the incidents described in the report, the so-called Rome Laboratory incident caused the most worries: during March and April 1994, more than 150 Internet intrusions were made into the systems of the Rome Laboratory, a research centre reporting to the Air Research and Development Command and specialising in electronic systems. The attackers used Trojan horses and sniffers to access and control Rome's operational network and were able to seize control of the facilities' support systems for several days. During this time, they copied and downloaded information such as systems data on air tasking orders. By masquerading as a trusted user, they were also able to successfully attack systems at other government facilities, including the National Aeronautics and Space Administration's (NASA) Goddard Space Flight Center, Wright-Patterson Air Force Base, some DoD contractors, and other private-sector organisations (Air Force Information Warfare Center 1995). During the investigation, while the two hackers were being observed by Computer Crime Investigators, one of the hackers accessed a system in South Korea, obtained all of the data stored on the Korean Atomic Energy Research Institute's system, and deposited it on the Rome Laboratory's system. Initially, it was unclear whether the Korean information belonged to North Korea or South Korea. The concern was that if it were North Korean, the North Koreans would think the transfer of data was the result of an intrusion by the US Air Force, which could be perceived as an aggressive act of war, especially since the United States was in sensitive negotiations with the North Koreans regarding their nuclear weapons programme at the time.

At this time, the 'foreign' intelligence threat was still considered the biggest threat in the spectrum. However, the development of the IW doctrine had now provided the framework and the vocabulary to think beyond the boundaries of this scenario. At first, Air Force officials feared that at least one of the hackers involved in the Rome Laboratory incident might have been working for a foreign country interested in obtaining military research data, or information on areas in which the Air Force was conducting advanced research. In addition, Air Force Information Warfare Center (AFIWC) officials thought that the hackers may have intended to install malicious code in software that could be activated years later, possibly jeopardising a weapons system's ability to perform safely and as intended, and even threatening the lives of the soldiers or pilots operating the system (GAO 1996). Both hackers, British teenagers going by the handles 'Datastream' and 'Kuji', were eventually caught (US Senate Permanent Subcommittee on Investigations 1996: Appendix B).

Similar intrusions included a system penetration of the US Naval Academy's computer systems in December 1994, when 24 servers were accessed and sniffer programmes were installed, files deleted, systems made inaccessible to authorised users, and over 12,000 passwords changed. In 1995 and 1996, an attacker from Argentina used the Internet to access a US university system and from there broke into computer networks at the Naval Research Laboratory, other DoD installations, NASA, and Los Alamos National Laboratory. Unknown persons accessed two unclassified computer systems at the Army Missile Research Laboratory at White Sands Missile Range and installed a sniffer programme (GAO 1996). As critics say, all reports about these incidents are full of 'coulds' and 'maybes', because what really scared the officials was not what actually happened but what *could* have happened. For example, since the Air Force did not know it was being attacked for at least three days, damage could potentially have been inflicted on Rome Laboratory systems and the information in those systems. In a sense, these incidents are more than mere scenarios, but the threat does not truly manifest itself either – it is the mere *potential* of what could have happened that is most frightening.

At around the same time (between January and June 1995), at the request of the Office of the Secretary of Defense for Command, Control, Communications and Intelligence, the RAND Corporation conducted exercises known as 'The Day After in Cyberspace' to simulate an IW attack, based on the Day After methodology, developed and used mainly to explore strategic planning options both for nuclear proliferation and counter-proliferation (Anderson and Hearn 1996). Senior members of the national security community and representatives from national security-related telecommunications and information systems industries participated in evaluating and responding to a hypothetical conflict between an adversary and the United States and its allies in the year 2000. In the scenario, an adversary attacks computer systems throughout the Unites States and allied countries, causing accidents, crashing systems, blocking communications, and inciting panic. For example, automatic tellers at large banks are attacked. The attacks create confusion and panic when the automatic tellers wrongfully add and debit thousands of US dollars to customers' accounts. A freight train is misrouted when a logic bomb is inserted into a railroad computer system, causing a major accident involving a high-speed passenger train. Meanwhile, telephone service is sabotaged in Washington, a major airplane crash is caused in Great Britain, and Cairo, Egypt, loses all power service. An all-out attack is launched on computers

82 *Asymmetric vulnerabilities*

at most military installations, slowing down, disconnecting, or crashing the systems. Weapons systems designed to pinpoint enemy tanks and troop formations begin to malfunction due to electronic infections (Molander *et al.* 1996).

The exercises were designed to assess the plausibility of IW scenarios and to help define key issues to be addressed in this area. They highlighted some defining features of the threat, including the fact that attack mechanisms and techniques could be acquired with relatively modest investment (Hamre 2003). The exercises also revealed that no adequate tactical warning system existed for distinguishing between IW attacks and accidents. Perhaps most importantly, the link between cyber-threats and infrastructures was already built into the scenario. Therefore, the study naturally demonstrated that because the US economy, society, and military relied increasingly on a high-performance networked information infrastructure, this infrastructure presented a set of attractive strategic targets for opponents possessing IW capabilities. The fears everybody had were thus substantiated by this exercise.

Apart from 'Day After', an exercise named 'Eligible Receiver', undertaken in 1997, also considerably shaped the perception of the threat. 'Eligible Receiver' was a no-notice Joint Staff Exercise designed to test DoD planning and crisis action capabilities when faced with attacks on DoD information infrastructures. A 'red team' of hackers from the National Security Agency (NSA) was organised to infiltrate the Pentagon systems. The team was only allowed to use publicly available computer equipment and hacking software. Although many details about 'Eligible Receiver' are still classified, it is said that the hackers were able to infiltrate and take control of the Pacific Command Center's computers, as well as of power grids and 911 emergency systems in nine major US cities. They intruded computer networks, denied services, changed, removed, and read e-mails, and disrupted phone services. The team gained super user access to over 36 computer systems, which meant they could create new accounts, delete accounts, turn the system off, or reformat the server hard drives. In addition, this disclosed several human vulnerabilities in the virtual world/cyberspace, including the ease with which the NSA team 'socially engineered' DoD personnel and the vast amount of valuable information they were able to collect from the Internet on a daily basis (Gertz 1998; Computer Science and Telecommunications Board 1999: 132; Hamre 2003).

Such exercises did not stop real hackers from gaining access to the government networks, however. In February 1998, more than 500 electronic break-ins into computer systems of the US government and the private sector were detected. The hackers got access to at least 200 different computer systems of the US military, the nuclear weapons laboratories, the Department of Energy, and NASA. The DoD established a 24-hour emergency watch, installed intrusion detection systems on key nodes, and assisted law enforcement in computer forensics and investigation. The incidents confirmed earlier Eligible Receiver findings, namely: the DoD had no effective system of indications and warnings, intrusion detection systems were insufficient, the DoD was not organised effectively for IO, and identifying the threat group and motives was a problem. At precisely the same time, the US forces in the Middle East were being built up because of tensions with Iraq over UN arms inspections. The fact that some of the intrusions could be traced back to Internet service providers in the Gulf region led to the initial conclusion that the Iraqi government had to be behind the attacks (GAO 1999). A closer investigation of the case later brought up the real attackers: two teenagers from Cloverdale in California and another teen from Israel. Thus, the earlier pattern is repeated: electronic break-ins are erroneously linked to an enemy state, but the real perpetrators are youths playing games of one-upmanship.

Shortly after this incident, dubbed 'Solar Sunrise', US officials accidentally discovered a pattern of probing of computer systems at the Pentagon, NASA, the Energy Department, private universities, and research labs. The highly classified incident, called 'Moonlight Maze', had obviously been going on for nearly two years before it was discovered in March 1998. The invaders were systematically prowling through tens of thousands of files – including maps of military installations, troop configurations, and military hardware designs. The Defense Department traced the trail back to a mainframe computer in the former Soviet Union, but the sponsor of the attacks remains unknown, and the Russian government denied any involvement (Vatis 1999).

All these incidents were often cited in hearings over the years as examples of how vulnerable the United States was and were excessively exploited by the media (Smith 1999a, 1999b). But the incidents also had different implications: the characteristics of the incidents led to the consensus that the military could not take the lead when it came to this new threat, despite its influence in framing the threat in the 1990s. It became clear that in the case of most cyber-attacks, neither the identity nor the objective of the perpetrator was known during the attack. As then FBI Director Louis Freeh told the Senate after 'Solar Sunrise' in a hearing: 'Solar Sunrise […] demonstrated to the interagency community how difficult it is to identify an intruder until facts are gathered in an investigation, and why assumptions cannot be made until sufficient facts are available' (Freeh 2000). Due to the nature of cyber-attacks, it is often impossible to determine at the outset whether an intrusion is an act of vandalism, computer crime, terrorism, foreign intelligence activity, or some form of strategic attack. The only way to determine the source, nature, and scope of the incident is to investigate. And the authority to investigate such matters and to obtain the necessary court orders or subpoenas clearly resides with law enforcement (Vatis 1998a).

John Hamre, then deputy secretary of defence, also made a clear statement on the role of the DoD and on the blurring of lines between responsibilities in a 1998 hearing. He said that one problem with cyber-attacks against infrastructure targets was that they could be the culmination of long-term, subtle, systematic intrusions. The preparatory phase could take place over several years, making it very hard to collate curious, seemingly unrelated events into a coherent picture. An attack may also take place over multiple jurisdictions, e.g. by targeting power grids or air traffic control nodes in several states. In this context, the boundary between national security and law enforcement, according to Hamre, was blurred, as was the border between public- and private-sector responsibility. In such an event, he said:

> DoD must be very careful in the roles it plays, and for which it prepares. We have neither the authorities, nor the organization for police activities. [...] Rather, DoD should be involved when an attack is targeted directly against national security assets, is more widespread and not localized, or when special technical expertise is required.
>
> (Hamre 1998)

US domestic law also gave the armed forces' lawyers headaches, because an attack on US infrastructures could originate in Iraq as well as in the United States. A military counter-strike through cyberspace might therefore unwittingly constitute an operation of US armed forces on domestic territory, which is prohibited by the *Posse Comitatus* Act of 1878 (Section 1385 of Title 18, United States Code).

Bound to lead? The military roles in protecting the nation against cyber-threats

As we have shown, the DoD was the driving force behind threat framing in the early 1990s. For the Pentagon and the intelligence community, IW offered a new vista in the post–Cold War era of diminishing military budgets, a paucity of conventional threats, base closures, and reductions in the numbers of both military and civilian employees. Its officials convinced the administration that it was necessary to defend the infrastructures of the United States in order to further offensive and defensive IW contingencies. Their approach was naturally two-pronged: on the one hand, actual war-fighting activities were of interest, but on the other, the United States' own vulnerability, linked to the notion of asymmetry, became a major topic.

'Computers at risk: safe computing in the information age'

The 1980s threat frame as identified in the NSDD 145 and NSD 42 already began to undergo change in the late 1980s. We find a new one in a document that is not a policy document but the outcome of a request from the Defense Advanced Research Projects Agency (DARPA) in 1988 to address the security and trustworthiness of US computing and communications systems as a reaction to the Morris Worm: the Computer Science and Technology Board's 1990 Report 'Computers at Risk: Safe Computing in the Information Age' (National Academy of Sciences 1991). Though it is not linked to the military in the strict sense, this study is of tremendous importance for the later development of the threat frame, as it was the first to link cyber-threats to the critical infrastructure protection (CIP) debate, which elevated the issue to prime position on the national security agenda in the 1990s and gave it another level of urgency.

In the report, the threat subject remains the same, but a differentiation between criminal elements and hackers is introduced for the first time. The report also very clearly links IT to society as a whole: as computer systems become more prevalent, sophisticated, embedded in physical processes, and interconnected, it argues, society becomes more vulnerable to poor system design, accidents that disable systems, and attacks on computer systems (National Academy of Sciences 1991: 1). The report even speaks of 'potential disasters that can cause economic and even human losses' (National Academy of Sciences 1991: 2). The new aspect is the link it makes to other so-called 'infrastructures' (National Academy of Sciences 1991: 2), though it still lacks the terminology of later years: 'For example, new vulnerabilities are emerging as computers become more common as components of medical and transportation equipment or more interconnected as components of domestic and international financial systems' (National Academy of Sciences 1991: 2). In addition, the document equates national security with economic interests. This is not a new development but important insofar as the broadening of the scope of national security opened the door for the subsequent reasoning: the report states that computers have become such an integral part of US business that computer-related risks cannot be separated from general business risks (National Academy of Sciences 1991: 11). The concentration of information and economic activity in computer systems, according to the report, makes those systems an attractive target to hostile entities, which raises questions about the intersection of economic and national-security interests and the design of appropriate security strategies for the public and private sectors (National Academy of Sciences 1991: 8), a question that would become increasingly prevalent in later years. In an even further step, the document forecasts a shift from conventional military conflict to economic competition in future years and thus attributes even more importance to information infrastructures. This link between the two realms can be interpreted as a necessary discursive legitimation for expanding security into 'new' areas; the proposed countermeasures could only be legitimised on the basis of a convincing argument to the effect that the interests of the national security apparatus and the private sector were one and the same.

In the report, we find a very strong motivational framing and call for action: the trends that the report identify suggest to the authors that whatever trust was justified in the past will not be justified in the future 'unless action is taken now' (National Academy of Sciences 1991: 11). Basically, it is argued that society has reached a 'discontinuity' and that what lies ahead is new terrain that requires new thinking. This urgency is also due to the fact that the threat is bigger and growing, due to a) the proliferation of computer systems into ever more applications, especially applications involving networking; b) the changing nature of the technology base; c) the increase in computer system expertise within the population, which increases the potential for system abuse; d) the increasingly global environment for business and research; and e) the global reach and interconnection of computer networks, which multiply system vulnerabilities (National Academy of Sciences 1991: 1). As we will see below, these factors, a mixture of technological change and proliferation of knowledge due to this change, remain the key reasons for processes of threat politics in later years. Again, these points are used to make a strong case that the state as protector of society needs to act. The prognostic frame is slightly enlarged in comparison to the earlier threat frames. Even though there still is a strong emphasis on technical security measures, attaining increased security is also labelled a management issue and a social problem. This threat frame would become the winning threat frame of the 1990s. The persuasiveness of this threat frame and the kind of link it establishes to the potential destruction of the entire society were likely decisive for its considerable success. Its emergence at this particular time is due to a rapidly changing technological substructure, as described in the report, and is based on the observation that infrastructures were becoming more and more dependent on information and communication technology and complex networks.

Early studies in the military

Apart from this report, various military reports from the early 1990s listed the same broad range of adversaries and referred to the whole nation as being endangered due to its dependence on the information infrastructure. In fact, the only variations in this threat frame can be found in the prognostic part of the frame. In the 'Redefining Security' report by the Joint Security Commission (JSC) to the secretary of defense and the director of central intelligence (28 February 1994), for example, we find further clear fault lines between government and the private sector, an issue that had become virulent in connection with the encryption debate, as we have shown. The document asks basic, but nonetheless, acute questions, such as what exactly the government's role should be in helping to protect information assets and intellectual capital that are in private hands or how and whether technology should be developed by the government to protect classified information, and how it should be provided to the private sector for the protection of sensitive but unclassified information (Joint Security Commission 1994: 2).

The overall focus of the report, reducing costs for security, is reflected in a strong economic reasoning. 'Redefining Security' argues, for example, that just the economic consequences of a successful attack on the telephone system or the National Information Infrastructure (NII) would be significant or even disastrous 'if instead of attacking our military systems and data bases, an enemy attacked our unprotected civilian infrastructure' (Joint Security Commission 1994: 80). Before the bombing of the Alfred P. Murrah Federal Building in Oklahoma City in April 1995, there had been less focus on terrorism and more on the economy, but the bottom-line reasoning is the same:

> The United States is increasingly dependent on information systems and networks. Information systems control the basic functions of the nation's infrastructure, including the air traffic control system, power distribution

Asymmetric vulnerabilities 87

and utilities, phone system, stock exchanges, the Federal Reserve monetary transfer system, credit and medical records, and a host of other services and activities.

(Joint Security Commission 1994: iv)

The threat subject is described as being 'increasingly sophisticated' and is characterised as coming from both insiders and outsiders. Specifically, there is an emphasis on foreign intelligence services again, including those of 'allies'. It is even claimed in the report that some of them are known to target US information systems and technologies, using techniques that can 'give them access to information without ever coming into our work spaces or approaching our people' (Joint Security Commission 1994: 81). An 'old' threat frame, that of the foreign intelligence threat, and a 'new' one, concerned with critical infrastructures, can be found in this document.

The call for action is linked to the novelty of the threat. In general, the word 'new' is used rather frequently: the nature of the threats is 'new' (they are diffuse, multifaceted, and dynamic), and therefore, a 'new' defence paradigm is needed, specifically because providing total security is impossible and because overall costs are too great to patch all of the safety gaps. The report proposes a number of remedies, including a new policy structure and a classification system designed to manage risks better, as well as methods of improving personnel security policies in both the government and the industry, a measure tailored against the 'insider' threat, which is assessed as being considerable. Apart from bringing the issue of information security to the attention of a broad range of actors in the national security community, in September 1994, the recommendations of the JSC led to the promulgation of Presidential Decision Directive 29 on 'Security Policy Coordination', which established the Security Policy Board (SPB), to handle these concerns (Clinton 1994b).

Another report that was mentioned above, the 1994 Summer Study 'Report of the Defense Science Board Summer Study Task Force on Information Architecture for the Battlefield' (Defense Science Board 1994), also proposed a threat frame. When it comes to characterizing the threat, we find that the DSB on the one hand describes information superiority as being as important as nuclear deterrence and dominance during the Cold War (Defense Science Board 1994: B-4). On the other, it stresses that the loss of control over the attack capabilities makes it both hard to define the threat and hard to understand it (Defense Science Board 1994: B-2). The reason for this, according to the report, is that the technology for IW is developed in the open commercial market, which clearly differentiates it from the Cold War and the nuclear threat, which was relatively easy to monitor. On the side of the threat subject, the paper establishes that IW attacks can be carried out by a spectrum of adversaries ranging from teenage hacker to sophisticated wide-ranging attacks (Defense Science Board 1994: 24), thus postulating a wide range of potential adversaries, a feature that is familiar from the 1980s. Particularly, the report states that:

88 *Asymmetric vulnerabilities*

> There is mounting evidence that there is a threat that goes beyond hackers and criminal elements. This threat arises from terrorist groups or nation states, and is far more subtle and difficult to counter than the more unstructured but growing problem caused by hackers. The threat causes concern over the specter of military readiness problems caused by attacks on Defense computer systems, but it goes well beyond the Department. Every aspect of modern life is tied to a computer system at some point, and most of these systems are relatively unprotected.
>
> (Defense Science Board 1994: 24)

Basically, this reflects the practice of partitioning the wide range of actors into two groups with fluent boundaries, based on organizational complexity: the first contains recreational or institutional hackers and organised crime, and the second contains terrorists and nation-states. The first is sometimes described as an 'unstructured' threat, while the latter is considered a 'structured' threat (National Academy of Sciences 1991; Minihan 1998). The unstructured threat is random and relatively limited. It consists of adversaries with limited funds and organisation and short-term goals. These actors have limited resources, tools, skills, and funding to accomplish a sophisticated attack and also lack the motivation to do so. The unstructured threat is not considered a danger to national security and is not usually the concern of the national security community. Nonetheless, such attacks could cause considerable damage mainly in the economic realm. The structured threat, on the other hand, is considerably more methodical and better supported. Adversaries from this group have all-source intelligence support, extensive funding, organised professional support, and long-term goals. Foreign intelligence services, criminal elements, and professional hackers (crackers) involved in IW, criminal activities, or industrial espionage are also included in this threat category. Unfortunately, the boundaries between the two categories are not always clear: even though the unstructured threat is not of direct concern for national security, it is still feared that a structured threat actor could masquerade as an unstructured threat actor or that structured actors could seek the help of technologically apt individuals from the other group.

In another major report, called 'Information Warfare – Defense (IW-D)' (Defense Science Board 1996), particular attention was paid to issues of protection. Established at the direction of the under-secretary of defense for acquisition and technology on 4 October 1995, the objective of the study was to make recommendations regarding the creation and maintenance of specific aspects of a national IW defence capability. This specific focus was a result of parallel and closely related activities in the civil domain after Oklahoma City; given the activities of the President's Commission on Critical Infrastructure Protection (PCCIP) study group, which are analysed in the next sub-chapter, the Task Force decided to address IW defence issues and provide conclusions mainly from the DoD's point of view. The report appeared a couple of months before the PCCIP report. However, we find in it the exact same diagnostic threat frame. The DSB task force – chaired by two former assistant secretaries of defence for command, control, communications, and intelligence – viewed the IW problem as so severe that it urged the Pentagon to embark immediately on a crash course to protect its networks against this new form of warfare by providing detailed policy funding and legal recommendations. To defend DoD and critical non-governmental systems against IW, the report recommended new legal authorisation that would allow 'DoD law enforcement and intelligence agencies to conduct efficient coordinated monitoring of attacks on the critical civilian information infrastructure...' (Defense Science Board 1996: 6–30).

In carving out a position for the DoD to take on this role in the civil sector, the report summed up the problem as follows: 'We should not forget that IW is a form of warfare, not a crime or an act of terror.' (Defense Science Board 1996: Exhibit 3–1) Subsequently, it adopted a rather blunt approach as to how the Pentagon should respond to such an attack or intrusion: 'The response could entail civil or criminal prosecution, use of military force [...] diplomatic initiatives or economic mandates' (Defense Science Board 1996: ES-4). These recommendations included a controversial call to give the Pentagon the legal power to protect non-governmental portions of the infrastructure in the name of defence and national security. Further recommendations included establishing the assistant secretary of defense (Command, Control, Communications, & Intelligence) (ASD/C3I) as the single focal point for Information Warfare-Defense (IW-D) within the department. According to this plan, the Defense Information Systems Agency (DISA) would have taken on a pivotal IW-D role, based on the recommendations in the report. It called for DISA to set up an IW operations centre to provide tactical warning, attack assessments, and emergency response, with infrastructure restoration capabilities.

Because the authors of the report see the DoD as taking the lead, they also promulgate a strategy of deterrence. In their view, deterrence is the first line of defence in the information age as much as during the nuclear age. The deterrence they envisage

> must include an expression of national will as expressed in law and conduct, a declaratory policy relative to consequences of an information warfare attack against the United States, and an indication of the resilience of the information infrastructure to survive an attack.
> (Defense Science Board 1996: ES-3)

In order to be able to deter, tactical warning is needed. The essence of tactical warning is monitoring, detection of incidents, and reporting of the incidents. Next, premeditated responses to the intrusions or attacks must be in place to deter future intrusions or attacks. This response, the authors say, could entail civil or criminal prosecution, the use of military force, perception management, diplomatic initiatives, or economic mandates and might also involve offensive IW.

In addition to this volley of possible countermeasures, they offer the usual technical and organizational remedies. In thus arguing, they use the rationale of risk management: because absolute security is not possible – a notion adapted from the JSC report – it is technically and economically impossible to design and protect the infrastructure to withstand any and all disruptions, intrusions, or attacks. The logical consequence is that one has to manage the existing risks (Defense Science Board 1996: ES-3). This can be done by protecting selected portions of the infrastructure that support critical functions and activities necessary for maintaining political, military, and economic interests. In this view, it should be possible to repair the infrastructure and to perform critical functions in the case of IW attacks (Defense Science Board 1996: ES-3). The beginning of this particular story can be called the 'managerial security story' (Aradau 2001b), which we will turn to in more detail below.

Developments in the military domain as described in this chapter are ambiguous. On the one hand, the RMA appears to further enhance the already unique military power of the United States: the development of the US military's system of systems, along with capabilities for precision strikes, dominant manoeuvre, and focused logistics, as well as massive investments by the US DoD in advanced technology, generally served to further broaden the gap between the United States and its allies as well as its foes (Johnson and Libicki 1995). On the other hand, there was a growing concern that the proliferation of technologies in the globalised marketplace might be counterproductive to US military security, constituting the primary security paradox in the information age. The fear that other nations might develop IW capabilities and doctrines of their own stands in strange contrast to the openness with which the United States promotes its new ideas globally by putting its entire doctrine online. While the documents analysed in this chapter were influential both in shaping threat perceptions and in bringing the issue of cyber-threats to the attention of a broad audience, they did not establish the winning threat frame. Basically, the role of the private sector in the CIP debate was becoming so important that it would have been simply impossible in practical terms to give the military a very dominant role. In the aftermath of the PCCIP's report, the DoD became less influential in the debate – to some extent, at its own request.

Due to the cyber-crime paradigm, the Federal Bureau of Investigation (FBI) was already involved in investigating computer crimes and had set up a special Computer Crime Squad in the early 1990s. On the basis of the Computer Fraud and Abuse Act of 1986, this unit investigated more than 200 cases until the mid-1990s and thus occupied the strongest position within government. Apart from the distribution of resources and practical reasons of investigation, legal norms prevented a more important role for the armed forces in the protection of critical infrastructures. As one report notes:

> the Defense Department is legally prohibited from taking action beyond identification of a cyber-attacker on its own initiative, even though the ability of the United States to defend itself against external threats is compromised by attacks on its C4I infrastructure, a compromise whose severity will only grow as the US military becomes more dependent on the leverage provided by C4I.
> (Computer Science and Telecommunications Board 1999: 176)

5 Critical infrastructures and homeland security

Despite the prominent role of the military in shaping the threat perception, a different track emerged when a particular event gave a distinct face to cyber-threats: the Oklahoma City bombing of April 1995. In its aftermath, the issue of cyber-threats was interlinked with the concept of critical infrastructure protection (CIP) – critical infrastructures being defined as those assets whose destruction or disruption would have a crippling impact on the heart of the US society – and the threat of terrorism. The threat frame that emerged from this premise made military options seem unsuitable, despite the military's great interest in the topic until at least the mid-1990s and despite the fact that terms like 'information warfare', 'cyber-war', or 'electronic Pearl Harbor' helped to hoist the problem firmly onto the security political agenda (Bendrath 2001).

In the years that followed the event, the foundations for the current policies were laid. The inter-agency Critical Infrastructure Working Group (CIWG), set up by President Bill Clinton and his Attorney General Janet Reno, two months after the Oklahoma City attack (Freeh 1997; PDD 39), was tasked with studying the infrastructural vulnerabilities of the United States to terrorist attacks. In January 1996, the CIWG issued its report, which in turn led to the establishment of the President's Commission on Critical Infrastructure Protection (PCCIP 1997). The PCCIP report of 1997 finally led to Presidential Decision Directives (PDD) 62 and 63 in May 1998 (Clinton 1998a, 1998b) and a more elaborate version of the same document, the National Plan for Information Systems Protection, in January 2000 (Clinton 2000). This is the focus of the first sub-chapter.

The PCCIP report and the subsequent PDDs established a threat frame that prevails until today and solidified enduring countermeasures. The years 1997 and 1998 in particular were a watershed in terms of the views on cyber-threats: when comparing open hearings concerning national security or the annual defence reports over the years, we see how the issue takes a quantum leap in 1998; there is a great quantitative increase in the time and space devoted to the topic in public hearings. The space allotted to cyber-threats related issues in the National Security Strategies (NSS) of the United States grew incrementally around the same time. In addition, cyber-threats came to be depicted as one of the prime dangers among the 'new' threats. Central Intelligence Agency (CIA) Director John Deutch, for example, had regularly warned of threats to national security from cyber-attacks since the mid-1990s. Asked in a Senate hearing to compare the danger of cyber-threats with the threat emanating from nuclear, biological, or chemical weapons, he answered, 'it is very, very close to the top' (Deutch 1996). In the PCCIP report, cyber-threats are described as being even more dangerous than other 'new' threats, especially because the necessary weapons are so easy to acquire (PCCIP 1997: 14). The threat also made its way into the general broad debate and the public mind through excessive media coverage.

In the year 2000, the issue of CIP remained a high priority on the political agenda; the events of 11 September 2001 merely served to further increase the awareness of vulnerabilities and the sense of urgency in protecting critical infrastructures (Bush 2001a, 2001b). However, while the threat frame as promoted by the PCCIP remained the same, the attention given to the cyber-threat aspect diminished. The attacks of 9/11 ensured that the topic of CIP turned into the nucleus of homeland security, though with a slightly different angle than under Clinton. While the Clinton administration viewed cyber-threats as one of the key dangers of the twenty-first century, the focus under Vice President George W. Bush administration shifted from a very strong focus on cyber-tools and methods towards integration of the physical aspects of terrorism, shown in the second sub-chapter. Other important developments took place in the military domain once again, where the debate centred on the Revolution in Military Affairs (RMA) and the transformation of the military more generally. Aspects of information warfare and the ability to prevail in the information domain were once again key issues.

Cyber-threats are linked to the CIP debate

The US government has viewed terrorism as a national security concern at least since the late 1960s, when intercontinental airline travel and global media brought the spectacle of terrorist hijackings to US living rooms. At the beginning of the Reagan administration, Secretary of State Alexander Haig had announced that opposition to terrorism would replace the Carter administration's focus on advancing human rights throughout the world (Ray and Schaap 2003: 5). Although opposition to terrorism never really became the primary focus of the Reagan administration, counter-terrorism policy was first formalised with President Reagan's National Security Decision Directive (NSDD) 207, issued in 1986 and based on the findings of Bush's 1985 Task Force on Terrorism (Pollard 1998; Richelson and Evans 2001). NSDD 207 reaffirmed and institutionalised federal jurisdiction in cases of terrorism in two categories: the Department of Justice through the Federal Bureau of Investigation (FBI) was responsible for domestic terrorism, and the Department of State for international terrorism.

For the Clinton administration, counter-terrorism became a top priority. One main reason for this was the new threat perception after the first World Trade Center attack in February 1993 and the Oklahoma City bombing in 1995.

Oklahoma City, on the one hand, showed that terrorism was no longer something that only happened overseas. On the other, and more importantly for our topic, Oklahoma City made government officials realise that an attack on a seemingly insignificant federal building, outside the 'nerve centre' of Washington, DC, was able to set off a chain reaction that impacted an area of economy that would not have normally been linked to the functions of that federal building. The idea was that, beyond the loss of human lives and physical infrastructure, a set of processes controlled from that building had also been lost (i.e. an FBI office and a payroll department), thereby impacting other agencies, employees, and/or the private sector further down the supply chain and far away from the physical destruction of the building in previously unimagined ways (Critical Infrastructure Protection Oral History Project 2005).

A direct outcome of the bombing was PDD 39, issued in June 1995. The 12-page, partly classified directive focuses on reducing US vulnerabilities and on deterring and responding to terrorism and weapons of mass destruction, especially proliferation. The PDD directed the FBI to expand its counter-terrorism programme, ordered the secretary of transportation to reduce vulnerability affecting the security of airports in the United States, instructed the director of central intelligence to lead 'an aggressive program of foreign intelligence collection, analysis, counterintelligence and covert action', and compelled the Federal Emergency Management Agency (FEMA) to coordinate consequence management activities. Terrorism was thus established as an issue that had to be addressed across the board of agencies (Clinton 1995b).

In addition, PDD 39 directed the attorney general to lead a government-wide effort to re-examine the adequacy of infrastructure protection. As a result, Reno convened the CIWG, chaired by Deputy Attorney General Jamie Gorelick and various other officials, to scope out the issue and report back to the cabinet with policy options. The CIWG's interim report was completed in early February 1996 (USSPSI 1996: 42). The attorney general's review particularly highlighted the lack of attention that had been given to protecting the cyber-infrastructure: critical information systems and computer networks. In this way, the topic of cyber-threats was linked to the topics of CIP and terrorism by (involuntary) referencing.

Responding to the working group's recommendations, the president issued Executive Order (EO) 13010 on 15 July 1996 (Clinton 1996b). With this EO, Clinton established a special study group, the PCCIP, whose task was to deliver a comprehensive report on the security of all infrastructure systems in the United States. The PCCIP included representatives of all relevant government departments, not only from the traditional security policy establishment. Additionally, the private sector was equally involved. This involvement was based on the assumption that security policy in the information technology (IT) field was no longer only a duty of the government, but a 'shared responsibility' (Clinton 1996b). Together with the PCCIP, Clinton set up the Infrastructure Protection Task Force (IPTF) to deal with the more urgent problems of coordination in infrastructure protection until the report was published. The members of the

IPTF were drawn exclusively from the country's classic security policy institutions – the FBI, the Pentagon, and the National Security Agency (NSA) (Clinton 1996b). To this extent, the IPTF can be regarded as a compromise between the cooperative (PCCIP) approach – including the private sector and other departments – and a classical security policy approach, namely giving the task to the FBI or the Department of Defense (DoD). The IPTF was chaired by and located at the Department of Justice to enable it to make use of the Computer Investigations and Infrastructure Threat Assessment Center (CITAC), which had been set up shortly before at the FBI (Tritak 1999). Obviously, the institutional resources of the FBI, which emerged from the cyber-crime debate as a strong player, constituted the decisive factor for this decision.

The PCCIP presented its report in the fall of 1997 (PCCIP 1997). The international impact of this document was such that it led to the topic of CIP being firmly established on the security agenda of various countries (Dunn and Wigert 2004). While the study assessed a list of critical infrastructures or 'sectors' – for example, the financial sector, energy supply, transportation, and the emergency services – the main focus was on cyber-risks. There were two reasons for this decision: first, these were the least known because they were basically new, and second, many of the other infrastructures were seen to depend on data and communication networks. The PCCIP thus identified a gap, or a 'new' problem, and linked the cyber-threats discourse even more firmly to the topic of critical infrastructures than it had been before.

Clinton followed most of the commission's recommendations in May 1998 with his PDD 62 and 63 (Clinton 1998a, 1998b). He created the position of a National Coordinator for Security, Infrastructure Protection and Counter-Terrorism at the National Security Council, who was supported by the newly founded Critical Infrastructure Assurance Office (CIAO). The Office of Computer Investigations and Infrastructure Protection (OCIIP), which had been assembled at the FBI on the basis of the CITAC, was expanded to become the inter-agency National Infrastructure Protection Center (NIPC). The NIPC was located at the FBI headquarters and was mainly staffed with FBI agents, with some representatives and agents from other departments and the intelligence agencies. The NIPC was made responsible for early warning as well as for law enforcement and was in charge of coordinating the various governmental and private-sector activities. The NIPC, therefore, had the most central role in the cyber-security policy under Clinton. Responsibility for the coordination of different high-level branches of the government rested with the new Critical Infrastructure Coordination Group (CICG) (Clinton 1998b). The close cooperation with the private sector that had begun with the PCCIP was continued and even enhanced.

National security strategies and cyber-threats

These developments also left their mark on the NSS of the United States. In general, the growing importance of cyberspace for national security becomes evident from comparison over the years. The 1990 edition of the NSS was the first one to specifically mention the growing criticality of 'super computers, microelectronics and telecommunications' in the newly emerging post–industrial era (quoted in Lloyd *et al.* 1990: 50). Though it strongly focused on positive aspects of the information revolution in connection with the economy, aspects of what later would be termed information warfare can already be found; specifically, it continued the Reagan administration's focus on the 'Contest of Ideas' and the need for a programme of public information to reach into closed societies (Reagan 1988; Bush 1990a; Kuehl 2000b). While this effort had been based on use of the radio and predated the rapid rise and spread of the Internet by a few years, it clearly emphasised goals that the coming technologies would make far more attainable: the wielding of 'soft power'. These goals were stated even more explicitly in the next NSS, published in August 1991, just a few months after the Persian Gulf War. In the face of the global explosion of information, the NSS of 1991 declared, the United States could leverage its advantages in IT to influence this evolving global community (Bush 1991). We will see below that the topic of 'public diplomacy' has recently risen to the top of information warfare efforts again.

President Clinton's NSS of 1995 mainly focused on praising the vast opportunities of an ICT-dominated age in terms of economic development and democratisation. There was an appreciation for the relationship between information and economics, with specific reference to the 'global economy linked by an instantaneous communications network'. But the report also noted that 'economic and security interests are increasingly inseparable' and established the goal of improving information networks as a means of meeting those interests (Clinton 1995a: 19). Furthermore, we find the observation that 'the threat of intrusions to our military and commercial information systems poses a significant risk to national security and must be addressed' (Clinton 1995a: 8). This short sentence was the beginning of a trend that would propel cyber-threats to the level of a vital national interest. The 1996 NSS continued in the same vein, but it specifically mentioned the need for intelligence on current and emerging IT or infrastructure that might potentially threaten US interests at home or abroad. It said that the intelligence community must 'provide worldwide capabilities to gather timely intelligence on current and emerging information technologies or infrastructure that may potentially threaten U.S. interests at home or abroad' (Clinton 1996a).

The Clinton administration marked the beginning of its second term of office with a new national security strategy, entitled 'A National Security Strategy for a New Century', issued in May 1997 (Clinton 1997). In accordance with the preceding report, it repeated the need to identify threats to modern information systems, and it repeated the warning contained in earlier reports about the danger from 'intrusions in our critical information infrastructures' (Clinton 1997: Chapter II, transnational threats). However, the importance of this issue seems to have grown distinctly since it was first raised in the 1995 report: First of all, it now came under a separate heading of 'Information Infrastructure', and a full paragraph was devoted to the issue. This paragraph states in particular that:

> The national security posture of the United States is increasingly dependent on our information infrastructures. These infrastructures are highly interdependent and are increasingly vulnerable to tampering and exploitation. Concepts and technologies are being developed and employed to protect and defend against these vulnerabilities; we must fully implement them to ensure the future security of not only our national information infrastructures, but our nation as well.
>
> (Clinton 1997: Chapter II)

This is clearly the most extensive and comprehensive statement of the strategic importance of the information infrastructure yet seen in a NSS (Kuehl 2000b). In 1998, the watershed year in terms of cyber-threats, the topic became even more elaborate: the NSS of 1998 declared that information and infrastructure constituted vital national interests, 'an intrinsic and essential element of our security strategy' (Clinton 1998c), and the report devoted an entire section of three full paragraphs to the need to protect critical infrastructures. In agreement with the PCCIP report, and even availing itself of the PCCIP's vocabulary, the NSS report argued that:

> Threats to the national information infrastructure, ranging from cyber-crime to a strategic information attack on the United States via the global information network, present a dangerous new threat to our national security. We must also guard against threats to our other critical national infrastructures – such as electrical power and transportation – which increasingly could take the form of a cyber-attack in addition to physical attack or sabotage, and could originate from terrorist or criminal groups as well as hostile states.
>
> (Clinton 1998c)

Clinton's sixth NSS document of December 1999 stated that 'protection of our critical infrastructures' was a vital national interest and that the United States would 'do what we must to defend these interests, including, when necessary and appropriate, using our military might unilaterally and decisively' (Clinton 1999). This powerful statement clearly implied that any nation or even non-state group that interfered with the US's critical infrastructures risked being the target of a traditional response based on kinetic firepower (Kuehl 2000b). While the previous report had mentioned asymmetric warfare, the 1999 report not only repeated the goal of fighting and winning under conditions in which an opponent might employ asymmetric means such as information operations (IO), it also again cited the potential threat from such operations if they were conducted against critical infrastructure. To a degree unmatched by any previous NSS, the 1999 report also emphasised the growing role of information in military operations, probably as a result of the experiences gained during the Kosovo conflict.

The PCCIP had explicitly described its 1997 report as a 'beginning' (PCCIP 1997: 101), and the presidential directives of May 1998 also acknowledged that there was no master plan for CIP yet (Clinton 1998a: 3). Thus, a number of government departments, agencies, and committees jointly worked on a comprehensive national strategy at the time after the release of these documents. Finally, on 7 January 2000, Clinton presented the first version of such a national strategy to the public under the headline 'Defending America's Cyberspace' (Clinton 2000). By the dawn of the new century, it was agreed that cyber-threats constituted a high-priority issue with high relevance for national security, linked to asymmetric threats, critical infrastructures, and terrorism. The plan reinforced the perception of cyber-security as a responsibility shared between the government and the private sector and made government agencies responsible for protecting their own networks against intruders. The National Plan definitely set in stone the key parameters of the threat frame that would remain unchanged in the years to come.

'Defending America's Cyberspace. National Plan for Information Systems Protection – An Invitation to Dialogue, Version 1.0' (Clinton 2000) is a clear documentation of the Clinton administration's policy and is clearly the most important in the hierarchy of policy papers at the time. Clinton's master plan adopted a twofold response to cyber-threats: on the one hand, the intelligence community and the law enforcement agencies together built up further capacities for investigations of cyber-crimes, like computer forensics tools or close surveillance of the hacker community. On the other hand, because of the amorphous nature of these non-state actors and unknown enemies, a lot of effort was put into hardening the critical infrastructures (Bendrath 2001). Within the government, we find a decentralised and cooperative policy similar to the one pursued between the government and the private infrastructure service providers. The government only protects itself and passes a great deal of the onus on to private actors.

Three new institutions were founded to work together for the security of the state's computer systems. The Federal Computer Incident Response Capability (FedCIRC), part of the General Services Administration (GSA), was tasked with building a central analysis cell to investigate incidents in all of the government's non-military computer networks. For military computers, this is done by the Joint Task Force – Computer Network Defense (JTF-CND), which was set up as early as 1999. The JTF-CND is located at the Defense Information Systems Agency (DISA) near the Pentagon, but it is subordinated to the Space Command in Colorado Springs (Clinton 2000: 39–42). The NSA's National Security Incident Response Center (NSIRC) provides support to FedCIRC, JTF-CND, DISA, NIPC, and the National Security Council (NSC) in case of attacks against systems that are part of the national security apparatus (Clinton 2000: 49). The FBI's NIPC was responsible for incident warnings, strategic analyses, and law enforcement (Clinton 2000: 42). In short, the construction of the threat as being 'new' forced the government to react by creating 'new' and more suitable government bodies. The FBI had emerged as the strongest player in the 1980s, equipped with an operational infrastructure for cyber-crime investigations and endowed with much symbolic capital. Even though the issue of cyber-threats was clearly linked to national security, no measures resulted that would traditionally fall in the purview of the national security apparatus. The nature of the issue and the discursive involvement of the private sector played a decisive role in this development.

The second part of the National Plan deals with the security of privately run infrastructures. It starts by stating that 'the Federal Government alone cannot protect US critical infrastructures' (Clinton 2000: 104). The state and local governments are also called 'partners' of the federal government, but the emphasis is placed on private companies. The goal is a close public private partnership. To ease concerns on the part of the infrastructure service providers, the plan goes to great lengths to emphasise fundamental principles such as 'voluntary' cooperation or 'trust' and advocates safeguarding the companies' own interests through protective measures (Clinton 2000: 106). In general, the distribution of resources and of the technical and social means for countering the risk was decisive: because the technology generating the risk makes it very difficult to fight potential attackers in advance, in practice, the measures focused on preventive strategies and on trying to minimise the impact of an attack when it occurs.

The dominant threat frame emerges: cyber-threats, terrorism, and CIP

During the Clinton years, we find some continuation of topics and threat frames established under Reagan and Bush on the one hand, but also considerable change on the other. The variety in terms of the threat subject ranging from hackers to states had already been established in NSDD 145, and there is only a slight variation of this spectrum after the end of the Cold War. In contrast to earlier years, however, the threat is frequently called 'new' in order to indicate the inadequacy of dealing with it using established structures and instruments. On the whole, there is far less emphasis on the foreign intelligence threat, though it still remains a concern, especially since many of the cited incidents seem to be intrusions perpetrated by foreign intelligence services. Among the far more virulent topics are scenarios of states using means of information warfare or sub-state actors using the information infrastructures for their attack. This development was accompanied by an expansion of the vocabulary to incorporate new terminology such as 'cyber-war', 'cyber-terrorism', or 'electronic Pearl Harbor', terms that are frequently used in hearings, interviews, and press articles.

While the threat subject remains more or less static, the referent object on the other hand undergoes substantial change: even though the Computer at Risk report had already spoken of dependency and critical infrastructure, the magnitude of the threat was expanded considerably when it was linked to the possible destruction of the whole of society. As a consequence, cyber-threats are treated as being equally dangerous as nuclear weapons. The reason for this change in the referent object is that the technological substructure begins to rapidly change in the 1990s, and the mass-phenomenon 'internet' emerges. This technical development and the threat perception are closely intertwined: suddenly, there is a very broad range of potential adversaries, because the weapons are at everybody's easy disposal. The weapons are not kinetic ones, but software and knowledge; the environment in which the attacks occur is not physical, but virtual; the possible attackers are unknown and can conceal themselves effectively even during an attack.

The dominant threat frame of the Clinton administration can be found in the 1997 PCCIP report. The report is such a milestone in the history of cyber-threats that not only the time and space dedicated to the issue grows considerably in subsequent hearings and statements but that we also find little variation from the PCCIP threat frame thereafter. Actors with prior conflicting threat frames, most notably two branches of the intelligence community, the Defense Intelligence Agency (DIA) and the CIA, adapted their views to the PCCIP threat frame. Due to the wide range of potential perpetrators in the threat frame, a basic question crystallised during this time: Are terrorists, enemy states, or ordinary criminals the most dangerous actors? In other words: Will we have to deal with 'cyber-terrorism,' 'cyber-war,' or just 'cyber-crime'? This question is not only one of prioritising defences, but ultimately about who was to have the lead to counter the new threat.

The PCCIP presented its report to the president in October 1997. The PCCIP report, the subsequent PDDs, and the National Plan set in stone a very distinct threat frame that became and stayed the prominent one. The report mainly stressed that dependence on the information and communications infrastructure had created new cyber-vulnerabilities (PCCIP 1997: 5) and that potential adversaries included a very broad range of actors 'from recreational hackers to terrorists to national teams of information warfare specialists' (PCCIP 1997: 15). In addition, the report lists natural disasters, component failures, human negligence, and wilful human misconduct among the threats. On the referent object side, it was clearly established that 'the nation is so dependent on our infrastructures that we must view them through a national security lens. They are essential to the nation's security, economic health, and social well being' (PCCIP 1997: vii). The dependence of society on the information and communication infrastructure, on the one hand, and ever-more complex interdependencies between infrastructures, on the other, were established as creating a new dimension of vulnerability, 'which, when combined with an emerging constellation of threats, poses unprecedented national risk' (PCCIP 1997: ix).

The threat is presented as 'new', so new that old defences become utterly useless, and new ways of thinking and new ways of protecting become indispensable, an idea that again had already been propagated in the Joint Security Commission (JSC) report of 1994. National defence is no longer the exclusive preserve of government, and economic security is no longer just about business. Again and again, the PCCIP stresses the evaporation of boundaries and the high degree of interdependency between single infrastructures, which creates overwhelming complexity. These vulnerabilities are exacerbated by several business trends within the infrastructures: extensive use of information automation; deregulation and restructuring; physical consolidation; globalisation; and adoption of a 'just-in-time' operational tempo (PCCIP 1997).

Again, the commission's single most important decision was to foster cooperation and communication between the private sector and the government. Most importantly, the report states that the interdependent nature of infrastructures creates a shared risk environment and that managing that risk will require a public–private partnership. Therefore, owners and operators of critical infrastructures are now on the front lines of security efforts, as they are the ones most vulnerable to cyber-attacks. They must focus on protecting themselves against the tools of disruption, while the government helps by collecting and disseminating the latest information about those tools and the way they are used. The federal government must lead the way into the information age by example, tightening measures to protect the infrastructures it operates against physical and cyber-attack; but it does not interfere with private matters. This new logic of security, already advanced by the JSC's report of 1994, was to become the answer to a changing threat environment.

Both the PDD 62 and 63 follow the PCCIP's reasoning and transform the winning and dominant threat frame into countermeasures. After that date, all the threat frames that are enunciated in public hearings and other documents resemble the PCCIP's threat frame: particularly, there is no variation on the threat subject and the referent object – the diagnostic threat frame is established and stable. Previous models that conflict with this view are brought into line; actors like the CIA or the DIA, which had traditionally focused their attention mainly on states, adhered to the PCCIP's threat frame after 1997. For example, Patrick M. Hughes (1998), director of the Defense Information Agency, said in his 1998 statement before the Senate Select Committee on Intelligence (SSCI) that threats to critical infrastructure included hazards emanating from nation-states, state-sponsored sub-national groups, international and domestic terrorists, criminal elements, computer hackers, and insiders, after his testimony had focused on state actors exclusively for two years in a row.

The consequence of the very broad prognostic threat frame is, however, that officials in various agencies struggle to identify the most dangerous actors or to decide whether states or non-state actors are more likely to become a threat. A general consensus has emerged that states are the ones to worry about, because they have greater capabilities – but it is more *likely* that terrorists or criminals will attack. As DIA Director Thomas Wilson said in 2000:

> Foreign states have the greatest potential capability to attack our infrastructure because they possess the intelligence assets to assess and analyze infrastructure vulnerabilities, and the range of weapons – conventional munitions, WMD, and information operations tools – to take advantage of vulnerabilities.
>
> (Wilson 2000)

If we look back at the discussion about structured and unstructured threats in the previous chapter, states are clearly counted among the structured threats. However, certain terrorist organisations are also considered to be structured (PCCIP 1997: 20). In addition, officials admit that it is very difficult to determine who is attacking, why, how, and from where. This difficulty stems from the ease with which individuals can hide or disguise their tracks by manipulating logs and directing their attacks through networks in many countries before hitting their ultimate target (Vatis 1999). The intelligence services therefore encounter considerable difficulties in understanding the threat, as we can see from the following statement by Ken Minihan in 1998:

> We do not have a clear or complete understanding of the threat to our information systems. Unstructured attacks are occurring against our networks every day, but unfortunately, most are not even detected. Of those that are detected, even fewer are reported. We are only seeing the tip of the iceberg. [...] Consequently we have no indication how many of the attacks we experience may actually be structured attacks.
>
> (Minihan 1998)

The distinct image of the cyber-terrorist also appears during these years. First mentioned in a public hearing in 1998, 'cyber-terror' quickly became one of the catchphrases of the debate. Poor definitions and careless use of terminology by many government officials is a major obstacle for meaningful discussion of the cyber-terror issue. A statement of Clinton, who was very influential in shaping the perception of the issue, can serve as an example of this semantic ambiguity. In his foreign policy farewell lecture at the University of Nebraska at Kearney in December 2000, he identified the need to pay attention to new security challenges like cyber-terrorism and said that:

> One of the biggest threats to the future is going to be cyberterrorism – people fooling with your computer networks, trying to shut down your phones, erase bank records, mess up airline schedules, do things to interrupt the fabric of life.
>
> (Bowman 2000)

His careless use of the term is an excellent example of how 'cyber-terrorism' is turned into an empty 'scarecrow' catchphrase for a very fuzzy phenomenon.

More of the same and still different: continuation of Clinton's policies and 9/11

When Bush came into office in 2001, cyber-security and interlinked topics had lost some of their initial drive, and the implementation of Clinton's National Strategy was a slower process than many had expected. For example, a General Accounting Office (GAO) report in April 2001 pointed out the significant deficiencies in progress made by the FBI's NIPC. In that report, the GAO (2001) identified several impediments to progress, including staffing shortfalls and inconsistent interpretations of the NIPC's role and responsibilities among other entities involved in CIP. In addition, Congress had withheld funding for many of the initiatives proposed by the Executive Branch to implement elements of Clinton's National Plan.

Also, it generally seems that the incoming Bush administration was less interested in the topic of cyber-threats than its predecessors, whether as an effect of this slow-down described above or by its own volition. For example, in his first National Security Presidential Decision (NSPD 1), promulgated on 5 March 2001, Bush emphasised that national security also depends on America's opportunity to prosper in the world economy. In sharp contrast to his predecessor, who had equated the information revolution with economic prosperity, the president did not mention cyber-security or the information infrastructure in this document even once (Bush 2001d). Nonetheless, Bush continued to support the activities begun by the Clinton administration. As part of its overall redesign of White House organisation and assignment of responsibilities, the incoming administration spent the first eight months reviewing its options for coordinating and overseeing CIP. The White House (2001a) published a report on CIP in February 2001, in which it attests to the state of the respective programs and does not include a change in strategy.

The Bush administration's review of CIP policy was influenced by two parallel debates. On the one hand, the NSC underwent a major streamlining: all groups within the NSC established during previous administrations were abolished, and their responsibilities and functions were consolidated into 17 Policy Coordination Committees (PCC) (Bush 2001d; White House 2001b). The activities associated with CIP were assumed by the counter-terrorism and national preparedness PCC (Moteff 2003: 8), reflecting the notion that cyber-security and infrastructures were closely linked to terrorism. Second, there was the continuing debate about how best to defend the country against terrorism more generally. In this domain, the work of the Gilmore Commission, an advisory panel formed in 1999 to assess domestic response capabilities for terrorism involving weapons of mass destruction (WMD), was particularly influential. At first, a strict interpretation of the panel's enabling legislation, and related federal statutes that provide definitions of 'weapons of mass destruction', seemed to indicate that the issue of cyber-terrorism was not within the purview of the panel's mandate (Gilmore 1999: v). Nevertheless, the panel concluded that the issues of cyber-terrorism and the forms of terrorist activities that the panel had considered were so interrelated that the panel could not ignore the issue (Gilmore 1999). In their second report in 2000, the Gilmore Commission noted that cyber-attacks inside the US could have 'mass disruptive' consequences, though not 'mass destructive' or 'mass casualty' effects, and referred to cyber-attacks during the Israeli–Palestinian conflict in the Middle East and the Distributed Denial of Service attacks in early 2000 as demonstration of the vulnerabilities of the 'e-commerce' infrastructure (Gilmore 2000: 40–2). In doing so, they reacted to the particular fuzzy cyber-terrorism image that had been created under the Clinton administration.

Rather surprisingly, they concluded that the most likely perpetrators of cyber-attacks against critical infrastructures were terrorists and criminal groups rather than nation-states (Gilmore 2000: 40). The Gilmore Commission's focus on terrorism lacked one crucial element: the essential question of whether there were any actors with the capability and motivation to carry out cyber-attacks with a scope that might truly affect national security. In this, they fell prey to an analytically flawed approach that is typical of the entire debate: by looking only at the plethora of vulnerabilities in automated information systems and simply assuming that terrorist organisations are willing to exploit these vulnerabilities, because these weaknesses might provide terrorists with a strategic advantage over the United States (Center for the Study of Terrorism and Irregular Warfare 1999: vii), the inevitable conclusion had to be that cyber-terrorism was unavoidable. The Gilmore Commission's statement can be taken as another example of the general state of the debate. Even after a considerable number of years, the threat image remained extremely fuzzy, and solid proof was still lacking.

9/11

The attacks of 11 September 2001 did not bring many changes for the overall strategy. The attacks, however, highlighted the fact that terrorists could cause enormous damage by attacking critical infrastructures directly and physically and thus demonstrated the need to re-examine physical protections (Moteff 2003: 3). As Marcus Sachs, who served in the White House Office of Cyberspace Security and was a staff member of the President's Critical Infrastructure Protection Board, expressed it in an interview in 2003:

> We were very shocked in the federal government that the attack didn't come from cyberspace [...]. Based on what we knew at the time, the most likely scenario was an attack from cyberspace, not airliners slamming into buildings [...]. We had spent a lot of time preparing for a cyber attack, not a physical attack.
>
> (Poulsen 2003)

Some observers believed after the 9/11 attacks that the undue prioritisation of the cyber-dimension had contributed to a shift of focus from the virtual to the physical domain. Securing the nation's critical infrastructure became a vital component of a post-9/11 homeland security strategy, but with a new focus on the integration of physical protections into the existing critical infrastructure policy. Thus, even though cyber-threats remained on the agenda of decision-makers, the phenomenon got less attention as a threat in its own right in the post-9/11 world. This change is also plainly visible in the 2002 NSS; while there had been a strong commitment to cyber-threats in the previous NSS as shown above, the 2002 edition does not mention the prefix 'cyber-' even once (Bush 2002).

Despite this, the threat frame established by the PCCIP report remained in place after 9/11. No new discourse strands can be identified, but through the strengthening of the discourse on terrorism/asymmetrical vulnerability and the coincident weakening of the cyber-dimension, a new threat image was produced: the idea of homeland security became the key concept. First and foremost, the attacks of 9/11 provided a reason to restructure the overall organisational framework of CIP in the United States. In the immediate aftermath of 9/11, Bush signed two EOs affecting CIP. With EO 13228, entitled 'Establishing the Office of Homeland Security and the Homeland Security Council' of 8 October 2001, Bush (2001a) set up an 'Office of Cyberdefense' at the White House, as part of the new Homeland Security Office, which in turn was part of the NSC. The mission of this office was to 'develop and coordinate the implementation of a comprehensive national strategy to secure the US from terrorist threats and attacks'. The second EO, EO 13231, 'Critical Infrastructure Protection in the Information Age', established the President's Critical Infrastructure Protection Board, whose responsibility was to 'recommend policies and coordinate programs for protecting information systems for critical infrastructure' (Bush 2001b). Furthermore, the EO established the National Infrastructure Advisory Council (NIAC).

USA PATRIOT Act

A significant change after 9/11 occurred on the legal floor. The 'Uniting and Strengthening America by Providing Appropriate Tools Required to Intercept and Obstruct Terrorism Act' [USA PATRIOT Act; P.L. 107–56, §506(a)], which became law on 26 October 2001, contains some of the most substantial changes to US federal cyber-crime laws since the last major revisions of 1996 and amended the Computer Fraud and Abuse Act (CFAA 18 USC, §1030) in several critical, and highly controversial, areas. Examples are enhanced minimum prison terms for all offences, state convictions counting for prior offences for determining recidivist sentencing, and special new protections for computers used for national security and criminal justice. The PATRIOT Act was a compromise version of the Anti-Terrorism Act of 2001 (ATA). The ATA contained several provisions vastly expanding the authority of law enforcement and intelligence agencies to monitor private communications and access personal information. The first draft of the Justice Department for a new ATA, which had been presented on 23 September 2001, treated most cases of computer crime as 'terrorism' and proposed lifelong imprisonment as the appropriate punishment. Even harmless activities most likely perpetrated by teenagers, like defacing websites, were to be treated as cyber-terrorism under this act. The PATRIOT Act followed the ATA's definition of cyber-terrorism but reduced the maximum penalty for hacking to ten years in jail where damage of at least US$5,000 had been caused. But it now criminalised break-ins into any computer outside the United States 'that is used in a manner that affects interstate or foreign commerce or communication of the United States' (US Code, §1030, Fraud and related activity in connection with computers).

The PATRIOT Act also significantly expanded the authority of law enforcement agencies to survey and capture communications. It amended and clarified the Computer Abuse Act by adding that the FBI has primary authority to investigate offences where espionage or national security is involved, except for offences affecting the duties of the US Secret Service. In general, it intended to merge the efforts of law enforcement and intelligence services and thus acted on the mantra that inside and outside threats were no longer clearly discernible. According to critics, the price of this plethora of legislative changes, which significantly increased the surveillance and investigative powers of law enforcement agencies in the United States, was the loss of a system of checks and balances that traditionally safeguards civil liberties in the face of such legislation (Electronic Privacy Information Center 2005). While Clinton had particularly stressed the need for the protection of civil liberties in National Plan 1.0, this caution was abandoned in the face of the supposedly looming terrorist threat, fuelling a new and vigorous privacy debate. Like many sweeping reform laws, the first version of the PATRIOT Act had a sunset clause to ensure that Congress would need to take active steps to re-authorise it, and indeed, the reauthorisation resolution passed in 2006 contained many civil liberties protections, the so-called 'Safeguards'. Nonetheless, controversies will continue as problems such as FBI misuse of the PATRIOT Act come to light: in March 2007, an audit by Justice Department Inspector General Glenn Fine found that the FBI had 'improperly and, in some cases, illegally used the USA PATRIOT Act to secretly obtain personal information' about US citizens (Fine 2007).

The establishment of the Department of Homeland Security

The most important change for the cyber-threats issue, however, was the establishment of the Department of Homeland Security (DHS 2004). The establishment of such an agency had been advocated by the United States Commission on National Security/21st Century, commonly referred to as the Hart-Rudman Commission, a couple of months before 9/11. The commission's final report, completed in February 2001, identified the possibility of tragic occurrences such as that of 9/11 and had said that the United States was increasingly vulnerable to attacks on its territory:

> [...] attacks may involve weapons of mass destruction and weapons of mass disruption. As porous as US physical borders are in an age of burgeoning trade and travel, its 'cyber borders' are even more porous – and the critical infrastructure upon which so much of the US economy depends can now be targeted by non-state and state actors alike. America's present global predominance does not render it immune from these dangers.
> (Hart-Rudman Commission 2001: 10)

Starting from this premise, the commission attached primary importance to homeland defence and recommended that a separate agency be developed to address homeland security. The new organisation was to include a directorate responsible for CIP (Moteff 2003: 9). Furthermore, it created the vocabulary and a framework for such an undertaking. The Homeland Security Act of 2002 established such an organisation. And indeed, CIP is one of six critical mission areas to reduce vulnerability for the homeland: as one of the major divisions of the DHS, the Directorate for Information Analysis and Infrastructure Protection (IAIP) was made responsible for identifying and assessing current and future threats and vulnerabilities to the homeland, issuing timely warnings, and taking preventive and protective action. The IAIP was tasked to unify and focus the key cyber-security activities of the CIAO, formerly part of the Department of Commerce; the FBI's NIPC; and the FedCIRC, formerly part of the General Service Administration (Dunn and Wigert 2004; Abele-Wigert and Dunn 2006).

In September 2002, the President's Critical Infrastructure Protection Board released a draft version of the 'National Strategy to Secure Cyberspace' for public comment, in which a general strategic overview, specific recommendations and policies, and the rationale for these actions were described. After a vetting process that signalled that cyberspace security was viewed as a public–private partnership, the final version appeared in February 2003 (Bush 2003a). It was closely followed by a 'National Strategy for the Physical Protection of Critical Infrastructures and Key Assets' (Bush 2003b), which ensured that the physical aspects of CIP were not forgotten. These two documents together were intended to serve as implementing components of the National Strategy for Homeland Security. The cornerstone of the strategy, again, is the implementation of a public–private partnership. 'In general, the private sector is best equipped and structured to respond to an evolving cyber threat', the report reads. 'A federal role [...] is only justified when the benefits of intervention outweigh the associated costs. This standard is especially important in cases where there are viable private sector solutions for addressing any potential threat or vulnerability' (Bush 2003a: ix). As under Clinton, the rationale for the strategy is that it avoids regulation and government-imposed standards to ensure that US companies can continue to innovate, remain productive, and compete in world markets.

To sum up these developments, the Bush administration developed a lot of activity in connection with the protection of critical infrastructures in the aftermath of 9/11. But in many respects, the Bush administration's policy regarding CIP represented a continuation of PDD-63: the fundamental policy statements are essentially the same, as are the infrastructures identified as critical, although they were expanded and emphasis was placed on targets that would result in large numbers of casualties (Moteff 2007: 12). There was one primary difference, however. First, the Office of Homeland Security was given overall authority for coordinating CIP against terrorist threats and attacks. Those responsibilities associated with information systems of critical infrastructures were delegated to the President's Critical Infrastructure Protection Board. Furthermore, the Board's responsibilities for protecting the physical assets of the nation's information systems were to be defined by the assistant to the president for national security and the assistant to the president for homeland security. While Clinton's PDD-63 focused primarily on cyber-security, it gave the national coordinator responsibility to coordinate the physical *and* virtual security for all critical infrastructures. The above-mentioned EOs not only segregated responsibility for protecting the nation's information infrastructure, but also considerably strengthened the physical aspect vis-à-vis the aspect of cyber-attacks.

Slow down

As a result of this, many critical voices were heard disapproving of the extent of the attention given to the cyber-dimension. The fact that Amit Yoran, the government's cyber-security chief, abruptly resigned after one year with the US DHS raised serious questions in the press about the Bush administration's ability to quickly improve the nation's cyber-security (cf. Gross 2004; Mark 2004; Verton 2004). Apparently, Yoran was frustrated with his post's limited authority and budgets that did not allow him to do this job effectively. And the troubles continued: top cyber-security officials continued to resign, another of them also publicly complained about his lack of authority (Krebs 2006). Negative press was part of the reasons why the second secretary of homeland security, Michael Chertoff, proposed to restructure the IAIP Directorate and rename it the Directorate of Preparedness as one of his Second Stage Review recommendations in 2005 (Chertoff 2005). Afterwards, the Information Analysis function was merged into a new Office of Intelligence and Analysis. The Infrastructure Protection function, with the same missions as outlined in the Homeland Security Act, remained, but was joined by other existing and new entities. In addition, the restructuring established the position of an assistant secretary for cyber-security and telecommunications, which had long been advocated by many within the cyber-security community, and of an assistant secretary for infrastructure protection (Moteff 2007: 15).

Generally speaking, the Bush administration rapidly became bogged down in the details of implementing its own strategy. Shortly before the beginning of Operation Iraqi Freedom in 2003, as part of Operation Liberty Shield, a comprehensive national plan to protect the homeland during operations in Iraq, the DHS identified a list of 160 assets or sites that it considered critical to the nation, based on their vulnerability to attack and potential consequences. During the course of the year, that list grew to include 1,849 assets or sites. According to a testimony by then Under-secretary for IAIP Frank Libutti before the House Appropriations Committee in 2004, the DHS intended to visit each of these sites to assess their vulnerabilities to various forms of attack (Libutti, quoted in Moteff 2007: 25) Over time, according to the DHS inspector general, this initial priority list evolved into what is now called the National Asset Database, which, as of January 2006, contained over 77,000 entries (Moteff 2006; Moteff 2007: 25). While the DHS has reportedly made progress on improving the reliability of the information contained in the database, it continues to draw criticism for including thousands of assets that many believe have more local importance than national importance (Moteff 2007: 26).

A DHS report summarising the results of 'Cyber Storm', a four-day exercise designed to test how industry and the government would respond to a concerted cyber-attack on key information systems, was seen as another indicator for insufficient progress made (DHS 2006). Cyber Storm was described as the first government-led, full-scale cyber-security exercise of its kind and took place from 6 to 10 February 2006. It was designed to test communications, policies, and procedures in response to various cyber-attacks and to identify where further planning and process improvements were needed. One of its special characteristics is its focus on the interconnectedness of cyber-systems with physical infrastructure and on coordination and communication between the public and the private sectors, as well as the fact that it was an international exercise. Like previous exercises – such as the ones described further above or the more recent Internet war games 'Silent Horizon' or 'Livewire' – Cyber Storm suggested that government and private-sector participants had trouble recognising the coordinated attacks, determining whom to contact, and organizing a response (DHS 2006). All in all, the exercise seemed to provide evidence that the administration was no better prepared for responding to a major cyber-attack than it had been for dealing with Hurricane Katrina, implying that the information systems that support large portions of the national economy, from telecommunications networks to power grids to chemical manufacturing and transportation systems, remained vulnerable.

The transformation of the military and offensive cyber-war

In a parallel development, we can again observe important progress in the military domain. During the presidency of Bush, the revolution in military affairs, closely linked to the development of information warfare capabilities, continued to be a major topic. Bush had already declared his intentions to transform the US military to meet the challenges of a new century one year before his actual election (Thompson 2005). And shortly after Secretary of Defense Donald Rumsfeld took office, he initiated a series of 11 panels to examine everything from US grand strategy to the personnel system, with the aim of accelerating the transformation of capabilities and forces to make them better suited to the security environment (Krepinevich 2001). In this debate, technology was once more presented as the great enabler and less as a source for vulnerabilities. In this mindset, Bush observed in a speech at Norfolk Naval Air Station on 13 February 2001 that:

> We are witnessing a revolution in the technology of war. Power is increasingly defined not by size but by mobility and swiftness. Advantage increasingly comes from information [...]. Safety is gained in stealth and force is projected on the long arc of precision-guided weapons.
>
> (Bush 2001c)

These and other statements revealed that issues of 'soft power', defined as the ability to achieve goals through attraction rather than coercion (Nye 1990, 2002,

2004; Keohane and Nye 1998), were no longer at the vanguard in the information warfare domain. Military technology and weapon systems, the hardware of any operation, became the new focal point.

In March 2001, the Defense Science Board (DSB) issued a report 'Protecting the Homeland', concerned with Defensive Information Operations and the US' vulnerability to cyber-attacks. The report called the Pentagon's 'Global Information Grid' a 'weapons system' and concluded that the United States was in an 'arms race' over information systems for warfare (Defense Science Board 2001: ES-2). The Task Force states that the DoD was unable to defend itself from an IO attack by a sophisticated nation-state adversary. It also stated that the vulnerability of the United States was greater than in 1996 and that more than 20 countries had or were developing computer attack capabilities (Defense Science Board 2001: ES-2). The chairman of the DSB study group explicitly warned of China as one such country (Wright 2001). Likewise, a Congressional Research Service (CRS) report on cyber-warfare in June 2001 reported that a number of nations were incorporating cyber-warfare as a new part of their military doctrine. Countries listed as having discussed the subject more or less openly were the United Kingdom, France, Germany, Russia, and China. The report stated that many of these countries were developing views towards the use of cyber-warfare that were different from those of the United States and might in some cases represent national security threats (Hildreth 2001). However, none of these reports presented any new evidence for the threat from other states except the fact that they were engaged in the idea of information warfare.

This, in fact, was no different from earlier reports on the topic. In the summer of 1995, the National Intelligence Council had reported on the information warfare capabilities of other state actors for the first time. Produced at the request of the Pentagon, the report focused on foreign efforts to attack the US public switched telephone network and the so-called Supervisory Control and Data Acquisition (SCADA) systems – the computers that control electric power distribution, oil refineries, and other similar utilities (Deutch 1996). The document remains classified, but in 1996, John Deutch, at the time the director of central intelligence, talked about the report in an unclassified hearing before the Senate Governmental Affairs Committee Permanent Subcommittee on Investigations. He said that the NSA had acknowledged that potential adversaries were developing a body of knowledge about the DoD's networks and other US systems and about methods to attack these systems. According to his estimate, more than 120 countries had established computer attack capabilities. Also, most countries were believed to be planning some degree of information warfare as part of their overall security strategy (Deutch 1996).

This figure is astoundingly high, and it is unclear what kind of evidence existed for this claim. Deutch himself mentioned that the report had a specific focus on 'rogue' states and on the question of whether they were developing plans or programmes to develop an offensive information warfare capability, but he also states that evidence was highly elusive. He called these countries 'very difficult intelligence targets' and said such programmes, by their nature, were 'almost certainly highly covert and difficult to uncover' (Deutch 1996). The countries most often cited as having an offensive information warfare capability, or as being likely to develop such capabilities in future years, are the classic strategic rivals like China and Russia. In one hearing, it was speculated that North Korea and Iran might have cyber-war capabilities (Shelby 1998), and once, later, even Cuba is named as having such capabilities (Stapleton 2000).

When studying the evidence that is given for these allegations, it is striking that advances in computer connectivity and information systems technology alone were taken as a sign that a country could have offensive capability. In addition, government officials use anecdotal evidence as sources for the intelligence, but also the fact that some nations had begun to include information warfare in their military doctrine and in their war college curricula. Among the frequently cited examples is a book published by two Chinese military officers that calls for the use of unconventional measures, including the propagation of computer viruses, to counterbalance the military power of the United States (Minihan 1998; Tenet 1998). Therefore, in order for nations to be suspected of developing such programmes, it was apparently enough that they recognised the value of attacking a country's computer systems.

The difficulty on the part of the intelligence community to produce accurate estimates of the cyber-threat got some specific attention in the mid-1990s: The 150-page Brown Commission Report on the Roles and Capabilities of the United States Intelligence Community (the 'Brown Report') stated in 1996 that the protection of computer networks in the private sector would necessarily exceed the roles and capabilities of US intelligence agencies, making reference to the earlier debates about the role of the NSA, but that collecting information about 'information warfare' threats posed by other countries or by non-governmental groups to US systems was a legitimate mission of the intelligence community (Brown Report 1996: 27). However, the commission noted that a better definition of this mission was urgently needed, because the existing activity in the domain appeared to be neither well-coordinated nor responsive to an overall strategy (Brown Report 1996: 27). The intelligence community's ability to handle information warfare came in for a similar assessment by the DSB Task Force, which called information warfare 'a non-traditional intelligence problem [that is] not easily discernible by traditional intelligence'. Traditional intelligence skills 'are largely irrelevant in the information warfare environment' (Defense Science Board 1996: 33). The inability to estimate the threat increased a sense of frustration and even powerlessness in the face of 'new' threats. The situation is not much different today.

In 2001, threat estimates and reports with belligerent vocabulary have a clear link to the ongoing transformation of the military. As said, information warfare as a vast umbrella concept remained a key aspect of this transformation. In March 2001, Deputy Defense Secretary Paul Wolfowitz testified before Congress that the United States had to develop new strategies to defend itself against, among other things, cyber-warfare (Garamone 2001). And just prior to Bush's June 2001 visit to Europe, National Security Adviser Condoleezza Rice indicated the president would consult with European leaders on developing a new framework to deal with common threats, such as information warfare (Rice 2001). On 7 June 2001, Bush referred to the 'true threats of the 21st century,' in a speech in Iowa, one of which was 'informational warfare' (White House 2001c). Also, the Bush FY2001 Defense Supplemental request included a non-disclosed amount for classified information warfare programs 'to enhance the intelligence community's ability to detect terrorist threats' (Department of Defense 2001b: 2). More than before, information warfare, as part of the strategic toolbox, was an issue for not only the United States but also for its allies. In his speech at the North Atlantic Treaty Organisation (NATO) Council in Brussels on 6 June 2001, Rumsfeld told the allies that not only the United States was threatened by attacks from cyberspace but also the other NATO countries and therefore the alliance as a whole. Among the 'future challenges' for NATO, Rumsfeld named not only traditional terrorism, high-tech weapons and missiles with WMD, but also 'cyber-attacks' (Gilmore 2001).

Perception management

Not surprisingly, the US' so-called 'War on Terror' and the occupation of Iraq had a great effect on the topic. Shortly after the attacks of 9/11, the issue of 'perception management', also called 'public affairs operations', received a lot of attention in connection with the Office of Strategic Influence (OSI). The OSI was a department created by the DoD on 30 October 2001 to support the 'War on Terror' through psychological operations in targeted countries (Dao and Schmitt 2002). The OSI was planned to be a centre for the creation of propaganda material for the stated purpose of misleading enemy forces or foreign civilian populations. After the creation of the office was reported in the United States and foreign media in mid-February 2002, intense discussions on purpose and scope of the office started. The discussions culminated in an unconvincing public statement by Rumsfeld (2002a) in late February 2002 that the office had been closed down.

The most recent document on these and similar aspects is the Information Operations Roadmap, a 30 October 2003 document approved personally by Rumsfeld (2003) and declassified in January 2006. It was developed by an oversight panel led by the deputy assistant secretary of defense (Resource and Plans) and representatives from the Joint Chiefs of Staff, the Office of the Secretary of Defense, and Special Operations Command, among other organisations. The document calls on the DoD to enhance its capabilities in five key IO areas: electronic warfare (EW), Psychological Operations (PSYOPS), Operations Security (OPSEC), military deception, and computer network operations (CNO). More graphically, the document states that: 'We Must Fight the Net [...] We must improve PSYOP [...] We must improve Network and Electro-Magnetic Attack Capability' (Rumsfeld 2003: 6). The phrase 'We must fight the Net', which appears more than once in the heavily redacted document, appears to refer to the possibility of the Internet and other networks being used as a weapon of attack.

The authors warn that US networks are very vulnerable to attacks by hackers, enemies seeking to disable them, or spies looking for intelligence. As a consequence, the document talks about the Internet as being equivalent to an enemy weapons system. While the idea is not entirely new, it still seems like a very radical, if not foolish, exaggeration of cyber-fears.

The document also recognises the legal conundrum presented by the use of overseas propaganda in the information age. One of the Roadmap's recommendations is the need to 'Clarify Lanes in the Road for PSYOP, Public Affairs and Public Diplomacy' (Rumsfeld 2003). These statements can be put in relation to the fact that the Pentagon had paid a private company, the Lincoln Group, to plant hundreds of stories in Iraqi newspapers, a fact that had become public in 2005. The stories – all supportive of US policy – were written by military personnel and then placed in Iraqi publications (see Bamford 2005; Hedges 2005), but of course they also made their way into US media outlets. That information put out as part of the military's psychological operations is finding its way onto the computer and television screens of ordinary Americans is also acknowledged in the Roadmap: 'Information intended for foreign audiences, including public diplomacy and Psyops, is increasingly consumed by our domestic audience [...] Psyops messages will often be replayed by the news media for much larger audiences, including the American public' (Rumsfeld 2003). It concludes that the distinction between foreign and domestic audiences becomes more a question of *intent* rather than actual information dissemination practices (Rumsfeld 2003: 6; National Security Archive 2006). This is of no small matter. The Smith-Mundt Act of 1948, amended in 1972 and 1998, prohibits the US government from disseminating propaganda to the American public using information and psychological operations directed at foreign audiences; and several presidential directives, including Reagan's National Security Directive (NSD) 77 in 1983, Clinton's PDD 68 in 1999, and Bush's NSPD 16 in July 2002 (the latter two still classified), have set up specific structures for carrying out public diplomacy and IO.

According to some newspaper articles, National Security Presidential Directive No. 16, signed by Bush in July 2002, orders the government to develop, for the first time, national-level guidance for determining when and how the United States would launch cyber-attacks against enemy computer networks (Graham 2003). Similar to strategic doctrine that has guided the use of nuclear weapons since the Second World War, the cyber-warfare guidance would establish presidential rules for deciding the circumstances under which such attacks would be launched, who should authorise and conduct them, and what targets would be considered legitimate. Bush's action highlights the administration's keen interest in pursuing a new form of weaponry that, according to many specialists, has great potential for altering the means of waging war. As we have pointed out above, the ongoing transformation of the armed forces was based on a vision of high-tech weaponry. The 'Rumsfeld Doctrine' promised that a technologically advanced military could easily win battles anywhere around the world with relatively small numbers of soldiers on the ground, based on mobility, stealth, and technology (Rumsfeld 2002b; O'Hanlon 2002). It argued that the power and accuracy of the latest weapons more than compensated for the reduced number of troops, relieving the United States from the constraints of needing allies to help supply large numbers of soldiers, which, as a side note, ultimately made it less difficult for the United States to bypass the United Nations (UN) and NATO in projecting power overseas and provided the military rationale for the administration's foreign policy of unilateral pre-emption (Slocombe 2003; Freedman 2003).

The National Cyberspace Strategy, viewed in the context of the underlying option of pre-emption detailed in the National Security Strategy of 2002, presents the identical possibility of future use of force by the United States in response to potential cyber-attacks (Gibson 2004). This strategy document seeks to 'prevent cyber-attacks against America's critical infrastructures, reduce national vulnerability to cyber-attacks, and minimise damage and recovery time from cyber-attacks that do occur' (Bush 2003b: viii). By reserving the right to respond in a manner other than criminal prosecution, the United States may potentially resort to force in response to actual or potential cyber-attacks. Thus, the language contained in the National Cyberspace Strategy appears to follow the same principles inherent in the National Security Strategy, which is that of a broad right of response. The strategy of pre-emption expanded to cyberspace corresponds well with offensive cyber-war ideas. In the previous administration, as shown during the Kosovo conflict (Eriksson A. 1999; Dunn 2002), there had been concern about using techniques of cyber-warfare that would then be emulated by others. The Bush administration, on the other hand, was suggesting that defeating terrorism required action across the full spectrum of capabilities. This can be seen as admission, if only a tacit one, that cyberspace-based means of warfare are an essential part of the global 'campaign against terrorism' (Gibson 2004). While the future of cyber-warfare is yet to be determined, it is certainly going to play a major role in the United States and international arsenals in the twenty-first century. The prospects of fast, cheap, devastating attacks on an enemy with a small chance of collateral damage provide the kind of combat more civilians would permit their government to commit.

Changes in the threat frame: Oklahoma City and critical infrastructures

In comparison to the first phase, policy windows play a different role after a threat is on the agenda: they are no longer necessary to get the issue onto the agenda, but they are more influential in triggering a re-framing of the threat frame. Above, we stated that the condition that was identified as problem for national security in the 1980s was the spread of information technologies and their link to automated systems. This changed with a change in the technological substructure: what had previously been a localised problem that only concerned a few people, mostly professionals, turned into a mass phenomenon in the 1990s. The underlying conditions, which became the problem to which those policy makers reacted, were the proliferation of information systems into all

114   *Critical infrastructures and homeland security*

aspects of life and the problems that emerged from dependency on these information and communication technologies.

At the core of the cyber-threat debate lie the malicious use of the information infrastructure, on the one hand, and the inherent insecurity of these technologies, on the other. In order to understand the emergence of the specific threat frame of the 1990s, it is therefore crucial to understand the characteristics of the information infrastructure, and especially the perception thereof. Apart from its development into an unbounded system, another factor that seemed to contribute to the vulnerability of the Internet was the rapid growth and use of the network, accompanied by the rapid deployment of new network services involving complex applications. In addition, experts left no doubt that the security problems of the technical sub-systems would further aggravate. A glimpse into the future revealed an ongoing dynamic globalisation of information services, which in connection with technological innovation would lead to a dramatic increase in the connectivity and complexity of systems, leading to ill-understood behaviour of systems, as well as barely understood vulnerabilities (Strogatz 2001). Not only was the global information infrastructure likely to provide constant connection through multiple devices embedded in all aspects of business, public, and personal life – becoming not only inter-dependent but rather *super*-dependent (Rathmell 2001) – but the mutual interaction between systems and networks was also likely to increase, thus creating ever more complex structures. As was well known from information sciences, the more complex an IT system is, the more bugs it contains – and the more complex it is, the harder it becomes to manage or control the security of an IT system (Näf 2001).

In the period under discussion, there is one instance that substantially changed the threat frame: the Oklahoma City bombing. It served as a 'wake-up call' and was the precipitating event that led the Clinton administration to rethink the vulnerabilities of the nation's infrastructure. Thereafter, the discourse changed significantly. Much as in Phase I, events in the world of information technology sounded alarms for the cyber-security community but mainly served to further strengthen the PCCIP's threat frame. The most prominent of these – most of which have already been described above – were indicators for the perceived vulnerability:

- *1990/91, Dutch hackers*: On the one hand, the incident happened during a time of war, while on the other, it was difficult to identify the perpetrators and their intentions. The incident showed how vulnerable the military had become due to its dependency on the civilian (information) infrastructure.
- *1994, Rome Lab incident*: The *incident*, well-documented by the DoD, was seen to be of particular concern because the attack showed how a small group of, as it later turned out, underage hackers could easily and quickly take control of defence networks.
- *1996, RAND 'The Day After' Exercise*: The exercises highlighted the fact that mechanisms and techniques for information attacks could be acquired with relatively modest investment. Furthermore, due to its design, the study

seemed to demonstrate that because the US economy, society, and military rely heavily on a high-performance networked information infrastructure, this infrastructure presents a set of attractive strategic targets for opponents who possess information warfare capabilities.

- *1997, Eligible Receiver*: This *exercise* demonstrated how easy it was to infiltrate the Pentagon systems and take control of power grids and municipal emergency ('911') systems (PCCIP 1997; Minihan 1998; Vatis 1998b). For defence officials, it also showed that no adequate protection was in place and exposed a lack of awareness about cyber-warfare (Hamre 2003).
- *1998, Solar Sunrise*: This incident caused fears similar to those that arose after the Rome Laboratory incident. Hackers got access to at least 200 different computer systems of the US military, the nuclear weapons laboratories, the Department of Energy, and National Aeronautics and Space Administration (NASA). At precisely the same time, the US forces in the Middle East were being built up because of tensions with Iraq over UN arms inspections (PCCIP 1997: 8; Minihan 1998; Vatis 1998b, 1999). The fact that some of the intrusions could be traced back to Internet service providers in the Gulf region initially led experts to believe that the Iraqi government had to be behind the attacks (GAO 1999). The incident provided a major impetus for the formation of a Joint Task Force on Computer Network Defense (JTF-CND) later in the year.
- *1998, Moonlight Maze*: The *intrusion* was noteworthy mainly due to two reasons: a) The DoD traced the attack back to a mainframe computer in the former Soviet Union and b) the attacks had been going on for a long time before they were detected. This was reminiscent of the Cuckoo's Egg incident.

As we have shown, US defence and intelligence officials had expressed concern not only about the security of classified data but also about the possibility that foreign countries or terrorists might use cyber-attacks to counter the overwhelming military superiority of the United States. Concerns about the second scenario increased after the PCCIP report. Starting from 1998, the examples listed above were cited more often to show that critical infrastructures were at risk due to their dependency on the information infrastructure, while the focus on the foreign intelligence threat further decreased. Furthermore, the entire subject also became less focused: while the theft of classified data has a fairly straightforward link to national security, it became less clear thereafter what exactly the threat to national security was, except for the *potential* damage that these incidents might have caused.

In fact, very often, real or imagined economic damage seems to be sufficient for an issue to be designated a national security threat, as the following examples demonstrate: the malfunction of a communications satellite in 1998 was referred to in a variety of hearings in order to demonstrate the nation's dependency on information technologies (Hamre 1998; Kerrey 1998). In addition, the distributed denial-of-service attacks in 2000 gave rise to a series of hearings. The attacks targeted the websites of Amazon, Microsoft, eBay, CNN, Yahoo, E*Trade, and ZDNet, which were offline for a while. About 50 computers at Stanford University, as well as computers at the University of California at Santa Barbara, were amongst the computers sending pings in these Denial-of-Service (DoS) attacks. Again, a teenage hacker was the source of the attacks, which, in the end, were nothing more than a petty annoyance.

A special case, which we will only fleetingly touch upon in this book, is 'Y2K', the Year 2000 problem. A major global fear arose that critical industries and government functions would stop working at 12 A.M. on 1 January 2000, since computer programmes would break down or produce erroneous results. Because they stored years using only two digits, and because the year 2000 would be represented by 00, it was feared that this value would be misinterpreted by software as representing the year 1900. This fear was fuelled by extensive press coverage and other media speculation, as well as corporate and government reports.

The preparation for Y2K was a significant boon for the computer industry as companies and organisations checked and upgraded their computer systems all over the world. Some individuals stockpiled canned or dried food in anticipation of food shortages. A few pundits predicted the collapse of civilisation or at least protracted economic depression and technological breakdown on a wide scale (cf. Yourdon and Yourdon 1998). Starting in around 1997, the Y2K problem became an issue in US policy circles PCCIP 1997: 11–12; Tenet 1999). The Senate formed a Special Committee on the Year 2000 Technology Problem, which held numerous hearings on the readiness of key economic sectors. In a way, the Y2K challenge was again seen to have served as a wake-up call to many who were previously unaware of extensive dependency on computers. In addition, Y2K efforts forced agencies to identify systems that were mission-critical (Mussington 2002).

The interesting thing about the Y2K threat frame is that, although in reality it was linked to an anticipated technical failure in the information infrastructure, the issue was also frequently linked to potentially malicious human agency in congressional hearings: it was believed that because many people, such as the technicians who updated computers to make them 'Y2K-safe', had been given access to programs as well as the authority to modify them and place them in service, there was a considerable threat from an insider or foreign contractors (PCCIP 1997: 12; Tenet 1999). This is an interesting case demonstrating that securitising actors have the tendency to 'actorise' threats. Apparently, the spectre of failures or accidents did not convey enough urgency in the threat politics process, so that the problem was 'spiced up'. Not only that, the issue was again linked to a classical foreign 'enemy' problem. This practice is also apparent from the above hacker incidents. As one sober analyst noticed in 1999: 'If your system goes down, it is a lot more interesting to say it was the work of a foreign government rather than admit it was due to an American teenage "script-kiddy" tinkering with a badly written CGI script' (Ingles-le Nobel 1999).

The most relevant of all the government or government-funded reports that acted as formal or informal feedback have been described in the earlier chapters. The 1994 JSC report, 'Redefining Security', set the stage for the security debate on threats in the 1990s; its strong focus on questions of information security helped to elevate the problem in the minds of government circles. The National Research Council's 'Computers at Risk' report of 1991 is referred to often (cf. PCCIP 1997: A-8), as it was one of the first studies to describe the growing vulnerability of networked computers and to outline a series of core principles to improve security. The DSB published several influential studies that were widely read (Defense Science Board 1994, 1996). In addition, a variety of GAO (1989, 1991) reports are frequently referred to, and their number increased over the years, which is an indicator for the growing relevance allotted to the topic. The most influential of all studies, however, was the PCCIP report, which not only set in motion the CIP debate in the United States but also triggered infrastructure protection efforts in many countries around the world (Dunn and Wigert 2004; Abele-Wigert and Dunn 2006).

Again, semi-academic publications and RAND publications figure prominently in the dispute. Apart from military writings (Libicki 1994, 1995, 1997a, 1997b, 1999; Johnson and Libicki 1995; Owens 1995, Cebrowski and Garstka 1998), popular books like Alvin and Heidi Toffler's *War and Anti-War* (1993), in which an 'electronic Pearl Harbor' is said to be just waiting to happen (Toffler and Toffler 1993: 149), or Alvin Toffler's *Third Wave* (1980) were widely read. The RAND studies written by Arquilla and Ronfeldt (1996, 1997a, 1997b, 1999), Campen's (1992) *The First Information Warfare*, or Schwartau's (1994) *Information Warfare* are other examples of books on this topic that established important terms like 'cyber-war' and 'net-war', or 'electronic Pearl Harbor'.

The third category in Kingdon's model – indicators, which includes statistics – gained momentum in this phase. The media in particular began to operate with numbers, focusing on the number of attacks or the amount of financial damage done by viruses. All the statistics clearly showed that the frequency of new worms and viruses was increasing and was likely continue to do so in future. In addition, the costs associated with them are significant: a market intelligence firm estimated a loss of US$8.8 billion due to the LoveLetter virus, US$2.6 billion in productivity loss for the Code Red worm, and US$9 billion due to the Klez virus (Clarke and Zeichner 2004; ICSA Labs 2003, 2004). Viruses like Michelangelo (JSC 1994), Melissa (GAO 1999), Explore.Zip, CIH (Vatis 1999), or SoBig (Clinton 2000: 43) were also referred to in order to stress the need to act.

Thus, we find that a variety of policy windows did play a role in the further consolidation of cyber-threats as a prime national security threat. But of all the examples in this chapter, only the Oklahoma City bombing lead to a reframing, or at least a change in the discourse, by firmly linking cyber-threats to critical infrastructure. All the other incidents or statistics are mainly cited to support a call for action and are used to demonstrate the high degree of vulnerability and dependency. It seems that, once an awareness of the problem had been created, there was little need for additional incidents to prove the point. 9/11, on the other hand, did not lead to reframing. However, this policy window diminished the virulence of cyber-threats and shifted the focus of most officials from the cyber-realm to the realm of physical terrorism. In that sense, 9/11 acted as a 'reality check': the high priority given to cyber-security in previous years suddenly seemed a mistake to many officials. The attacks on US territory marked the end of virtual threats and potentially grave consequences and provided a concrete threat to act upon.

The fact that there was no reframing merits some specific attention: Why did 9/11 not change the threat frame or countermeasures, but nonetheless changed aspects of the cyber-threats debate? The reason for this, we believe, is twofold: on the one hand, the prevalent threat frame was widely accepted and obviously highly stable due to congruence with overall beliefs. In EO 13231 of 16 October 2001, for example, we find the shorthand version of the PCCIP threat frame:

> It is the policy of the United States to protect against disruption of the operation of information systems for critical infrastructure and thereby help to protect the people, economy, essential human and government services, and national security of the United States, and to ensure that any disruptions that occur are infrequent, of minimal duration, and manageable, and cause the least damage possible. The implementation of this policy shall include a voluntary public-private partnership, involving corporate and nongovernmental organizations.
>
> (Bush 2001b)

Even when cyber-threats were downscaled, there was no need to change this threat frame. In addition, all the turf battles had been fought in the 1990s, so that this specific threat occurred in a more 'settled' phase. The lead of the law enforcement community and the crucial importance of public private partnerships were widely accepted by all actors involved. The establishment of the DHS, propagated as a step towards pulling down the artificial walls between institutions that deal with internal threats and others that deal with external ones, did not fundamentally change this perception: it merely changed parts of the organisational setting.

Not surprisingly, we find that, at least initially, one main focus in public hearings was on the possibility of terrorists using cyber-means for attacks. In addition, a number of studies were conducted in the aftermath of 9/11 that focused on Muslim terrorists and their cyber-capabilities (OCIPEP 2001; Vatis 2001; NIPC 2002; Technical Analysis Group 2003). At this time, the focus of attention shifted from hackers depicted as terrorists towards terrorist hackers, and specifically Muslim ones (Conway 2008). Needless to say, the mass media also immediately jumped on the subject. Two days after the attacks, *USA Today* wrote about cyber-attacks in the near future – 'another wave of terrorism' – and quoted a former Pentagon official's warning of an 'electronic Pearl Harbor' (Schwartz 2001). Soon after, the debate centred on Osama bin Laden and al-Qaida. In December, an alleged member of al-Qaida who had been caught in India was quoted by Newsbytes as saying that his organisation had infiltrated Microsoft and manipulated the source code for their new operating system Windows XP (McWilliams 2001). This report quickly made its way around the world, though it just relied on a single and somehow sketchy source: the information came from Indian IT security entrepreneur Ravi Visvesvaraya Prasad, known for his sensationalist op-eds on the 'threat' of Chinese information warfare in Indian newspapers (Prasad 2000, 2001).

But it was not only the media that focused on terrorist attackers; officials also focused their attention on terrorists. The few examples cited below again show how volatile and unfounded the cyber-threat assessments still were. In his Senate testimony on 'The Terrorist Threat Confronting the United States' in February 2002, Dale L. Watson, the FBI's executive assistant director on counter-terrorism and counterintelligence, talked about 'an emerging threat':

> Beyond criminal threats, cyber space also faces a variety of significant national security threats, including increasing threats from terrorists. [...] Cyberterrorism – meaning the use of cyber tools to shut down critical national infrastructures (such as energy, transportation, or government operations) for the purpose of coercing or intimidating a government or civilian population – is clearly an emerging threat.
>
> (Watson 2002)

In March 2002, the intelligence community's new 'global threat' estimate was presented to Congress. CIA Director George J. Tenet, when discussing possible cyber-attacks, mostly talked about terrorists, after having focused his attention on the whole range of actors in previous years (Tenet 1997, 1998, 1999):

> We are also alert to the possibility of cyber warfare attack by terrorists. [...] Attacks of this nature will become an increasingly viable option for terrorists as they and other foreign adversaries become more familiar with these targets, and the technologies required to attack them.
>
> (Tenet 2002)

In the 'CIA Answers to Questions for the Record', dated 8 April 2002, it is further specified that:

> Various terrorist groups including al-Qa'ida and Hizballah are becoming more adept at using the Internet and computer technologies, and the FBI is monitoring an increasing number of cyber threats.... These groups have both the intentions and the desire to develop some of the cyberskills necessary to forge an effective cyber attack modus operandi.
>
> (Central Intelligence Agency 2002)

Others, too, feared that al-Qaida had these abilities: for example, Vice Admiral Lowell E. Jacoby, Director of the DIA, stated that members of al-Qaida had spoken openly of targeting the US economy as a way of undermining US global power. As proof for this claim, he stated that al-Qaida was using publicly available Internet websites to reconnoitre US infrastructure, utilities, and critical facilities (Jacoby 2003). Again others, such as Robert S. Mueller (2003), Director of the FBI, feared that though current attacks were mere nuisances such as denial-of-service attacks, their options might increase.

Again, one wonders about these intelligence estimates. The assessment of the threat is still largely anecdotal, with threat assessments revealing a general weakness that by that time had become a trend, not an exception. To make things worse, the focus on cyber-terrorists proved to be a fairly temporary phenomenon, too. About a year after 9/11, Richard Clarke, the then head of the White House Office for Cyber Security, told the press that the government had again begun to regard nation-states rather than terrorist groups as the most dangerous threat. He said:

> There are terrorist groups that are interested [in conducting cyber-attacks]. We now know that al Qaeda was interested. But the real major threat is from the information-warfare brigade or squadron of five or six countries.
> (Cha and Krim 2002)

Detached from all of this, the cyber-threat frame as developed under Clinton remained in place. Not only was the diagnosis – a very wide range of potential perpetrators – accepted, but so was the prognosis: whether cyber-terror or cyber-warfare, the countermeasures as laid out in the National Plan and Bush's National Strategy to Secure Cyberspace seemed to satisfy decision-makers.

To sum up, during the Bush administration, the already existing CIP package was expanded by adding the concept of homeland security. Critical infrastructures, defined as assets whose destruction or disruption would have a crippling impact on the heart of the US society, became the core of what needs to be protected in homeland security, while vulnerabilities, be they physical or virtual, abound. However, while the threat frame as promoted by the PCCIP remained the same, the attention given to the cyber-threat aspect diminished. The events of 9/11 focused many minds in that direction. In 1998, the then Deputy Secretary of Defense John Hamre said in a hearing that the question was not whether the United States would suffer an 'electronic Pearl Harbor', but when (Hamre 1998). One year later, Hamre was quoted as saying: 'We are at war-right now. We are in a cyberwar' (Donnelly and Crawley 1999). In a recent interview, this once eager cyber-advocate said:

> I spend hours a day worrying about biological warfare. I spend hours a day worrying about nuclear warfare. I do not spend minutes a day worrying about cyber warfare as a means of mass destruction. In the scale of things you want your government to worry about that can really cause existential threats to society, biological warfare and nuclear warfare are far, far bigger than cyber warfare.
> (Hamre 2003)

After 9/11, 'critical infrastructures' became a synonym for 'the homeland'. But despite the fact that cyber-threats still figure in these observations, the tangible aspects began to displace cyber-threats from the limelight. As we have pointed out, the National Security Strategy of 2002 is virtually devoid of any mention of information age–related issues: there is no mention of any concerted national approach or strategy for protecting the information society, no indication that the global economy of the twenty-first century is a cyber-economy, and no indication of the need for international cooperation in this arena (Bush 2002).

6 Securing the information age
Failed securitisation or a new logic of security?

In the last three chapters, we traced the emergence of cyber-threats as a model of threats in modern times and analysed the political process that moved the threat onto the political agenda and led to subsequent alterations of its appearance. In order to see how cyber-threats are constructed, we introduced the concept of threat frames with three distinct parts (according to Snow and Benford 1988: 199–202): *diagnostic framing*, which is the act of defining a problem and assigning blame for the problem to an agent or agencies (this is the equivalent of designating the threat subject and referent object of security; Buzan *et al.* 1998: 32); *prognostic framing*, which deals with elaborating solutions and proposing specific strategies, tactics, and objectives by which these solutions may be achieved; and *motivational framing*, which means to rally the troops behind the cause or a 'call for action'. The content of the threat frame – formulated by professionals of security – must appeal to the existing values and beliefs of the target audience (in our particular case, top-level decision-makers) to become effective. At the same time, many different aspects influence the conditions in which such a framing takes place, such as the beliefs and resources of the framing actors as well as institutions and the broader environment, all of which influence the framing process. The observable impact of the threat politics process is the establishment of countermeasures or policies.

This chapter revisits previous assumptions and examines the variables of the framework for analysis: policy windows, securitisation/framing actors, threat frames, and countermeasures. Furthermore, we want to focus on the impacts of the impacts, namely, on the new logic of security that becomes obvious from our analysis of countermeasures.

When conditions turn into problems

Two factors explain the reasons for threat construction: on the one hand, I looked at 'policy windows', understood as opportunities to move a certain issue to the fore in the political process, and on the other hand, there is bureaucratic competition between agencies, aggravated by the loss of the external enemy after the end of the Cold War. The rise of cyber-threats to the top of the security political agenda can thus be seen as an outcome of the major re-orientation of security policies that took place when the Cold War ended. As traditional security problems lost their urgency, governments turned to advisors, specialists, analysts, and researchers not only in order to receive advice on policy alternatives but also for identifying new challenges and problems, which led to a multitude of 'new' issues being added to the security agenda (Eriksson 1999b, 2001a). By creating an environment in which it became possible to construct new threats, this geopolitical development played a pivotal role in the whole process of threat framing and could itself be considered a kind of policy window.

Our case studies only provided one instance of Phase I, which is a very thin basis for theorising. In addition, we have found that it is rather difficult to identify the exact point in time when the first threat framing occurred, but such identification would be necessary in order to convincingly link policy windows to the securitisation/initial threat-framing process. This is due to vagueness in the definition of what 'securitisation' actually is; and even if we seek to identify the first instance of when an issue was successfully framed as a national security threat, the task does not become substantially easier. In our specific case, the definition of cyber-threats as the malicious use of information and communication technologies either as a target or as a weapon gives the issue some additional focus, but it is still not altogether clear when the first cyber-threat frame was created. This is the result of an empirical problem: How far back would we have to go to identify the first threat frame? And, for that matter, how else but in hindsight would it be possible to identify policy windows – i.e. if there is a (re-) framing, there must have been a policy window somewhere – as we have done it? Methodological prowess mainly depends on very careful definitions of both the phenomena we address and the political process we are looking for; however, both are difficult to provide. On the one hand, the phenomenon itself, as we have argued in Chapter 1, is highly elusive and is also constantly evolving as the technological substructure changes. On the other, even though the original concept of securitisation was clarified by focusing on security as a practice with an outcome in Chapter 2, we still have difficulties in clearly identifying acts of threat framing. What we can identify, though, is a period when a condition turned into a problem: this happened when cyber-crime came to be perceived as a serious issue, a development mainly brought about by an increase in incidents and mounting economic losses.

In contrast to the single case for Phase I, there are various instances of reframing to be found in Phase II. Among all the identified policy windows, event windows clearly appear as the most prominent. It seems as if political windows had not played any role at all, at least not overtly: cyber-threats were never an election theme; neither were they highly politicised in general, probably because the fear of them did not mobilise the electorate at any time. We have identified only two policy windows with discernible impact on the reframing of threat frames: the Oklahoma City bombing and the 9/11 attacks. Both are so-called event windows, and both are real incidents in the physical world that are, in fact, related to terrorism. According to theory, beliefs are relatively stable, so that it is not surprising that only incidents with a comparatively great overall impact, including psychological impact, are capable of initiating a change in the belief system. Despite this similarity, the roles of the two incidents in reframing issues are different. The Oklahoma City attack brought a new issue – that of interdependencies – to the attention of decision-makers and perhaps had the biggest influence on the entire debate. 9/11, on the other hand, served as a reality check that did not change the threat frame per se, but changed the tone of the discourse by strengthening one of the discourse strands, namely that of terrorism and, more specifically, Muslim terrorism.

How much explanatory power does the 'policy window' variable actually have? Is it possible that without policy windows, there would have been no cyber-threat framing? To put the question differently, are policy windows needed at all for reframing, or can we identify instances of reframing that are independent of policy windows? For example, the subtle reframing of national security decision directives (NSDD) 145 in national security directive (NSD) 42 does not seem connected to a policy window, even though it is also debatable whether this can actually be counted as reframing. Then again, it is possible that certain forces saw the change in administration as a good opportunity to reintroduce their particular views of the problem. Also, and most importantly, the emergence of the broader threat frame in the National Academy of Sciences (NAS) study of 1990 is not connected either to any identifiable policy window. It is true that the document did not create any new countermeasure, but it set the stage for the future debate and provided part of the vocabulary taken up by military documents and studies in the early 1990s. In this particular instance, certain individuals with specific ideas are likely to have played the most significant role. With our approach, however, the origin or flow of ideas cannot be uncovered. All these examples reveal an additional weakness in our approach: not only do we have difficulties in identifying the first instances of threat framing, but there are also difficulties associated with identifying instances of reframing; it is in fact unclear what constitutes an act of reframing or to which degree two frames have to differ from each other to qualify as a new threat frame.

At the same time, the case studies make clear that all of Kingdon's categories (indicators, focusing events, and feedback) become intermingled – events and statistics are mentioned in official reports, and then, these reports in turn act as feedback. Furthermore, apart from instigating cases of reframing, problem windows are used to underscore arguments. In that sense, they are turned into stories to prove the need for action. Not surprisingly, we can identify the following traits of these stories (see also Smith 1999a): we find a great reliance on hypotheses upon what might happen and not what has happened, because there are no incidents that provide an easily discernible link to a national security threat. In addition and closely connected to this fact, scores of generally insignificant computer security incidents are accumulated as anecdotal evidence, mainly shown in the chapter on virtual attacks against the Department of Defense (DoD), and delivered out of context or in an exaggerated manner, always insinuating that something awful is about to happen in the barely anticipated future. Moreover, we can observe an absurd vicious circle of news generation: the evidence that is presented in hearings is often based on (true or false) stories in the media (one example is the incident involving dam floodgates that was described in the introduction). Media outlets, in turn, quote government officials on the exact same stories to give their reporting more weight (Conway 2008). Thus, the media, even though not directly involved in threat framing, is responsible for creating a kind of 'hyperreality' (Baudrillard 1983), a condition that occurs when the media depicts something as more true to life than the object it is purporting to represent (see also Derian 1995: 37–41). With this practice, the standard of proof becomes malleable.

As for the variable of policy window, the evidence indicates that policy windows (or at least something resembling them) play a certain role in threat politics, despite the fact that some of the assumptions about causality (policy windows come prior to the framing process) might be faulty. It is also obvious that policy windows in Phase II play a different role than the ones in Phase I. Their primary role in the framing process is to give the issue a new direction by changing either the beliefs or the resources of key actors. We can further argue that not all events, indicators, or instances of feedback are turned into policy windows, but that they are necessary for initiating the process of threat framing and as an affirmation of existing threat perceptions, and that they serve as steady fuel for the process of threat politics. At the same time, various observations point to the assumption that the variable might be too limited in its current form. In fact, 'policy window' might be a misleading concept altogether. Returning to Kingdon's theory, he argues that a window opens because of change in the political stream or when a new problem comes to the attention of officials. However, this does not answer *why* it comes to the attention of officials or *why* the political stream changes. The first question is partially answered by looking at indicators, focusing events, or formal and informal feedback; this has indeed been central for our approach but happens prior to the opening of a policy window. Therefore, we should perhaps replace the variable 'policy window' with 'problem recognition' for Phase I and 'disturbing event' for Phase II – an approach that does not, however, resolve some of the empirical problems that were described.

Professionals of security and epistemic communities

The question of who is involved in the process of threat framing and threat politics is not easily answered. Probably, the biggest impediment was that we were not able to link specific actors to threat frames or vice versa; only in hearings can threat frames be attributed to individuals, but even then, we do not know where these frames originated from. It is therefore almost impossible to designate an individual or group that came up with the first threat frame or to identify the group that moved it onto the agenda for the first time. The same is true for Phase II – neither we can identify with any certainty the characteristics of the actors who have been influential in re-framing the issue of cyber-threats, nor can we therefore say anything about the differences between the actors in the two phases. Nevertheless, there are certain statements we can venture to make.

It can be shown that specific actors or actor constellations develop a specific threat frame, which is deductible from their statements and can be identified from official documents. Notions of cyber-threats have originated among military as well as civilian actors. In the law enforcement community, cyber-crime has become a particularly salient threat image. Within the military bureaucracy, the perceived threats have been framed as 'information warfare', 'information operations', and 'cyber-war'. Both communities refer to 'cyber-terror', a threat image that has remained very fuzzy. Among computer scientists, technicians, and network operators, the threat images are usually much narrower, with an emphasis on attacks, exploits, and disruptions perpetrated against computer networks, software conflicts, and other bugs which can lead to systems crashes, for example, the Year 2000 (Y2K) computer bug and its perceived implications. We have argued that the securitising and framing actors are most likely to emerge from the so-called professionals of security, which are endowed with both symbolic capital and the capacity to inter-link heterogeneous discourses in the security domain. This is based on the belief that there are specific positions within the state that have a privileged capacity to transform non-security issues into security questions (Bigo 1994, 1998), in contrast to assuming that in principle everyone can speak for society (Wæver 1995). The transformative capacity of security professionals is a direct result of their institutional position, which empowers them to produce credible knowledge about threats. That successful threat frames are in some ways linked to professionals of security can be confirmed, but again, we have no way of knowing where these frames originally originated from.

From the very beginning of the almost 20-year period that we have investigated, the law enforcement community played a strong role in the process due to existing resources, norms, and institutions. Members of the military took the place of a framing but not of an executing actor: they gave cyber-threats a new face but then had to cede responsibility and admit that they could not provide the answer to them. As a result, they became more or less marginalised in the broader debate after a certain point. Only in the domain of information warfare, framed as a traditional military task, did they retain primary responsibility and strive to advance developments in the domain. However, it would be wrong to argue that they did not try to retain some influence in countering the threat initially, as our discussion of the conflicting prognostic threat frames has shown. The (perceived) nature of the threat as well as restraints stemming from norms and institutions made such a bigger role of the military establishment unfeasible. Therefore, we can learn that the question of who wins, why, and when is not only dependent on the content of a threat frame but also on the position and the determination of actors, as we can learn from the voluntary ceding of power due to failure in the face of the threat. What we need, however, are more details and a better methodological approach to learn more about actors.

Though we do not want to consider methodological issues in too much depth here, it is clear that some of the open questions concerning the attribution of threat frames to actors could best be answered by conducting expert interviews. Even further insights into actor constellations could be gained from the advocacy coalition framework (ACF) developed by Paul Sabatier (1988) as well as Paul Sabatier and Hank Jenkins-Smith (1993, 1999), which focus on the role of beliefs in the policy-making process. The framework emphasises the beliefs of policy-makers and the networks of these actors that develop within policy domains or subsystems. The ACF says that during periods of subsystem stability, one coalition, or more specifically, its beliefs, will define policy. Policy redesigning occurs when subsystems change, which is to say that the set of prevailing beliefs change due to policy-oriented learning or due to turnover of participants in the subsystem or, alternatively, due to a change in the external environment. We have to be aware, however, that even though this approach would greatly enhance our knowledge concerning actors, such a detailed analysis of coalitions would shift the focus of analysis away from threat framing as such.

Other questions remain to be answered. For example, if an issue is already on the agenda, is it necessary for a top politician to be in position each time the issue is reframed, according to the framework? Or, is the act of securitisation or threat framing always a conscious, wilful act, or do 'accidental' securitising actors exist? Put differently, do these actors always want to give a specific topic a higher degree of urgency, or do threat politics occur automatically? The material collected in the previous chapters does not provide any answers to these questions. The assumption that a top decision-maker is needed to shift an issue onto the decision-making agenda seems fairly straightforward, but there is no empirical evidence for this. This turns our attention to the audience question once more: we can argue that who accepts the securitisation argument is not relevant, but what matters is that it *is* accepted and turned into countermeasures. Therefore, the issue of frame resonance conveniently replaces the 'audience' in securitisation theory and is rather independent of any actor specification. We have also speculated about possible policy entrepreneurs who would profit from the outcome of threat politics. In our case studies, none were discernible, and it seems as if that factor was generally negligible. Probably, no policy entrepreneur is needed in threat politics because a call for urgency is enough.

Another difficulty that was revealed was the distinction between hidden and visible participants in the framing process. The influence of hidden actors in creating ideas and also in generating threat frames is undisputed, but we were not able to identify any with our approach. Due to this, they have been marginalised in the entire discussion of threat politics process to the point where they seem irrelevant. However, there is one approach that would help to enhance our understanding of the creation and specifically the diffusion of ideas: the epistemic communities approach, which – like the ACF approach – is a useful add-on for clarifying some points in the framework.

The concept of epistemic communities was introduced into international relations theory by John Ruggie in 1972 (Ruggie 1972). His understanding of epistemic communities as a cognitive level of international institutionalisation that 'delimit for their members the proper construction of reality' (Ruggie 1998: 69) was influenced by the idea of the *episteme*, derived from Michel Foucault

(1970), and by the concept of epistemic communities as used by Burkhard Holzner (Holzner 1968; Antoniades 2003: 23). Thereafter, the concept lay dormant until the early 1990s, when it was re-introduced in a special issue of 'International Organization' edited by Peter Haas (1992: 3), who defined epistemic communities as a 'network of professionals with recognized expertise and competence in a particular domain and an authoritative claim to policy-relevant knowledge within that domain or issue-area'.

The major question driving the inquiry was how decision-makers define state interests and develop solutions if they are unfamiliar with the technical aspects of a specific problem due to uncertainty (Haas 1992: 1). It was assumed that there is a direct link between the way in which the problems are understood by the policy-makers or, more specifically, the way they are represented by those to whom they turn for advice and how states identify their interests in specific issue-areas (Haas 1992: 2). Therefore, the approach focuses particularly on the role that networks of knowledge-base experts play in articulating the cause-and-effect relationship of complex problems, in framing the issues for collective debate, in proposing specific policies, and in identifying salient points for negotiation (Adler and Haas 1992: 372).

In a more recent discussion of epistemic communities, Antoniades (2003) distinguishes between two generic types of epistemic communities: *ad-hoc coalitions* aiming at the solution of a particular policy problem; and *constant groupings* with a holistic character, which aim at the establishment and perpetuation of beliefs and visions as dominant social discourses (Antoniades 2003: 28). In addition, he looks at two interrelated levels of action: a *cognitive one*, in which the role of mainly holistic epistemic communities is a reproduction of social reality in a real-world environment, and a *practical one*, which looks at how epistemic communities, mainly ad-hoc groups, intervene in the policy process.

Cognitive level of action. Constant epistemic communities have the power to impose particular discourses and particular worldviews on societies, which includes the ability to influence the self-conception of peoples and collectives, and therefore their understanding about their desires and interests (Antoniades 2003: 29). Therefore, epistemic communities exercise a 'cognitive authority' as far as knowledge is concerned. By virtue of their strategic role in the construction of social reality, epistemic communities also have an important role in the construction of the language that is used to describe and depict this reality, which becomes particularly important in the context of discourse analysis (Antoniades 2003: 29–31). Naturally, discursive struggles also take place among epistemic communities. At a given time, there is not one epistemic community but many that exist alongside each other. Some of them are likely to have adverse normative beliefs and visions about society and world politics or the solution to a specific policy problem. Because they have an interest in dominating the construction of social reality, these communities struggle with each other in their effort to establish their discourses and visions of societies.

Practical level of action. By influencing social reality, epistemic communities influence the conceptual framework in which every policy process is embedded. Members of epistemic communities can participate either directly or indirectly in the policy process: if key decision-makers are themselves part of the epistemic communities, it is particularly easy to show a link between them and policy decisions. When epistemic communities are involved more indirectly, they can act as advisors or sources of information and might influence agents' policy and interests, they can have agenda-setting function, and they can work out the details of a policy (Antoniades 2003: 32–3).

Though in-depth empirical analysis would be needed to specify our assumptions, it looks as if epistemic communities might help us to further explain mainly two aspects of threat politics: first, the range of choices available to decision-makers, by defining the parameters of the issue and thus ultimately the selection of policy options (agenda-setting); and second, the diffusion of ideas to other countries, which is not the concern of this book (policy diffusion). It is likely that this concerns both ad-hoc groups and more holistic and permanent thought communities, at both the cognitive and the practical level of action. For threat politics, the agenda-setting aspect is particularly interesting. In theory, epistemic communities exert influence on the political process of threat construction by defining the alternatives available for selection and by framing the range of political parameters of an issue (Adler and Haas 1992: 375). This is similar to Kingdon's (2003: 117, 199–201) idea of hidden participants, a group that he sees as encompassing specialists in government, academics, and special-interest groups that define the policy stream and propose solutions to various societal conditions. At the top level, as described above, members of the epistemic community could also be visible participants, including top-level decision-makers.

Framing a threat through analogies and metaphors

As specified, the framework answers the *how* question by looking at attributes of threat frames. This generates insights into how the threat is discussed, i.e. how cyber-incidents are 'constructed' as a threat to national security. In general, it has been very useful to focus on threat frames to explain the process of threat politics. Difficulties in identifying different, dominant, and less dominant threat frames can be attributed to impeding factors that we have already identified: first of all, the approach is weak when it comes to identifying framing actors, and second, it is empirically impossible to identify all threat frames existing at a given time. In addition, we do not have a vetting tool to differentiate between dominant and less dominant threat frames. A remedy to overcome this shortcoming was to look at the successful threat frames, which are easily identifiable from key policy documents, and then ask in retrospect why these threat frames asserted themselves.

In Phase I, there were only a few threat frames, but initially, none of them showed all the necessary characteristics of a true cyber-threat frame, defined as the use of the information infrastructure as weapon and target. The emergency response frame is one example of an early framing, but it only implicitly assumes a threat aspect. The electromagnetic pulse (EMP) discussion, on the other hand, lacks the dimension of the information infrastructure being used as a weapon. The winning threat frame in the 1980s was dominated by the cyber-crime discussion, but to elevate it to the necessary level of urgency, the every-day issue of cyber-crime was linked to the foreign intelligence threat. The practice of linking strands in a discourse to others in order to create a new discourse is called 'referencing'. In the case of threat politics, we can observe that certain issues are linked to those that are already accepted as national security issues.

In threat framing, government officials and experts use certain phrases and also certain types of stories to add urgency to their case. Specific uses of language dramatise the actual threat: the use of specific phrases and words make its construction as a national security threat possible in the first place. Since there is no real-world reference for the threat, constant persuasion is required to sustain the sense that it is a real danger. And, because the national security dimension is not completely obvious, it is necessary to use specific analogies (Cohn 1987; Chilton 1996). Within the cyber-threat discourse, the most prevalent analogy for many years has been the possibility of an 'electronic Pearl Harbor' (Smith 1998; Bendrath 2001), first used by Winn Schwartau (1994: 43), the founder of the 'infowarcon' conferences, in testimony before the US Congress as early as 1991, as he claims. This analogy links the cyber-security debate to a real and successful surprise attack on critical US military infrastructures during the Second World War while, at the same time, warning against the idea of the United States being invulnerable due to its geographical position, conjuring up visions of a danger coming from an enemy that is geographically and morally located outside of the United States (the foreign threat image).

An analogy to deadly weapons can also be found in the designation of cyber-threats as 'weapons of mass disruption', analogous to 'weapons of mass destruction' – i.e. nuclear, biological, or chemical weapons. In 1999, Congressman Curt Weldon (R-Pennsylvania) placed cyber-terrorism at the top of his list of modern threats to the American way of life, as we have already pointed out (Poulsen 1999). In September 2002, Richard Clarke, former Special White House Adviser for Cyberspace Security, told ABC News: '[Cyber-terrorism is] much easier to do than building a weapon of mass destruction. Cyber-attacks are a weapon of mass disruption, and they're a lot cheaper and easier' (Wallace 2002). The frequent use of the term cyber-terror is another such analogy. Detached from any academic definition of the issue, it is a spectre depicting a terrorist and a keyboard, wreaking havoc that can disrupt an entire society.

Why did the President's Commission on Critical Infrastructure Protection (PCCIP) threat frame prevail? According to our theory, the threat frame that has the highest frame resonance and appeals best to top-level decision-makers is most likely to prevail. In a historical perspective, we can show that the successful cyber-threat frame accumulated issues over the years; in other words, more and more issues were interlinked: first, there was the singular cyber-threat frame of cyber-crime. This was interlinked by referencing with foreign exploitation and espionage to elevate it to a national security issue. Then, it was linked to critical infrastructures and terrorism. The concept of homeland security is a more acute version of this last elevation. When we look at the threat subject specifically, we find that from the beginning, cyber-attacks were constructed as stemming from a very broad range of actors. Harmful attacks can be carried out in innumerable ways, potentially by anyone with a computer connected to the Internet, and for purposes ranging from juvenile hacking, organised crime, or political activism to strategic warfare. The new enemies are neither clearly identifiable, nor can they be associated with a particular state. The Internet makes it easy to acquire hacking tools, which have become both more sophisticated and more user-friendly. The idea is that the Internet has special qualities that are of particular relevance to national security matters: particularly the fact that it allows unauthorised users to invade critical computer facilities around the world; its capacity to empower individuals and small groups by allowing them to transmit information across the globe on a secure basis by means of encryption (Halperin 2000); and the fact that it gives everybody access to 'powerful' weapons.

In comparison to the threat subject, which was fairly stable from the beginning, the referent object has changed over the years. At first, it consisted mainly of government networks and the classified information residing in it that was threatened. This was not generally a problem for the wider public. But even though a link between the economy and national security was established very early on, cyber-crime by itself is not a threat to national security. The link to the intelligence debate was a prerequisite for elevating it to that level. Later, the link to critical infrastructures provided a far clearer need for national security: this way, cyber-threats are ultimately seen as a threat to society's core values and to the economic and social well-being of a nation.

The cyber-terror frame as a sub-theme of the general cyber-threat frame combines two of the great fears of the late twentieth century: the fear of random and violent victimisation and the distrust or outright fear of computer technology, both of which capitalise on the fear of the unknown (Pollitt 1997). Terrorism is feared, and is designed to be feared, because it is perceived as being random, incomprehensible, and uncontrollable. Technology, including information technology, is feared because it is seen as complex, abstract, and arcane in its impact on individuals. Because computers do things that used to be done by humans, there is a notion of technology being 'out of control', which is even strengthened by the increase in connectivity and complexity brought about by the information revolution.

The prognostic part of the frame remained far more contested than the diagnostic part during the entire debate. The question of how to counter the threat, mainly related to the question of responsibilities, was discussed until approximately 1997, when the PCCIP threat frame offered a solution that appealed to everyone. Motivational framing became a feature of threat frames in the 1990s, when the threat was attributed to new and poorly understood vulnerabilities, due to dependence of society on the information and communication infrastructure, on the one hand, and ever-more complex interdependencies between infrastructures, on the other. Threats to critical infrastructures are pictured as being disconnected from a state entity with a territorial base (Fisher 2001). Due to the global nature of information networks, attacks can be launched from anywhere in the world, and discovering their origin remains a major difficulty, if they are detected in time at all.

The PCCIP threat frame thus successfully amalgamated a number of issues that had been floating around in the security debate, such as terrorism, critical infrastructures, asymmetric vulnerabilities, and cyber-threats. The introduction of numerous non-state enemies as threat subjects dissolves the distinction between internal and external threats. Opening up this very wide range of potential adversaries underscores a perspective of vulnerability, uncertainty, and insecurity (Denning 2001a, 2001b). To put it differently, first, the broad range of adversaries was coined on the threat subject side. Then, broadening the referent object from government networks and computers to the entire society on the one hand and developing the very stable idea of public–private partnerships on the other created the PCCIP threat frame. Thus, the prevailing threat frame is very broad and also very vague, both in terms of what or who is seen as the threat and of what or who is seen as being threatened. This creates a certain degree of leeway in drafting countermeasures. Due to their very diffuse nature, these threats defy traditional security institutions and make it difficult to rely on a counterstrategy based on retaliation (Molander *et al.* 1996; Hundley and Anderson 1997).

Further, because the ownership, operation, and supply of the critical systems are largely in the hands of the private sector, the distinction between the private and public spheres of action is dissolved. In addition, due to the nature of cyber-attacks, it is often difficult until very late to know where an attack has ultimately originated (Serabian 2000). Furthermore, the characteristics of the threat to critical infrastructures imply that boundaries between the civilian and military spheres of action are dissolved. In the agent dimension, a danger has been constructed that emanates from an enemy who is located outside of the Unites States, both in geographical and in moral terms. This picture of a dangerous 'other' reinforces the idea of the nation as a collective self. The use of phrases like 'our computers' or 'our infrastructures' amplifies this effect. The reference object of security is the entire US society. The logical and political implication of this is that defence against cyber-attacks comes under the purview of national security policy.

Countermeasures: public–private partnerships and changing conditions of securing

Nevertheless, we can make the following general observation about countermeasures: even though the issue of cyber-threats is clearly linked to national security on a rhetorical level, generally, no exceptional measures are envisaged that would traditionally fall under the purview of the national security apparatus. Therefore, the cyber-threats debate is an example of failed securitisation (cf. Bendrath 2001), according to theory. Even though I have deliberately expanded the framework of analysis beyond questions of successful or unsuccessful securitisation, this point merits some additional attention.

One could argue that some of the measures in the Uniting and Strengthening America by Providing Appropriate Tools Required to Intercept and Obstruct Terrorism (USA PATRIOT) Act are exceptional, such as the fact that 'murder by computer' can be punished by life imprisonment. However, this is not an instance of securitisation but rather an expression of a kind of normalisation of information technology: a murder carried out in person could be punished by a death sentence. Similarly, a large number of government reports, even if they are related to national security, are not in themselves an argument for securitisation as long as these reports only contain wide-ranging political measures instead of extraordinary measures. George W. Bush's decision to develop a cyber-attack doctrine could be a more successful instance of securitisation. But again, the addition of this tool to the box could also be seen as a normalisation of information technology. In this case, the extraordinary measures consist in the specific instrumentalisation of cyber-attacks – not necessarily as a reaction to other cyber-attacks but, more generally, in the fight against terrorism.

Generally, national security countermeasures stress deterrence or the prevention of attacks and only attribute secondary importance to the investigation and pursuit of the attackers, since the concept of compensatory or punitive damage is rarely meaningful in the context of national security (National Academy of Sciences 1991: 19). Private-sector countermeasures, however, are frequently oriented towards detection, which means developing audit trails and other chains of evidence that can be used to prosecute attackers in court (National Academy of Sciences 1991). Technical measures exist in both domains, and the boundaries are often fluent. As is apparent when looking at the technical countermeasures laid out in the various policy documents, the US government became involved in developing technology for computer and communications security at a very early stage in the debate. Its efforts related largely to preserving national security and, in particular, to meeting one major security requirement, namely 'confidentiality', which means preserving data secrecy in accordance with the espionage threat frame of the 1980s.

These early programs paid little attention to the other two major requirements of computer security, namely 'integrity', understood as protective measures against improper data modification or destruction, and 'availability', or facilitating timely use of systems and the data they hold (National Academy of Sciences 1991: 3; Stoneburner 2001). We can observe that this began to change as the private sector became increasingly involved in protection measures and as control over countermeasures in general shifted away from government towards the private sector in the 1980s. Changing usage patterns, the increase of outside attacks, and expectation patterns moved availability to the top of this priority list. The first goal of modern information security has, in effect, become to ensure that systems are predictably dependable despite the existence of all sorts of malicious actors and, particularly, in the face of denial-of-service attacks. This means that technical countermeasures are geared towards preventing the disruption of the economy and, as a consequence, towards ensuring the functionality of society – the main goal of the contemporary Critical Infrastructure Protection (CIP) debate.

In the 1990s, critical infrastructures emerged as focal point in the debate. The concept of critical infrastructure protection includes very many different aspects, one of which is cyber-security. The protection of critical information infrastructures is considered an essential *part* of CIP. Despite the fact that the concept of CIP has undergone change during the years since its emergence under Clinton, the key issues have remained the same: at its core, we find the strategy of preparation, meaning the preventive protection of critical infrastructures by technical means. The concept of 'information security' takes centre stage. Clearly, technical measures are never exceptional. At the same time, however, technical measures are used to ensure national security. From this, it follows that national security measures do not always have to be exceptional.

Critical infrastructures are an inherently civil domain. Before 'critical infrastructure' became a term of great interest in the US national security debate, the topic of infrastructures was debated by public policy-makers in the 1980s. The focus of debate was on the nature, extent, and severity of poor physical condition and on decisions enacted by government at all levels on spending priorities to meet physical and management needs (Moteff *et al.* 2002: 14). Definitions of infrastructure at that time were, for example, related to public service and production facilities, which include a wide array of public facilities and equipment required to provide social services and support private-sector economic activity or facilities that provide a foundation or basic framework for the national economy, and in which federal policy plays a significant role. Already included were facilities that provide services that 'form the underpinnings of the nation's defense, a strong economy, and our health and safety' (Moteff *et al.* 2002: 14–16). Thus, we find that the national security dimension is present but not as a priority.

The usage of the term 'critical infrastructure' in today's sense evolved around the second half of the 1990s in connection with the Oklahoma City bombing. The PCCIP report defines 'critical infrastructure' as a

> framework of interdependent networks and systems comprising identifiable industries, institutions (including people and procedures), and distribution capabilities that provide a reliable flow of products and services essential to the defense and economic security of the United States, the smooth functioning of government at all levels, and society as a whole
>
> (PCCIP 1997: B-2)

Certain forms of infrastructure are deemed more essential than others; if any of these should cease to function for a prolonged period, it would be difficult for society as a whole to continue functioning. Therefore, these elements are regarded as 'critical'. The PCCIP designated certain 'sectors', such as telecommunications, electrical power systems, banking and finance, and emergency services, as critical. The choice of business sectors as units for lists of critical assets is a pragmatic approach that mirrors the fact that the majority of infrastructures is owned and operated by private actors. In his Executive Order of 8 October 2001, Bush expanded the sectors included in CIP to encompass nuclear material, agriculture, and 'special events' of 'national significance' (Bush 2001a: sec. e, §4). This was followed by other documents, which add the chemical industry, postal services, and shipping to the list (Bush 2002: 31). Some experts even argue that the debate should be enlarged to the whole of the 'built environment', which encompasses all human-made physical elements of society and where the average person spends 95 per cent of their lives (Yates 2003).

During the same time in which the criteria for 'critical' infrastructures have expanded over time, the very concept of criticality has also changed. We can distinguish between two different but closely interlinked ways of understanding criticality (Metzger 2004):

- *Criticality as systemic concept*: This approach assumes that an infrastructure or an infrastructure component is critical due to its structural position in the whole system of infrastructures, especially when it constitutes an important link between other infrastructures or sectors and thus reinforces interdependencies. This is a technically oriented understanding.
- *Criticality as a symbolic concept*: This approach assumes that an infrastructure or an infrastructure component is inherently critical because of its role or function in society; the issue of interdependencies is secondary – the inherent symbolic meaning of certain infrastructures is enough to make them interesting targets. The symbolic understanding of criticality allows the integration of non-interdependent infrastructures as well as objects that are not man-made into the concept of critical infrastructures, including significant personalities or natural and historical landmarks with a strong symbolic character.

Both conceptions have existed side by side for some time. But, it is the combination of both of these notions that has designated the protection of critical infrastructures a key challenge for national security today. The emphasis on the networked, interdependent, and interconnected nature of various sectors in connection with the symbolic understanding creates a specific set of problems: when the concept of criticality, and accordingly the notion of what is to be secured, is expanded from interconnected physical networks to include everything with an emotional attachment, almost everything becomes an infrastructure, and everything is potentially critical: even a minor event of little apparent significance could potentially trigger largely unpredictable cascading effects throughout a large number of sectors. In this way, the problem becomes in effect unmanageable: in the inherently binary logic of security, there are no grey areas.

Either one is secure or one is not. Seen from this viewpoint, it is simply impossible to provide absolute protection for all potentially critical assets.

The response to this dilemma has been to use the classic tool of the private sector, risk analysis. According to one standard definition of risk found in the technical domain, it is a function of the *likelihood* of a given *threat source* displaying a particular potential *vulnerability* and the resulting *impact* of that adverse event (Haimes 1998). Risk analysis refers to the processes used to evaluate those probabilities and consequences and also to the study of how to incorporate the resulting estimates into decision-making processes. As a decision-making tool for the security sector, risk assessment methodologies aim to assure that the priority or appropriateness of measures used to counter specific security threats is adequate for the existing risks. Outcomes of the risk assessment process are used to provide guidance on the areas of highest risk and to devise policies and plans to ensure that systems are appropriately protected (Dunn 2004). Risk assessment methodologies are step-by-step approaches. At the end of these processes, one usually arrives at risk mitigation measures, which involves prioritising, evaluating, and implementing the appropriate risk-reducing controls suggested by the risk assessment process. The underlying reasoning is that if one cannot secure everything, at least one can prioritise.

In contrast to the logic of security, the logic of risk is not binary but probabilistic. It is a constant process towards a desired outcome. Thus, managing risk is essentially about accepting one that is insecure, but also constantly patching this insecurity, and thus working towards a future goal of more security. As Kristian Kristensen puts it,

> The rationality of risk functions as a means to manage the present, and the goal of absolute security is moved into the future. The state can thus argue that it will live up to its constitutional commitments in the future by continuously arguing that it is minimizing the risk in the present. This gives the government the conceptual means to picture the reality of critical infrastructure protection as a constant 'work in progress'.
>
> (Kristensen forthcoming 2008)

More importantly, even a business rationale is not only forced upon governments by the mammoth task of securing everything, but is also due to the fact that the private industry owns and operates about 85–95 per cent of critical infrastructures and key assets in the United States, depending on the sources cited. Therefore, much of the expertise and many of the resources required for planning and taking better protective measures lie outside the federal government (Baird 2002; Goodman *et al.* 2002; Bosch 2002). As a result, it is necessary to delegate a large part of the responsibility for the protection of critical infrastructure to their private owners and operators. Whereas the traditional logic of national security suggests unilateral government action and policy, CIP policies are inevitably blurred by domestic considerations and other policy imperatives.

One could argue that this environment forces certain practices (like risk analysis) on the government. However, this does not necessarily have to be a negative development but could in fact also be seen as a convenient way out of a great dilemma. First, the responsibility for creating security can be and must be put on the shoulders of non-state actors, not least because the information revolution and economic growth are so closely interrelated, any involvement of the state in cyber-security matters is undesirable and subject to much scrutiny. Second, one can argue that in this community, it has long been acknowledged that absolute security is not possible but that one is nonetheless constantly striving towards more security.

Ultimately, all of this has led to failed securitisation: securitisation moves are only successful if they are taken out of the 'normal bounds of political procedure', which in turn amounts to a call for exceptional measures (Buzan *et al.* 1998: 24), and if an audience 'accepts' the security argument and extraordinary measures (Buzan *et al.* 1998: 25). What has evolved, however, is a new logic of security. Today, national security is also concerned with attempts to create resilience and redundancy in national infrastructure through cyber-security measures and other means. This means that measures that are generally regarded as being within the purview of information security may now also be included among measures to ensure national security. In this new logic of security, two formerly different notions of security merge as technical security, and safety and national security become one.

As a result of this, it has become questionable whether security policy can only be understood as a 'policy for extraordinary circumstances' or as a policy for existential threats that is removed from the realm of everyday politics (Buzan *et al.* 1998). Current definitions allow us to designate practically everything as an 'infrastructure'; and the CIP concept implies that everything is a concern for national security. Therefore, exceptional measures are highly contextual and subjective, so that they might not always be security measures in a restricted sense, and security measures might not always be exceptional. It seems that we are faced with both, a failed securitisation *and* a new logic of security. This reflects a changing and very broad concept of security for which securitisation theory might not have an answer. The fact that the maintenance of 'business continuity' for an individual, corporate, or local actor, and security efforts in terms of national or even international security often exist side by side (Demchak 1999) in the realm of CIP and homeland security seems to be a long-term trend rather than an exception and points to the changing nature of security practices in a world in which the state sees itself as being unable 'to go it alone'.

7 Cyber-threats and security in the information age

Issues and implications

This book has dealt with the political processes that have favoured the rise of cyber-threats to prominence and, occasionally, to a top place on the security political agenda in the United States. It has explored a fairly 'new' security issue in terms of the threat perceptions of key actors and the dynamic interaction between actor constellations, systemic conditions, and institutional settings. Threat frames, specific interpretive schemata about what counts as threat or risk and how to respond to it, were at the heart of the investigation – and have revealed a lot about how security in the information age is defined and ultimately practiced.

One of the main reasons why the issue of cyber-threats has gained so much attention in recent years is the fact that in the process of threat politics, US officials have convincingly argued that they threatened the very fabric of modern societies. The argument goes that increasingly, everything, including, for example, the delivery of energy to homes and businesses and the effectiveness of health care systems, is dependent on the reliability of information systems and networks. These critical information infrastructures are regarded as the backbone of critical infrastructures in general, given that the uninterrupted exchange of data is essential to government operations, emergency services, and commerce. This dependence on information – combined with increasing vulnerabilities resulting from the technical security gaps, the complexity of technology, ongoing market liberalisation, and the growing ability and willingness of malicious actors to conduct physical and cyber-attacks – makes telecommunications and information systems highly vulnerable targets, at least in theory.

Compared to more traditional security threats, which have usually been categorised in terms of the dimensions 'actor', 'intention', and 'capabilities', modern threats, which include, but do not only consist of, cyber-threats, can no longer be labelled that easily due to various levels of uncertainties. The possible use of information and communication technologies (ICT), either as a target or as a tool, by a wide range of malevolent actors defies traditional approaches to threat analysis. As we have pointed out in this study, the defining characteristic of cyber-threats is their unsubstantiated nature: none of the worst-case scenarios have ever materialised, not even in part. At the heart of the issue lies the fact that we are dealing with a threat whose dimensions remain altogether uncertain –

opening up a broad margin for political bargaining. One aspect of this is that various sorts of experts disagree on the gravity of the cyber-threats and grapple with the question of how likely they are and how soon an incident with a genuinely society-threatening impact might occur. In fact, the estimated probabilities range from 0 to 1, from never to tomorrow. This is not overly surprising because the question of 'how likely – how soon' is notoriously hard to answer at the best of times, for who knows the future?

Common wisdom has it that predictions of adverse future events such as cyber-attacks is considerably handicapped by the fact that the end of the Cold War not only brought the end of a relatively stable bipolar world order but also the end of the relatively bounded nature of threats – a statement that is of course oversimplified, for threats were never quite as clear as some like to claim. However, the argument is that in the realm of cyber-threats, there is no clearly identifiable actor who could become a possible enemy; in theory, cyber-attackers can be teenagers, 'rogue states', terrorists, or disgruntled insiders, even private companies or political activists. Further, this uncertainty implies that it is very hard to obtain verifiable information on the hostile intentions and capabilities of the possible attacker. In addition, even the assumption of an entire society's vulnerability has been repeatedly questioned: as pointed out in the introduction, our technology-based societies have learned to live fairly well with the many disruptions that occur daily. One could also argue that complex societies are both more adaptable and more redundant than others.

Some even say that the assumption of vulnerability is wrong, because automatically linking computer network vulnerability to critical infrastructure vulnerability is misleading: critical infrastructures, especially in large market economies, are more distributed, diverse, redundant and self-healing than a cursory assessment may suggest, rendering them less vulnerable to attack (Lewis 2002). Furthermore, there is a lot of guesswork involved at all levels: in order to know how vulnerable critical infrastructures truly are to cyber-attacks, we would need a detailed assessment of redundancy for each target infrastructure, normal rates of failure and response, the degree to which critical functions are accessible from public networks, and the level of human control, monitoring, and intervention in critical operations (Ezell *et al.* 2000; Haimes and Jiang 2001; Lewis 2002;). However, there is no public or even readily available data on how vulnerable critical systems are, since defence computers are buried under layers of secrecy and classification, and private companies are not likely to volunteer such information (Chapman 1998).

Hence, it looks as though we were dealing with a threat that is in essence unknowable and, by inference, in essence unmanageable. However, new avenues of reasoning are opened when unmanageable threats are treated as *risks*. Risks exist in a permanent state of virtuality and are actualised only through anticipation (Loon 2002: 2), leading to a state of 'no-longer-but-not-yet – no longer trust/security, not yet destruction/disaster' (Beck 1999: 137). This state of limbo permits promising new security practices. Cyber-threat politics take place in a security environment that is governed by the notion of risk management rather than traditional security practices, and the strategies and policies pursued to secure the information space change the role of government in providing security; providing security inside a society is not the same as on the outside, despite the fact that the ultimate goal remains the same. At the most fundamental level, while it remains the essential task of a government to provide the security of society, it has simultaneously become impossible for a government to achieve this by itself in the case of protection against cyber-threats, especially in the form of critical infrastructure protection (CIP).

Changed security practices and an evolving new logic of security were already discussed in the last chapter of this book, but this subject merits additional attention. As we have argued in Chapter 1, there is never a simple answer to the question of what has changed to what degree. Often, the question of change refers to systemic and sweeping phenomena, a fundamental type of change that transforms the practices and constitutive conventions of the entire system. One might argue that a fundamental change in the international system occurs when a significant amount of its constitutive norms or rules are altered (Kratochwil 1989: 64). Susan Strange (1988: 123) has argued similarly when stating that technological changes only change power structures if they are accompanied by changes in the basic belief systems that underpin or support the political arrangements that are acceptable to society. At the same time, we must be aware that change is inherently a question of perceptions. Not only is change an evolutionary process rather than a single event with clearly discernible beginning or end, it is also not universally given; it is rather a matter of scales and of arbitrarily chosen reference points. In a short term or microperspective, previous year was fundamentally different from present year – while in a long term or macro-perspective, a truly fundamental alteration of the persisting dynamics and patterns of power, authority, status, and nature of social institutions may be lacking (Holsti 1998: 4). In this context, the questions of discovery and innovation are of fundamental importance: How can we notice a 'pattern' we have never seen before (Crutchfield 1994, 2002)? In fact, there is always some ad hoc quality involved in the recognition of something new. While such patterns may merit consideration in their own right, the ontological validity of a perceived novelty remains unclear. Because patterns must be 'recognised' by the observer, any observed structure or patterns may be an artefact of the research question; other patterns may go unnoticed for the same reasons (Mihata 1997: 32).

In this book, the solution to this ontological difficulty has been to acknowledge that the perception of issues by key actors has the decisive impact on their beliefs and actions. In our analysis, we have not focused on the questions of 'change or no change' and 'more complex or not' as objective truth but rather on the implications of these developments. The argument is that it does not matter whether there actually is such a development, but it matters whether it is believed to be real and whether people act as if it were real. However, it seems of some value to attempt to go beyond the acknowledgment of the importance of perceived changes and to try to pinpoint what is new in today's security environment, even if this stands in some contrast to the constructivist framework we have developed to address threat politics.

As I have argued above, we can observe a qualitatively significant change in some of the means employed to achieve security today. The urgency of fighting cyber-threats was established by linking them to the concept of critical infrastructures. CIP is an important subset of the even wider-ranging concept of homeland security, and it is here that changes can best be exemplified. Security policy has traditionally been about policies of fortification, balancing, and a 'hardening' of the outer shell of the state. Unmistakeably, homeland security is part of national security, but it is still not entirely congruent with it, being more like a parallel concept than a derivative of national security. It is a manifestation consistent with the line of reasoning that the challenges faced 'inside' and 'outside' of the state have become blurred in the new threat environment to the point where they have become the same. One concrete consequence of this is that the tasks of the 'agents of security' have changed, as those traditionally concerned with security inside the state are increasingly involved in issues of 'international' security (Sjursen 2004) and vice versa. Part of this expansion has included a redefinition of law enforcement concerns as security concerns. As a result, the 'low politics' of policing has now in some instances become 'high politics' and vice versa (Bigo 2000; Andreas and Price 2001: 51).

Practices aiming to create security inside sovereign space, on the domestic territory, are not revolutionarily new practices: protection concepts for strategically important infrastructures and objects have been part of national defence planning for decades, though at varying levels of importance. Today, however, both the context and their significance have changed. It is indeed a 'new' phenomenon that certain practices in connection with cyber-threats and CIP have made grey zones of security possible, and a future state of potential security through risk management, a state that is never being but always becoming. Specifically, we have shown how the US administration applies the logics of probability and risk to CIP. Due to the nature of what is to be secured, these policies are conditioned on negotiation and shared responsibility with the private actors of domestic society. In this relationship, a domesticated version of security policy comes under the influence of an economic rationale.

It has even been convincingly argued that one solution to the problem of cyber-security is to focus on economic and market aspects of the issue rather than on suitable technical protection mechanisms (Andersson 2001). If we apply this viewpoint, we quickly realise that the insecurity of the Internet can be compared to environmental pollution and that cyber-security in fact shows strong traits of a 'public good' that will be underprovided or fail to be provided at all in the private market. Public goods provide a very important example of market failure, in which individual behaviour aimed at gaining profit from the market does not produce efficient results (Dunn Cavelty and Mauer 2007).

Clearly, looking at cyber-security as an economic problem means to 'desecuritise' the issue even further. Despite the fact that the securitisation of cyber-threats, as defined by securitisation theory, has failed, the rationale of national security is upheld on the rhetorical level. This is not necessarily desirable. A rhetorical 'desecuritisation' could help. Desecuritisation as the 'unmaking of security' has been considered a technique for defining down threats, in other words, a 'normalisation' of threats that were previously constructed as extraordinary. This normalisation is a process by which security issues lose their security aspect, making it possible to interpret them in multiple ways. Desecuritisation, therefore, allows more freedom both at the level of interpretation and in actual politics or social interaction (Aradau 2001b). While such a normalisation is not necessary on the level of countermeasures, it is necessary on the level of threat rhetoric. At the same time, a focus on market aspects of the issue can help create a market for cyber-security, which could reduce much of the insecurity of the information infrastructure, and thus also diminish the vulnerability of society (Suter 2007).

A strong economic perspective has not, however, prevented cyber-instruments from being added to the military toolbox. It is somehow ironic that new security practices geared towards the protection of cyber-threats go hand in hand with what I would like to call new threat practices by the United States. It is evident from our study that the birth of information warfare concepts focused security policy on the vulnerability of civil infrastructures in the first place and thus ultimately raised an array of questions about the nature, scale, and ultimately management of future international conflicts. A matter of great relevance in this context is the role of the US government in creating a sense of insecurity in this domain that subsequently has a negative impact on the perceptions of key actors within the United States. Specifically, there is an underlying tension between the desire of military establishments to exploit cyberspace for military advantages and to develop doctrines and capabilities within the broad rubric of 'information operations' and concerns about the dependency of militaries, governments, economies, and societies on the networked information systems that are emerging as the backbone of post-industrialised societies.

The doctrinal development observable today goes far beyond being a mere guideline for technology-supported military operations; it openly considers the use of non-military and asymmetrical alternatives in international conflicts as well as ways to exploit them as a tool for international politics detached from military battlefield operations – e.g. to conduct computer espionage and sabotage as well as 'truth projection' through electronic mass media at all times. The extant information operations concepts consider the targeting of civil targets on the physical, psychological, and virtual levels. When this tendency is added to the general trend towards asymmetric strategies, we seem to be heading towards warfare in which battlefields envelop entire societies, the distinction between civilian and military targets disappears, and military objectives shift from the destruction of discrete enemy lines to an erosion of popular support for the war within the enemy's society. Thus, information operations blur the boundaries between civilian and military objectives and systems and also between war and peace, since many aspects of information operations are conducted ceaselessly. Even though modern conflicts are often pictured as being less violent and bloody than former wars, the trend towards more civilian involvement is not encouraging. Suddenly, the frontlines are 'everywhere'.

What these state-led approaches to attack through cyberspace fail to recognise, however, is the nature of the globally interdependent network environment and, more surprisingly, the leading role in this domain of the private sector, whose key role in securing the homeland is emphasised in practically every public speech on the topic. Andrew Rathmell (2001) has argued, for example, that the notion of interdependencies is not appreciated by current military thinking. Constrained by a focus on delivering 'effects' to a particular geographic conflict zone, armed forces are trying to exploit electronic attacks for precise targeting of enemy infrastructures.

There is a severe disjunction between the emerging military doctrine on information operations and computer attacks, on the one hand, and the technological and market realities of a globalised, interdependent, and networked world, on the other. The features of the emerging information environment make it extremely unlikely that any but the most limited and tactically oriented instances of computer attacks could be contained, as current military doctrine would demand. More likely, computer-attacks by the military could 'blow back' through the interdependencies that characterise the environment. Even relatively harmless viruses and worms cause considerable random disruption to businesses, governments, and consumers. In addition, the routine use of computer network–attacks would most likely undermine the already brittle trust in cyberspace. Awareness that global information networks are routinely exploited by Western militaries would lead users to question whether data and systems were trustworthy and to wonder whether information was being polluted. The damage to consumer and business confidence could well undermine efforts to promote a reliable information society.

This said, the approach that we have chosen to analyse the issue of cyber-threats in this book does not help us to determine whether cyber-threats are fact or fiction. This reveals a vexing rift between theory and practice: cyber-threats have not (yet) become a reality, but the United States, and other governments in developed societies, still act as though they were a clear and present danger. Granted, this means that, in theory, it does not matter whether the threat is real or not: what matters is that decision-makers consider cyber-attacks a real threat and act accordingly. The question of whether the threat is real does matter in practice, however. Even though the analysis of threat frames can enlighten us as to why certain political solutions are preferred over others, the approach does not solve any of the problems decision-makers have with managing uncertainties. The dilemma is that decision-makers must act on the basis of objective truth and facts – they cannot constantly question their own actions and assumptions or focus their attention on political processes in which they are directly involved. But what if there are no objective truths or facts? As Douglas and Wildavsky (1983: 1) put it, 'can we know the risks we face now and in the future? No, we cannot; but yes, we must act as if we do'.

The most pressing issue with considerable direct impact is probably the question of how to establish a sustainable 'security threshold' in the face of such uncertainties. As Barry Buzan has argued: 'Setting the security trigger too low on the scale risks paranoia [...] setting it too high risks failure to prepare for major assaults until too late' (Buzan 1991: 115). The goal of CIP is to ensure that any disruption of the services provided by critical infrastructures will be infrequent, of minimal duration, and manageable. In theory, therefore, even a single attack – regardless of the nature of the attacker – could constitute a matter of national security. Clearly, this security threshold depends on the definition of criticality. As we have shown, the concept of criticality has been greatly expanded over the years and now theoretically encompasses all elements of the networked environment. Following this logic, everything is insecure and must be secured. But securing everything is something that cannot be done: it is not only physically impossible but even further complicated by the inclusion of psychological aspects in the definition – in this case, not even the private sector can help. The only way out of this problem is to employ a much narrower and more sensible concept of what is to be considered as critical.

All the evidence that we have seen in the last couple of years suggests that computer network vulnerabilities are an increasingly serious business problem, but that their threat to national security is overstated. We could even argue that positioning the topic on the national security agenda is not justified. Put simply, if a cyber-attack does not cause damage that rises above the threshold of the routine disruptions that every economy experiences, it does not pose an immediate or significant risk to national security. In fact, in the larger context of normal economic activity, where dozens or even hundreds of different systems provide critical infrastructure services, it may be a routine occurrence for service to be denied to customers for hours or even days during instances of water system failures, power outages, air traffic disruptions and other scenarios, which thus constitute routine events that do not affect national security at all.

However, the current threat frame is so persuasive that the inherently nebulous notion of cyber-threats will remain on the national security agenda in some form. Because of this, decision-makers must be careful not to foment 'cyber-angst' to an unnecessary degree, even if the threat cannot be completely dismissed. In seeking a prudent policy, the difficulty for decision-makers is to navigate the rocky shoals between hysterical doomsday scenarios and uninformed complacency. In the realm of cyber-threats, the issue is not really whether we will be attacked in the near or distant future. The focus should rather be on a far broader range of potentially dangerous occurrences involving cyber-means and targets, including failure due to human error, technical problems, and market failure apart from malicious attacks. This not only does justice to the complexity of the problem but also prevents us both from setting the security trigger too low and setting it too high.

Bibliography

Abele-Wigert, I. and Dunn, M. (2006) *The International CIIP Handbook 2006: An Inventory of Protection Policies in 20 Countries and 6 International Organizations* (Vol. I), Zurich, Switzerland: Center for Security Studies.

Adler, E. (1997) 'Seizing the middle ground: Constructivism in world politics', *European Journal of International Relations*, 3, 3, pp. 319–63.

Adler, E. and Barnett, M. (eds) (1998) *Security Communities*, Cambridge: Cambridge University Press.

Adler, E. and Haas, P.M. (1992) 'Conclusion: Epistemic communities, world order, and the creation of a reflective research program', *International Organization*, 46, 1, pp. 367–90.

Air Force Information Warfare Center (1995) *A Technical Analysis of the Rome Laboratory Attacks*, Kelly Air Force Base, Texas: US Government Printing Office.

Akdeniz, Yaman (1999) 'The regulation of Internet content in Europe: Governance control versus self-responsibility', *Swiss Political Science Review*, 5, 2, pp. 123–31.

Alberts, D.S. and Papp, D.S. (eds) (1997) *The Information Age: An Anthology of Its Impacts and Consequences* (Vol. I), Washington, DC: National Defense University Press.

—— (eds) (2000) *The Information Age: An Anthology of Its Impacts and Consequences* (Vol. II), Washington, DC: National Defense University Press.

—— (eds) (2001) *The Information Age: An Anthology of Its Impacts and Consequences* (Vol. III), Washington, DC: National Defense University Press.

Alberts, D.S., Papp, D.S. and Kemp III, W.T. (1997) 'The technologies of the information revolution', in Alberts, D.S. and Papp, D.S. (eds) *The Information Age: An Anthology of Its Impacts and Consequences* (Vol. I), Washington, DC: National Defense University Press, pp. 36–50.

Alexander, B. (2004) 'Out of the info loop: Why information networks are crucial to modern warfare', *Reason*, June 2004. Available online at www.reason.com/0406/cr.ba.out.shtml (accessed 14 May 2007).

Anderson, R.H. and Hearn, A.C. (1996) *An Exploration of Cyberspace Security R&D Investment Strategies for DARPA: "The Day After ... in Cyberspace II"*, Santa Monica: RAND.

Andersson, R. (2001) 'Why information security is hard: An economic perspective', in IEEE Computer Society (ed.), *Proceedings of the 17th Annual Computer Security Applications Conference*, Washington, DC: IEEE Computer Society, pp. 358–65.

Andreas, P. and Price, R. (2001) 'From war fighting to crime fighting: Transforming the American national security state', *International Studies Review*, 3, 3, pp. 31–52.

Bibliography

Anonymous (2003) *Maximum Security*, Indiana: Sams Publishing.

Antoniades, A. (2003) 'Epistemic communities, epistemes and the construction of (world) politics', *Global Society*, 17, 1, pp. 21–38.

Aradau, C. (2001a), 'Migration: The spiral of (in)security', *Rubikon*, March 2001. Available online at http://venus.ci.uw.edu.pl/~rubikon/forum/claudia1.htm (accessed 14 May 2007).

—— (2001b) 'Beyond good and evil: Ethics and securitization/desecuritization techniques', *Rubikon*, December 2001. Available online at http://venus.ci.uw.edu.pl/~rubikon/forum/claudia2.htm (accessed 14 May 2007).

Arkin, W.M. (1999) 'NATO's info strategy bombs', *Special to Washington Post*, 26 April 1999.

Armstrong, J.E. and Sage, A.P. (1999) *An Introduction to Systems Engineering*, New York: John Wiley and Sons.

Arquilla, J. and Ronfeldt, D.F. (1996) *The Advent of Netwar*, Santa Monica: RAND.

—— (eds) (1997a) *In Athena's Camp: Preparing for Conflict in the Information Age*, Santa Monica: RAND.

—— (1997b) 'Cyberwar is coming!', in Arquilla, J. and Ronfeldt, D.F. (eds) *In Athena's Camp: Preparing for Conflict in the Information Age*, Santa Monica: RAND, pp. 23–60.

—— (1999) *The Emergence of Noopolitik: Toward an American Information Strategy*, Santa Monica: RAND.

—— (eds) (2001) *Networks and Netwars: The Future of Terror, Crime, and Militancy*, Santa Monica: RAND.

Ashby, W.R. (1956) *Introduction to Cybernetics*, London: Methuen.

Austin, J.L. (1962) *How to Do Things with Words*, London: Oxford University Press.

Avizienis, A., Laprie, J.-C. and Randell, B. (2000) *Fundamental Concepts of Dependability*, UCLA CSD Report no. 010028. Available online at www.ece.cmu.edu/~ece749/docs/laprie.pdf (accessed 14 May 2007).

Axelrod, R. (1997) *The Complexity of Cooperation: Agent-Based Models of Competition and Collaboration*, Princeton: Princeton University Press.

Bacon, K.H. (1999) 'DoD news briefing', Monday, 29 March 1999. Presenter: Mr. Kenneth H. Bacon, ASD PA, Washington, DC, Department of Defense. Available online at www.defenselink.mil/transcripts/transcript.aspx?transcriptid=645 (accessed 14 May 2007).

Bailey, D. (1984) 'Attacks on computers: Congressional hearings and pending legislation', in *Proceedings of the 1984 IEEE Symposium on Security and Privacy*, Oakland: IEEE Computer Society Press, pp. 180–7.

Baird, Z. (2002) 'Governing the Internet: Engaging government, business, and nonprofits', *Foreign Affairs*, 81, 6, pp. 15–20.

Ball, D. (1981) 'Counterforce targeting: How new?, How viable?' *Arms Control Today*, 2, 2, pp. 1–6.

Bamford, J. (2005), 'The man who sold the war: Meet John Rendon, Bush's General in the propaganda war', *Rolling Stone*, 17 November 2005. Available online at www.rollingstone.com/politics/store/_/id/8798997 (accessed 14 May 2007).

Barbrook, R. and Cameron, A. (1995) 'The Californian ideology', *Science as Culture*, 26, 6, pp. 44–72.

Barlow, J.P. (1994) 'The Economy of ideas: Selling wine without bottles on the global net', *Wired Magazine*, 2.03, March 1994. Available online at www.wired.com/wired/archive/2.03/economy.ideas.html (accessed 14 May 2007).

—— (1996) *A Declaration of the Independence of Cyberspace*, Electronic Frontier Foundation Website, available at http://homes.eff.org/~barlow/Declaration-Final.html (accessed 14 May 2007).

Baudrillard, J. (1983) *Simulations*, New York: Semiotexte.

Beck, U. (1986) *Risikogesellschaft auf dem Weg in eine andere Moderne*, Frankfurt am Main Suhrkamp.

—— (1999) *World Risk Society*, Cambridge: Polity Press.

—— (2001) 'Risk society revisited: Theory, politics and research programmes', in Adam, Barbara, Beck, Ulrich and Loon, Joost van (eds) *The Risk Society and Beyond: Critical Issues for Social Theory*, London: Sage, pp. 211–29.

Beedham, C. (2005) *Language and Meaning: The Structural Creation of Reality*, Studies in Functional and Structural Linguistics 55, Amsterdam & Philadelphia: John Benjamins.

Beer, S. (2004) *History of Cybernetics – Chapter 2: The Coalescence of Cybernetics*, available at www.asc-cybernetics.org/foundations/history2.htm (accessed 14 May 2007).

Bellin, D. and Chapman, G. (1987) (eds) *Computers in Battle: Will They Work?* New York: Harcourt, Brace, Jovanovich.

Bendrath, R. (1999) 'Der Kosovo-Krieg im cyberspace. Cracker, infowar und medienkrieg', *Telepolis*, 19 July 1999. Available online at www.heise.de/tp/r4/artikel/6/6449/1.html (accessed 14 May 2007).

—— (2001) 'The cyberwar debate: Perception and politics in US critical infrastructure protection', *Information & Security: An International Journal*, Volume 7, pp. 80–103.

—— (2003) 'The American Cyber-Angst and the real world – Any link?' in Latham, R. (ed.) *Bombs and Bandwidth: The Emerging Relationship between IT and Security*, New York: The New Press, pp. 49–73.

Bendrath, R., Eriksson J. and Giacomello G. (2007) 'Cyberterrorism to cyberwar, back and forth: How the United States securitized cyberspace', in Eriksson, J. and Giacomello, G. (eds) *International Relations and Security in the Digital Age*, London: Routledge, pp. 57–82.

Bequai, A. (1986) *Technocrimes: The Computerization of Crime and Terrorism*, Lexington: Lexington Books.

Berger, P. and Luckmann, T. (1967) *The Social Construction of Reality: A Treatise in the Sociology of Knowledge*, New York: Anchor Books.

Berkowitz, B.D. (1997) 'Warfare in the information age', in Arquilla, J. and Ronfeldt, D. (eds) *In Athena's Camp: Preparing for Conflict in the Information Age*, Santa Monica, RAND, pp. 175–90.

—— (2003) *The New Face of War: How War Will Be Fought in the 21st Century*, New York: Free Press.

Berkowitz, B.D. and Hahn, R.W. (2003) 'Cybersecurity – who is watching the store', *Issues in Science and Technology*, 19, 3, Spring, pp. 55–62.

Berman, J.J. (1987) 'National security vs. access to computer databases: A new threat to freedom of information', *First Principles*, 12, 3, June 1987.

Berners-Lee, T. (1999) *Weaving the Web: The Original Design and Ultimate Destiny of the World Wide Web*, New York: Harper Collins.

Bertalanffy, L. von (1968) *General Systems Theory: Foundations, Development, Applications*, New York: George Braziller Publishing.

—— (1975) *Perspectives on General System Theory: Scientific-Philosophical Studies*, New York: George Braziller Publishing.

Beth, T., Frisch, M. and Simmons, G. (eds) (1992) *Public Key Cryptography: State of the Art and Future Directions*, Lecture Notes in Computer Science, No. 578, New York: Springer-Verlag.

Biddle, S. (1996) 'Victory misunderstood: What the Gulf War tells us about the future of conflict', *International Security*, 21, 2, pp. 139–79.

Biggiero, L. (2001) 'Sources of complexity in human systems', *Nonlinear Dynamics, Psychology, and Life Sciences*, 5, 1, pp. 3–19.

Bigo, D. (1994) 'The European internal security field: Stakes and rivalries in a newly developing area of police intervention', in Anderson, M. and den Boer, M. (eds) *Policing Across National Boundaries*, London: Pinter, pp. 161–73.

—— (1998), 'Sécurité et immigration: vers une gouvernementalité par l'inquiétude?' *Cultures et Conflits*, 31–2, pp. 13–38.

—— (2000) 'When two becomes one: Internal and external securitisation in Europe', in Kelstrup, M. and Williams, M.C. (eds) *International Relations Theory and the Politics of European Integration: Power, Security and Community*, London: Routledge, pp. 171–205.

Blank, S.J. (2003) *Rethinking Asymmetric Threats*, Carlisle: Carlisle Strategic Studies Institute.

Blondell, J. (1982) *The Organization of Governments*, Beverly Hills: Sage.

Boekle, H., Nadoll, J. and Stahl, B. (2000) *Identität, Diskurs und vergleichende Analyse europäischer Außenpolitiken. Theoretische Grundlegung und methodische Vorgehensweise*, PAFE-Arbeitspapier Nr. 1, Universität Trier.

—— (2001) *Nationale Identität, Diskursanalyse und Außenpolitikforschung: Herausforderungen und Hypothesen*, PAFE-Arbeitspapier Nr. 4, Universität Trier.

Borger, J. (1999) 'Pentagon Kept the lid on cyberwar in Kosovo', *The Guardian*, 9 November 1999. Available online at www.guardian.co.uk/Kosovo/Story/0,2763, 197391,00.html (accessed 14 May 2007).

Borgmann, A. (1999) *Holding on to Reality: The Nature of Information at the Turn of the Millennium*, Chicago: University of Chicago Press.

Bosch, O. (2002) 'Cyber terrorism and private sector efforts for information infrastructure protection', unpublished paper, presented at the ITU Workshop on creating trust in critical network infrastructures, Seoul, 20–22 May 2002.

Bowker, G. (1993) 'How to be universal: Some cybernetic strategies 1943–1970', *Social Studies of Science*, 23, 1, pp. 107–28.

Bowman, L.M. (2000) 'Cybercrime fighters: The feds want you!', *ZDNet News*, 11 December 2000. Available online at www.zdnet.com/zdnn/stories/news/0,4586, 2663288,00.html (accessed 14 May 2007).

Brandt, D. (1995) 'Infowar and disinformation: From the Pentagon to the net', *NameBase NewsLine*, 11, October–December 1995. Available online at www.namebase.org/news11.html (accessed 14 May 2007).

Brewin, B. (1999) 'Cyberattacks against NATO traced to China', *Federal Computer Week*, 2 September 1999. Available online at www.cnn.com/TECH/computing/9909/02/chinahack.idg/index.html (accessed 14 May 2007).

Brock, J.L. (1991) 'Computer security, hackers penetrate DOD computer systems statement', *Testimony of the Director Government Information and Financial Management Information Management and Technology Division Before the Subcommittee on Government Information and Regulation, Committee on Governmental Affairs, United States Senate*, 20 November 1991. Available online at www.globalsecurity.org/security/library/report/gao/145327.pdf (accessed 14 May 2007).

Brodie, B. (1973) *War and Politics*, New York: MacMillan Press.
Brown Report (1996) *Preparing for the 21st Century: An Appraisal of U.S. Intelligence*, Commission on the Roles and Capabilities of the United States Intelligence Community, Washington, DC: US Government Printing Office.
Burke, E.B. (2001) 'The expanding importance of the computer fraud and abuse act', *GigaLaw.com*, January 2001. Available online at www.gigalaw.com/articles/2001-all/burke-2001–01-all.html (accessed 14 May 2007).
Burns, R. (1999) 'Computer warfare used in Yugoslavia', *Associated Press*, 7 October 1999. Available online at http://transnational.org/SAJT/features/computerwarfare.html (accessed 14 May 2007).
Bush, G.H.W. (1990a) *A National Security Strategy of the United States*, Washington, DC: US Government Printing Office.
—— (1990b) *National Policy for the Security of National Security Telecommunications and Information Systems*, National Security Directive (NSD) 42, Washington, DC, 5 July 1990.
—— (1991) *A National Security Strategy for the United States*, Washington, DC: US Government Printing Office.
Bush, G.W. (2001a) *Executive Order 13228: Establishing the Office of Homeland Security and the Homeland Security Council*, Washington, DC, 8 October 2001.
—— (2001b) *Executive Order 13231: Critical Infrastructure Protection in the Information Age*, Washington, DC, 16 October 2001.
—— (2001c) *Remarks by the President to the Troops and Personnel*, Norfolk Naval Air Station, Norfolk, Virginia, 13 February 2001. Available online at www.whitehouse.gov/news/releases/20010213–1.html (accessed 14 May 2007).
—— (2001d) *Organization of the National Security Council System*, National Security Presidential Decision (NSPD 1), 5 March 2001.
—— (2002) *The National Strategy for Homeland Security*, Washington, DC: US Government Printing Office.
—— (2003a) *The National Strategy for Physical Protection of Critical Infrastructures and Key Assets*, Washington, DC: US Government Printing Office.
—— (2003b) *The National Strategy to Secure Cyberspace*, Washington, DC: US Government Printing Office.
Butts, C.T. (2001) 'The complexity of social networks: Theoretical and empirical findings', *Social Networks*, 23, pp. 31–71.
Buzan, B. (1991) *People, States and Fear: An Agenda for International Security Studies in the Post-Cold War Era*, 2nd edn, Brighton: Harvester Wheatsheaf.
Buzan, B., Wæver, O. and de Wilde, J. (1998) *Security: A New Framework for Analysis*, Boulder: Lynne Rienner.
Byrne, D. (1998) *Complexity Theory and the Social Sciences. An Introduction*, London: Routledge.
Çambel, A.B. (1992) *Applied Chaos Theory: A Paradigm for Complexity*, Boston: Academic Press.
Campbell, D. (1992) *Writing Security: United States Foreign Policy and the Politics of Identity*, Manchester: Manchester University Press.
Campen, A.D. (ed.) (1992) *The First Information War: The Story of Communications, Computers and Intelligence Systems in the Persian Gulf War*, Fairfax: AFCEA International Press.
Campen, A.D. and Dearth, D.H. (eds) (1998) *Cyberwar 2.0: Myths, Mysteries and Reality*, Fairfax: AFCEA International Press.

150 Bibliography

Campen, A.D., Dearth, D.H. and Goodden, T. (eds) (1996) *Cyberwar: Security, Strategy and Conflict in the Information Age*, Fairfax, AFCEA International Press.

Cashell, B., Jackson, W.D., Jickling, M., and Webel, B. (2004) *The Economic Impact of Cyber-Attacks*, Congressional Research Service Documents, CRS RL32331, 1 April 2004, Washington, DC: Congressional Research Service.

Castells, M. (1996) *The Rise of the Network Society*, Oxford: Blackwell.

Casti, J.L. (1979) *Connectivity, Complexity, and Catastrophe in Large-Scale Systems*, Chichester: Wiley and Sons.

Cebrowski, A.K. and Garstka, J.J. (1998) 'Network-centric warfare: Its origin and future, in *Proceedings of the Naval Institute*, 124, 1, pp. 28–35.

Center for Strategic and International Studies CSIS (1996) *The Information Revolution and International Security*, Robert F. McMormich Tribune Foundation Report, Washington, DC: Center for Strategic and International Studies.

Center for the Study of Terrorism and Irregular Warfare (1999) *Cyberterror: Prospects and Implications*, White paper, Monterey: Center on terrorism and irregular warfare. Available online at www.nps.navy.mil/ctiw/files/Cyberterror%20Prospects%20and%20Implications.pdf (accessed 14 May 2007).

Central Intelligence Agency (2002) *The Questions for the Record from the Worldwide Threat Hearing on 6 February 2002*. Available online at www.fas.org/irp/congress/2002_hr/020602cia.html (accessed 14 May 2007).

Cha, A.E. and Krim, J. (2002) 'White House officials debating rules for cyberwarfare', *Washington Post*, 22 August 2002. Available online at www.landfield.com/isn/mail-archive/2002/Aug/0088.html (accessed 14 May 2007).

Chapman, G. (1998) 'National security and the Internet', unpublished paper, presented at the Annual Convention of the Internet Society, Geneva, July 1998. Available online at www.utexas.edu/lbj/21cp/isoc.htm (accessed 14 May 2007).

Chertoff, M. (2005). *Statement of Secretary Michael Chertoff, U.S. Department of Homeland Security, Before the United States Senate Committee on Homeland Security and Government Affairs, Washington, DC*. Available online at www.homelandsecurity.ms.gov/docs/ChertoffTestimony_Senate_07142005.pdf (accessed 14 May 2007).

Chilton, P. (1996) *Security Metaphors – Cold War Discourse from Containment to Common House*, New York: Peter Lang.

Critical Infrastructure Protection Oral History Project (2005) 'Historical outline', School of Law's National Center for Technology & Law and organized by the Center for History & New Media at George Mason University. Available online at http://echo.gmu.edu/CIPP/essay/ (accessed 14 May 2007).

Clarke, R. and Zeichner, L. (2004) 'Beyond the moat: New strategies for cyber-security', *Bank Systems & Technology*, 27 January 2004. Available online at www.banktech.com/showArticle.jhtml?articleID=17501355 (accessed 14 May 2007).

Clinton, W.J. (1994a) *A National Security Strategy of Engagement and Enlargement*, Washington, DC: US Government Printing Office.

—— (1994b) *Security Policy Coordination*, Presidential Decision Directive 29, Washington, DC, 16 September 1994.

—— (1995a) *A National Security Strategy of Engagement and Enlargement*, Washington, DC: US Government Printing Office.

—— (1995b) *US Policy on Counterterrorism*, Presidential Decision Directive 39, Washington, DC, 21 June 1995.

—— (1996a) *A National Security Strategy of Engagement and Enlargement*, Washington, DC: US Government Printing Office.

—— (1996b) *Executive Order 13010 on Critical Infrastructure Protection*, Washington, DC, 15 July 1996.
—— (1997) *A National Security Strategy for a New Century*, Washington, DC: US Government Printing Office.
—— (1998a) *Protection Against Unconventional Threats to the Homeland and Americans Overseas*, Presidential Decision Directive 62, Washington, DC, 22 May 1998.
—— (1998b) *Protecting America's Critical Infrastructures: Presidential Decision Directive 63*, Washington, DC, 22 May 1998.
—— (1998c) *A National Security Strategy for a New Century*, Washington, DC: US Government Printing Office.
—— (1999) *A National Security Strategy for a New Century*, Washington, DC: US Government Printing Office.
—— (2000) *Defending America's Cyberspace: National Plan for Information Systems Protection. An Invitation to a Dialogue.* Version 1.0, Washington, DC: US Government Printing Office.
Cohen, E. (1996) 'A revolution in military affairs', *Foreign Affairs*, 75, 2, pp. 37–54.
Cohen, W.S. and Shelton, H.H. (1999) *Joint Statement on the Kosovo After Action Review (initial assessment)*, presented by Secretary of Defense William S. Cohen and Gen. Henry H. Shelton, Chairman of the Joint Chiefs of Staff, before the Senate Armed Services Committee, 14 October 1999. Available online at www.defenselink.mil/releases/release.aspx?releaseid=2220 (accessed 14 May 2007).
Cohn, C. (1987) 'Sex and death in the rational world of defense intellectuals', *Signs: Journal of Women in Culture and* Society 12, 4, pp. 687–718.
Committee on Science, Engineering, and Public Policy (1982) *Scientific Communication and National Security*, Washington, DC: National Academy Press.
Computer Emergency Response Team CERT (1988) 'Darpa establishes computer emergency response team' *Computer Emergency Response Team Press Release*, 13 December 1988. Available online at www.cert.org/about/1988press-rel.html (accessed 14 May 2007).
—— (2005) CERT/CC Statistics 1988–2005. Available online at www.cert.org/stats/cert_stats.html#incidents (accessed 14 May 2007).
Computer Science and Telecommunications Board (1989) *Growing Vulnerability of the Public Switched Network: Implications for National Security Emergency Preparedness*, Washington, DC: National Academy Press.
—— (1999) *Realizing the Potential of C4I, Fundamental Challenges*, Washington, DC: National Academy Press.
Connolly, W.E. (1983) *The Terms of Political Discourse*, Princeton: Princeton University Press.
Conway, M. (2008) 'The media and cyberterrorism: A study in the construction of 'reality', in Dunn Cavelty, M. and Kristensen, K.S. (eds) *The Politics of Securing the Homeland: Critical Infrastructure, Risk and Securitisation*, London: Routledge.
Cooper, J.R. (1997) 'Another view of the revolution in military affairs', in Arquilla, J. and Ronfeldt, D. (eds) *In Athena's Camp: Preparing for Conflict in the Information Age*, Santa Monica: RAND, pp. 99–140.
Copeland, T.E. (ed.) (2000) *The Information Revolution and National Security*, Carlisle Barracks: Strategic Studies Institute.
Cordesman, A.H. (2000) *Defending America. Redefining the Conceptual Borders of Homeland Defense. Critical Infrastructure Protection and Information Warfare*, Washington, DC: Center for Strategic and International Studies.

152 Bibliography

Covert, C. (1983) 'Seven curious teenagers wreak havoc via computer', *Detroit Free Press*, 28 August 1983, Section: WWL, p. 1F.

Cox, R. W. (1992) 'Towards a post-hegemonic conceptualization of world order: Reflections on the relevancy of ibn khaldun', in Rosenau, J.N. and Czempiel E.-O. (eds) *Governance Without Government: Order and Change in World Politics*, Cambridge Studies in International Relations Nr. 20, Cambridge: Cambridge University Press) pp. 132–58.

Creveld, M. van (1989) *Technology and War: From 2000 BC to the Present*, New York, Free Press.

—— (1991) *The Transformation of War: The Most Radical Reinterpretation of Armed Conflict Since Clausewitz*, New York, Free Press.

Crutchfield, J.P. (1994) 'Is anything ever new? Considering emergence', in Cowan, G., Pines, D. and Melzner, D. (eds) *Complexity: Metaphors, Models, and Reality*, SFI Series in the Sciences of Complexity XIX, Redwood City: Addison-Wesley, pp. 479–97.

—— (2002) 'What lies between order and chaos?' in Casti, J.L. and Karlqvist, A. (eds) *Art and Complexity*, Oxford: Oxford University Press.

Cukier, K.N. (1999) 'Internet governance and the ancien regime', *Swiss Political Science Review*, 5, 1, pp. 127–33.

Czempiel, E.-O. and Rosenau, J.N. (1989) *Global Changes and Theoretical Challenges: Approaches to World Politics for the 1990s*, Lexington: Lexington Books.

Daase, C. (1999) *Kleine Kriege – Grosse Wirkung: Wie unkonventionelle Kriegführung die internationale Politik verändert*, Baden-Baden: Nomos Verlagsgesellschaft.

Daase, C., Feske, S. and Peters, I. (eds) (2002) *Internationale Risikopolitik: Der Umgang mit neuen Gefahren in den internationalen Beziehungen*, Baden-Baden: Nomos Verlagsgesellschaft.

Dam, K.W. and Lin, H.S. (eds) (1996) *Cryptography's Role in Securing the Information Society*, Washington, DC: National Academy Press.

Dao, J. and Schmitt, E. (2002) 'Pentagon readies efforts to sway sentiment abroad', *New York Times*, 19 February 2002. Available online at www.commondreams.org/headlines02/0219–01.htm (accessed 14 May 2007).

David, N.C. (1997) 'An information-based revolution in military affairs', in Arquilla, John and Ronfeldt, David (eds) *In Athena's Camp: Preparing for Conflict in the Information Age*, Santa Monica: RAND, pp. 79–98.

Davis, J. (2002) 'Improving CIA analytic performance: Strategic warning', *The Sherman Kent Center for Intelligence Analysis Occasional Papers*, 1, 1, September 2002. Available online at www.au.af.mil/au/awc/awcgate/cia/strategic_warning_kent. htm (accessed 14 May 2007).

Debrix, F. (2001) 'Cyberterror and media-induced fears: The production of emergency culture', *Strategies: Journal of Theory, Culture & Politics*, 14, 1, May, pp. 149–68.

Defense Science Board (1994) *Report of the Defense Science Board Summer Study Task Force on Information Architecture for the Battlefield*, Washington, DC: Department of Defense.

—— (1996) *Report of the Defense Science Board Task Force on Information Warfare – Defense (IW-D)*, Washington, DC: Department of Defense.

—— (2001) *Protecting the Homeland. Report of the Defense Science Board Task Force on Defensive Information Operations*. 2000 Summer Study Volume II, Washington, DC: Department of Defense.

Deibert, R.J. (1997) *Parchment, Printing, and Hypermedia: Communication in World Order Transformation*, New York: Columbia University Press.

Dekker, M. (1997) 'Security of the Internet', in *The Froehlich/Kent Encyclopedia of Telecommunications*, 15, New York, pp. 231–55. Available online at www.cert.org/encyc_article/tocencyc.html (accessed 14 May 2007).

Demchak, C.C. (1999) '"New Security" in cyberspace: Emerging intersection between military and civilian contingencies', *Journal of Contingencies and Crisis Management*, 7, 4, pp. 181–98.

Denning, D. (2000) 'Cyberterrorism', testimony before the special oversight panel on terrorism. Committee on Armed Services U.S. House of Representatives, 23 May 2000.

—— (2001a) 'Is Cyber-terror Next?' essay for the social science research council, after September 11. Available online at www.ssrc.org/sept11/essays/denning.htm (accessed 14 May 2007).

—— (2001b) 'Activism, hacktivism, and cyberterrorism: The Internet as a tool for influencing foreign policy', in Arquilla, J. and Ronfeldt, D. (eds) *Networks and Netwars: The Future of Terror, Crime, and Militancy*, Santa Monica: RAND, pp. 239–88.

Denning, P. (ed.) (1990) *Computers Under Attack: Intruders, Worms, and Viruses*, New York: Addison-Wesley.

—— (1997) 'The Internet after thirty years', in Denning, Dorothy E. and Denning, Peter J. (eds) *Internet Besieged: Countering Cyberspace Scofflaws*, New York: ACM Press, pp. 15–27.

Department of Homeland Security (DHS) (2004) *Securing Our Homeland: US Department of Homeland Security Strategic Plan*, 24 February 2004, Washington, DC: US Government Printing Office.

—— (2006) *Cyber Storm: Exercise Report*, 12 September 2006, Washington, DC. Available online at www.dhs.gov/xlibrary/assets/prep_cyberstormreport_sep06.pdf (accessed 14 May 2007).

Department of the Air Force (1998), *Air Force Doctrine Document 2–5, Information Operations*, Washington, DC, Department of the United States Air Force: August 1998.

Department of the Army (1996) *Information Operations, Field Manual No. 100–6*, Washington, DC, Department of the Army.

Department of Defense (1999) *An Assessment of International Legal Issues in Information Operations*, Washington, DC: Department of Defense.

—— (2001a) *Directive Number 3600.1, Information Operations*, Revision One, October 2001. Available online at www.iwar.org.uk/iwar/resources/doctrine/DoD36001.pdf (accessed 14 May 2007).

—— (2001b) *FY2001 Defense Supplemental Request*, June 2001. Available online at www.dod.mil/comptroller/defbudget/fy2001/fy2001_supp.pdf (accessed 14 May 2007).

—— (2001c) *Department of Defense Dictionary of Military and Associated Terms*, Joint Publication 1–02, 12 April 2001 (As Amended Through 14 April 2006). Available online at www.dtic.mil/doctrine/jel/new_pubs/jp1_02.pdf (accessed 14 May 2007).

Der Derian, J. and Shapiro, M. (eds) (1989) *International/Intertextual Relations: Postmodern Readings of World Politics*, New York: Lexington Books.

Der Derian, J. (1995) 'The value of security: Hobbes, Marx, Nietzsche, and Baudrillard', in Lipschutz, Ronnie (ed.) *On Security*, New York: Columbia University Press, pp. 24–45.

Bibliography

Deutch, J. (1996) *Testimony of the Director of U.S. Central Intelligence Before the Senate Governmental Affairs Committee, Permanent Subcommittee on Investigations*, 25 June 1996. Available online at www.fas.org/irp/congress/1996_hr/s960625d.htm (accessed 14 May 2007).

Deutsch, K.W. (1957) 'Mass communications and the loss of freedom in national decision-making: A possible research approach to interstate conflicts', *Journal of Conflict Resolution*, 1, 2, pp. 200–11.

Devost, M.G. (1995) *National Security in the Information Age*, unpublished Master Thesis, University of Vermont, Burlington. Available online at www.devost.net/papers/national_security_in_the_information_age.html (accessed 14 May 2007).

Devost, M.G., Houghton, B.K. and Pollard, N.A. (1997) 'Information terrorism: Political violence in the information age', *Terrorism and Political Violence*, 9, 1, pp. 72–83.

Diffie, W. and Hellman, M.E. (1976) 'New directions in cryptography', *IEEE Transactions on Information Theory*, 22, 6, pp. 644–54.

Dodd, G.S. (1990) *The Computer Fraud and Abuse Act of 1986: A Measured Response to a Growing Problem*, New York: Random House.

Donati, P. (1992) 'Political discourse analysis', in Diani, M. and Ron E. (eds) *Studying Collective Action*, London: Sage, pp. 136–67.

Donnelly, J. and Crawley, V. (1999) 'Hamre to hill: "We're in a cyberwar"', *Defense Week*, 1 March 1999, p. 1.

Douglas, M. and Wildavsky, A. (1983) *Risk and Culture: An Essay on the Selection of Technological and Environmental Dangers*, Berkley: University of California Press.

Downes, L., Mui, C. and Negroponte, N. (1998) *Unleashing the Killer App: Digital Strategies for Market Dominance*, Cambridge, MA: Harvard Business School Press.

Drucker, P.F. (1989) *The New Realities: In Government and Politics, in Economics and Business, in Society and World View*, New York: Harper Collins Publishers.

Drummond, N. and McClendon, D.J. (2001) 'Cybercrime-alternative models for dealing with unauthorized use and abuse of computer networks', *Law and Internet*, September. Available online at http://gsulaw.gsu.edu/lawand/papers/su01/drummond_mcclendon/ (accessed 14 May 2007).

Dunn Cavelty, M. and Mauer, V. (2007) 'Concluding remarks: The role of the state in securing the information age – challenges and prospects', in Dunn Cavelty, M., Mauer, V. and Krishna-Hensel, S.-F. (eds) *Power and Security in the Information Age: Investigating the Role of the State in Cyberspace*, Aldershot: Ashgate.

Dunn, M. (2002) *Information Age Conflicts: A Study on the Information Revolution and a Changing Operating Environment*. Zürcher Beiträge zur Sicherheitspolitik und Konfliktforschung, No. 64, Zurich: Center for Security Studies.

—— (2004) 'Analysis of Methods and Models for CII Assessment', in Dunn, M. and Wigert, I. (2004) *The International CIIP Handbook 2004: An Inventory of Protection Policies in Fourteen Countries*, Zurich: Center for Security Studies, pp. 219–98.

—— (2005) 'The socio-political dimensions of critical information infrastructure protection (CIIP)', *International Journal for Critical Infrastructure Protection*, 1, 2/3, pp. 58–68.

—— (2007a) 'Securing the digital age: IR theory and the twin-forces of complexity and change', in Eriksson, J. and Giacomello, G. (eds) *International Relations and Security in the Digital Age*, London: Routledge, pp. 85–105.

—— (2007b) 'Cyber-terror – looming threat or phantom menace? The framing of the US Cyber-Threat debate', *Journal of Information Technology and Politics*, 4, 1.

Dunn, M. and Wigert, I. (2004) *The International CIIP Handbook 2004: An Inventory of Protection Policies in Fourteen Countries*, Zurich: Center for Security Studies.

Eichin, M. and Rochlis, J. (1989) *With Microscope and Tweezers: An Analysis of the Internet Virus of November 1988*. Available online at www.mit.edu/people/eichin/virus/main.html (accessed 14 May 2007).

Electronic Privacy Information Center EPIC (1998a) *Letter of the Computer Professionals for Social Responsibility (CPSR) to Representative Jack Brooks, Chairman, House Judiciary Committee*, 11 August 1992. Available online at www.eff.org/Privacy/Crypto/?f=cpsr_brooks.letter.txt (accessed 14 May 2007).

—— (1998b) *Critical Infrastructure Protection and the Endangerment of Civil Liberties An Assessment of the President's Commission on Critical Infrastructure Protection (PCCIP)*, Washington, DC: Electronic Privacy Information Center.

—— (1999) *Cryptography and Liberty: An International Survey of Encryption Policy*, Washington, DC: Electronic Privacy Information Center. Available online at www.gilc.org/crypto/crypto-survey-99.html (accessed 14 May 2007)

—— (2005) *The USA PATRIOT Act*, Washington, DC: Electronic Privacy Information Center, 24 May 2005. Available online at www.epic.org/privacy/terrorism/usapatriot/ (accessed 14 May 2007).

Ellison, R.J., Fisher, D.A., Linger, R.C., Lipson, H.F., Longstaff T. and Mead, N.R. (1997) *Survivable Network Systems: An Emerging Discipline*, Technical Report, CMU/SEI-97-TR-013, ESC-TR-97–013, November 1997. Available online at www.cert.org/research/97tr013.pdf (accessed 14 May 2007).

Ellul, J. (1964) *The Technological Society*, New York: Vintage.

Elmer-Dewitt, P. (1983) 'The 414 Gang Strikes Again', *Time Magazine*, 29 August 1983.

Erickson, J. (2003) *Hacking: The Art of Exploitation*, San Francisco: No Starch Press.

Eriksson, A.E. (1999) 'Information warfare: Hype or reality?' *The Non-Proliferation Review*, 6, 3, pp. 57–64.

Eriksson, J. (1999a) 'Agendas, threats, and politics. Securitization in Sweden', paper presented at the ECPR Joint Sesssions, workshop 'Redefining Security', Mannheim, 26–31 March 1999.

—— (1999b) 'Observers or advocates? On the political role of security analysts', *Cooperation and Conflict*, 34, 4, pp. 311–30.

—— (ed.) (2001a) *Threat Politics: New Perspectives on Security, Risk and Crisis Management*, Ashgate: Aldershot.

—— (2001b) 'Cyberplagues, IT, and security: Threat politics in the information age', *Journal of Contingencies and Crisis Management*, 9, 4, pp. 211–22.

Eriksson, J. and Giacomello, G. (2006) 'The information revolution, security, and international relations: (IR) Relevant Theory?' *International Political Science Review*, 27, 3, pp. 221–44.

Eriksson, J. and Noreen, E. (2002) *Setting the Agenda of Threats: An Explanatory Model*, Uppsala Peace Research Papers, 6. Available online at www.pcr.uu.se/publications/UPRP_pdf/uprp_no_6.pdf (accessed 14 May 2007).

Ezell, B.C., Farr, J.V. and Wiese, I. (2000) 'Infrastructure risk analysis of municipal water distribution system', *Journal of Infrastructure Systems*, 6, 3, pp. 118–22.

Feenberg, A. (1991) *Critical Theory of Technology*, Oxford: Oxford University Press.

Fine, G. (2007) Office of the Inspector General United States Department of Justice, *Statement of Glenn A. Fine, Inspector General, U.S. Department of Justice, Before the Permanent Select Committee on Intelligence U.S. House of Representatives concerning The FBI's Use of National Security Letters and Section 215 Requests for Business Records*, 28 March 2007. Available online at www.usdoj.gov/oig/testimony/0703b/final.pdf (accessed 14 May 2007).

156 Bibliography

Fisher, K. (1997) 'Locating frames in the discursive universe', *Sociological Research Online*, 3, 2. Available online at www.socresonline.org.uk/socresonline/2/3/4.html (accessed 14 May 2007).

Fisher, U. (2001) 'Information age state security: New threats to old boundaries', *Journal for Homeland Security*, November 2001. Available online at www.homelandsecurity.org/journal/articles/fisher.htm (accessed 14 May 2007).

Fitzpatrick, D. (2003) 'Cybersecurity Expert Warns of Post-9/11 Vulnerability', *Pittsburgh Post-Gazette*, 9 September 2003. Available online at www.post-gazette.com/pg/03252/219578.stm (accessed 14 May 2007).

Forrester, J.W. (1961) *Industrial Dynamics*, Massachusetts: Productivity Press.

Foucault, M. (1970) *The Order of Things*, New York: Random House.

Fredericks, B. (1997) 'Information warfare: The organizational dimension', in Neilson, B. (ed.) *Sun Tzu and the Art of War in Information Warfare: A Collection of Winning Papers from the Sun Tzu Art of War in Information Warfare Competition*, Washington, DC: National Defense University Press, pp. 79–102.

Freedman, L. (2003) 'Prevention, not preemption', *The Washington Quarterly*, 26, 2, pp. 105–14.

Freeh, L.J. (1997) 'Counterterrorism', *Statement of Louis J. Freeh, Director Federal Bureau of Investigation Before the Senate Appropriations Committee Hearing on Counterterrorism*, 13 May 1997. Available online at www.fas.org/irp/congress/1997_hr/ss970513f.htm (accessed 14 May 2007).

—— (2000) *Statement of Louis J. Freeh, Director Federal Bureau of Investigation Before the Senate Committee on Appropriations Subcommittee for the Departments of Commerce, Justice, State, the Judiciary, and Related Agencies*, 16 February 2000. Available online at www.milnet.com/infowar/cyber021600.htm (accessed 14 May 2007).

Freeman, C. and Louca, F. (2002) *As Time Goes By: From the Industrial Revolutions to the Information Revolution*, Oxford, Oxford University Press.

Froehlich, J.N., Pinter, E.M., and Witmeyer III, J.J. (1997) 'Computer viruses: Making the time fit the crime', *Legal Column Archives*. Available online at www.fmew.com/archive/ (accessed 14 May 2007).

Froomkin, A.M. (1995) 'The metaphor is the key: Cryptography, the clipper chip, and the constitution', *University of Pennsylvania Law Review*, 143, pp. 709–897.

—— (1996) 'It came from planet clipper: The Battle Over Cryptographic Key "Escrow"', *Law of Cyberspace issue of the University of Chicago Legal Forum*, 15, pp. 14–74.

Fuchs, D.A. and Kratochwil, F. (eds) (2002), *Transformative Change and Global Order. Reflections on Theory and Practice*, Münster: LIT-Verlag.

Fulghum, D. (1999), 'Security leaks and unknown bedeviled Kosovo commanders', *Aviation Week and Space Technology*, 151, 18, 1 November 1999, pp. 33–6.

Fursenko, A. and Naftali, T. (1997) *One Hell of a Gamble: Khrushchev, Castro, and Kennedy, 1958–1964*, New York: W W Norton & Co.

Galbraith, J.K. (1968) *The New Industrial State*, New York: Signet.

Gamson, W.A. (1992) *Talking Politics*, Cambridge: Cambridge University Press.

GAO (1985) United States General Accounting Office, *Communications Privacy: Federal Policy and Actions*, Report to the Honorable Jack Brooks, Chairman, Committee on the Judiciary, House of Representatives, GAO/OSI-94-2, 4 November 1993, Washington, DC: General Accounting Office.

—— (1989) United States General Accounting Office, *Computer Security Virus High-*

lights Need for Improved Internet Management, Report to the Chairman, Subcommittee on Telecommunications and Finance, Committee on Energy and Commerce House of Representatives, GAO/IMTEC-89–57, June 1989, Washington, DC: General Accounting Office.

—— (1991) United States General Accounting Office, *Computer Security: Hackers Penetrate DoD Computer Systems*, GAO/T-IMTEC-92–5, 20 November 1991, Washington, DC: General Accounting Office.

—— (1995) United States General Accounting Office, *The Potential Impact of National Security Decision Directive (NSDD) 145 on Civil Agencies*, Warren G. Reed before the Subcommittee on Transportation, Aviation, and Materials, Committee on Science and Technology, 17 June 1985, Washington, DC: General Accounting Office.

—— (1996) United States General Accounting Office, *Information Security: Computer Attacks at Department of Defense Pose Increasing Risk*, GAO/AIMD-96–84, 22 May 1996, Washington, DC: General Accounting Office.

—— (1999) United States General Accounting Office, *Critical Infrastructure Protection: Comprehensive Strategy Can Draw on Year 2000 Experiences*, GAO/AIMD-00–1, 1 October 1999, Washington, DC: General Accounting Office.

—— (2001) United States General Accounting Office, *Critical Infrastructure Protection: Significant Challenges in Developing Analysis, Warning, and Response Capabilities*, GAO-01–323, 25 April 2001, Washington, DC: General Accounting Office.

Garamone, J. (2001) 'Wolfowitz discusses DoD goals during testimony', *American Forces Information Service News Articles*, 7 March 2001.

Garreau, J. (2005) *Radical Evolution: The Promise and Peril of Enhancing Our Minds, Our Bodies – and What it Means to be Human*, New York: Doubleday.

Gellman, B. (2002) 'Cyber-attacks by Al qaeda feared: Terrorists at threshold of using internet as tool of bloodshed, Experts say', *Washington Post*, 27 June 2002, p. A01.

Gershwin, L.K. (2001) 'Cyber threat trends and US network security', *Statement for the Record, United States Congress, Joint Economic Committee Hearing 'Wired World: Cyber Security and the U.S. Economy*, 21 June 2001.

Gertz, B. (1998) 'NSA's operation eligible receiver', *The Washington Times*, 16 April 1998.

Giacomello, G. (1999) 'Taming the net? The issue of government control on the Internet', *Swiss Political Science Review*, 5, 2, pp. 116–22.

Giacomello, G. and Eriksson J. (eds) (2007) *International Relations and Security in the Digital Age*, London: Routledge.

Gibson, D.M. (2004) *A Virtual Pandora's Box: Anticipatory Self-Defense in Cyberspace*. Available online at www.uiowa.edu/~cyberlaw/csl03/dgcsl03.html (accessed 14 May 2007).

Gilmore (1999) Advisory panel to assess domestic response capabilities for terrorism involving weapons of mass destruction, 1st Report, *Assessing the Threat*, 15 December 1999, Washington, DC: RAND.

—— (2000) Advisory panel to assess domestic response capabilities for terrorism involving weapons of mass destruction, 2nd Report, *Toward a National Strategy for Combating Terrorism*, 15 December 2000, Washington, DC: RAND.

Gilmore, G. J. (2001) 'Rumsfeld to NATO: Prepare now for emerging threats', *American Forces Press Service*, 7 June 2001.

Goff, P. (ed.) (1999) *Kosovo News and Propaganda War*, Vienna: The International Press Institute.

Goldman, E.O. (2001) 'New threats, new identities and new ways of war: The sources of change in national security doctrine', *Journal of Strategic Studies*, 24, 3, pp. 12–42.

Gomez, P. (2001) 'Vom Umgang mit Komplexität: Denkfallen und Entscheidungshilfen', in Mey, H. and Lehmann Pollheimer, D. (eds) *Absturz im freien Fall – Anlauf zu neuen Höhenflügen: Gutes Entscheiden in Wirtschaft, Politik und Gesellschaft*, Zürich: Vdf Hochschulverlag AG, pp. 151–66.

Goodman, M.D. and Brenner, S.W. (2002) 'The emerging consensus on criminal conduct in cyberspace', *UCLA Journal of Law and Technology*, 10, 2, pp. 139–223.

Goodman, S.E., Hassebroek, P.B., King, D. and Azment, A. (2002) *International Coordination to Increase the Security of Critical Network Infrastructures*, Document CNI/04, paper presented at the ITU Workshop on Creating Trust in Critical Network Infrastructures, Seoul, 20–2 May 2002. Available online at www.itu.int/osg/spu/ni/security/docs/cni.04.pdf (accessed 14 May 2007).

Graham, B. (2003) 'Bush orders guidelines for cyber-warfare: Rules for attacking enemy computers prepared as U.S. weighs Iraq options', Washington Post, 7 February 2003, p. A01.

Green, J. (2002) 'The myth of cyberterrorism', *Washington Monthly*, November 2002. Available online at www.washingtonmonthly.com/features/2001/0211.green.html (accessed 14 May 2007).

Gross, G. (2004) 'U.S. Cybersecurity chief resigns: Amit Yoran, said to be Frustrated with progress, gives one-day notice', *IDG News Service*, 01 October 2004. Available online at www.infoworld.com/infoworld/article/04/10/01/HNchiefresigns_1.html (accessed 14 May 2007).

Guzzini, S. (2002) 'Constructivism and the role of institutions in international relations', *Copenhagen Peace Research Institute Working Papers*, 38, Copenhagen: Copenhagen Peace Research Institute.

Haas, P.M. (1992) 'Introduction: Epistemic communities and international policy coordination', *International Organization*, 46, 1, pp. 1–35.

—— (1993) 'Epistemic communities and the dynamics of international environmental co-operation', in Rittberger, V. (ed.) *Regime Theory and International Relations*, Oxford: Clarendon Press, pp. 168–201.

Hables Gray, C. (1997) *Postmodern War: The New Politics of Conflict*, New York: Guilford Press.

Hack FAQ (2004) Available online at www.nmrc.org/pub/faq/hackfaq/index.html (accessed 14 May 2007).

Haimes, Y.Y. (1998) *Risk Modeling, Assessment, and Management*, New York: Wiley and Sons.

Haimes, Y.Y. and Jiang, P. (2001) 'Leontief-based model of risk in complex interconnected infrastructures', *Journal of Infrastructure Systems*, 7, 1, pp. 1–12.

Halperin, D. (2000) 'The Internet and national security: Emerging issues', in Alberts, D.S. and Papp, D.S. (eds) *The Information Age: An Anthology of Its Impacts and Consequences* (Vol. II), Washington, DC: National Defense University Press, pp. 137–73.

Hamre, J.J. (1998) 'Critical infrastructure protection – Information Assurance', *Hearing on Intelligence and Security, Testimony of the Deputy Secretary of Defense* [accompanied by Mr. Linton Wells, II, Principal Deputy, Assistant Secretary of Defense for Command, Control, Communications & Intelligence, Department of Defense and Brigadier General John H. Campbell, USAF, Deputy Director for Information Operations (J-39), Department of Defense] 11 June 1998, House Military Procurement and Military Research & Development Subcommittees. Available online at www.fas.org/irp/congress/1998_hr/98-06-11hamre.htm (accessed 14 May 2007).

—— (2003) Frontline Interview with John Hamre, 18 February 2003. Available online at www.pbs.org/wgbh/pages/frontline/shows/cyberwar/interviews/hamre.html (accessed 14 May 2007).

Hart-Rudman (2001) *Road Map for National Security: Imperative for Change: The Phase III Report of the U.S. Commission on National Security/21st Century*, 15 February 2001, Washington, DC: US Government Printing Office. Available online at http://handle.dtic.mil/100.2/ADA387531 (accessed 14 May 2007).

Hedges, S.J. (2005), 'Media use backfires on U.S.; many ask if pentagon altered information to make case for war', *Chicago Tribune*, 11 December 2005.

Heider, F. (1944) 'Social perception and phenomenal causality', *Psychological Review*, 51, pp. 358–74.

—— (1958) *The Psychology of Interpersonal Relations*, New York: John Wiley & Sons.

Henry, R. and Peartree, E.C. (eds) (1998a) *Information Revolution and International Security*, Washington, DC: Center for Strategic and International Studies.

—— (1998b) 'Military theory and information warfare', *Parameters*, XXVIII, 3, pp. 121–35.

Herrera, G. (2003) 'Technology and international systems', *Millennium*, 32, 3, pp. 559–94.

—— (2007) 'Cyberspace and sovereignty: Thoughts on physical space and digital space', in Dunn Cavelty, M., Mauer, V. and Krishna-Hensel S.-F. (eds) *Power and Security in the Information Age: Investigating the Role of the State in Cyberspace*, Aldershot: Ashgate.

Hildreth, S.A. (2001) *Cyberwarfare*, Congressional Research Report for Congress, RL30735, 19 June 2001, Washington, DC: Congressional Research Service.

Hinsely, F.H. and Stripp, A. (2001) *Codebreakers: The Inside Story of Bletchley Park*, Oxford: Oxford University Press.

Hobart, M.E. and Schiffman, Z.S. (2000) *Information Ages: Literacy, Numeracy, and the Computer Revolution*, Washington, DC: Johns Hopkins University Press.

Hoffmann, L. (1999) 'U.S. opened cyber-war during Kosovo fight', *Washington Times*, 24 October 1999, p. C1.

Holmgren, J. and Softa, J. (2003) 'The functional security agenda in the Nordic States', *Threat Politics Project*, Opublicerad rapport, Utrikespolitiska Institutet, Sweden: University of Uppsala.

Holsti, K.J. (1998) *The Problem of Change in International Relations Theory*, Institute of International Relations, The University of British Columbia, Working Paper No. 26, December. Available online at www.iir.ubc.ca/site_template/workingpapers/webwp26.pdf (accessed 14 May 2007).

Holzner, B. (1968) *Reality Construction in Society*, Cambridge: Schenkman Publishing.

Homer-Dixon, T. (2000) *The Ingenuity Gap*, New York: Knopf.

Hughes, P.M. (1998) 'Global threats and challenges: The decades ahead', *Statement of the Director, Defense Intelligence Agency for the Senate Select Committee on Intelligence*, 28 January 1998. Available online at www.fas.org/irp/congress/1998_hr/s980128h.htm (accessed 14 May 2007).

Hundley, R.O. and Anderson, R.H. (1997) 'Emerging challenge: Security and safety in cyberspace', in Arquilla, J. and David R. (eds) *In Athena's Camp: Preparing for Conflict in the Information Age*, Santa Monica: RAND, pp. 231–52.

Hundley, R.O., Anderson, R.H., Bikson, T.K., Dewar, J.A., Green, J.D., Libicki, M.C., and Neu, C.R. (2000) *The Global Course of the Information Revolution: Political, Economic, and Social Consequences Proceedings of an International Conference*, Santa Monica: RAND.

Husain, K.N. (2003) 'The men behind the curtain', *Bulletin of the Atomic Scientists*, 59, 6, pp. 62–71.

Huysmans, J. (1998a) 'Security! What do you mean? From concept to thick signifier', *European Journal of International Relations*, 4, 2, pp. 226–55.

—— (1998b) 'Revisiting Copenhagen: Or, on the creative development of a security studies agenda in Europe', *European Journal of International Relations*, 4, 4, pp. 479–506.

—— (1998c) 'The question of the limit: Desecuritization and the aesthetics of terrorism in political realism', *Millenium*, 27, 3, pp. 569–89.

ICSA Labs (2003) *ICSA Labs 2002 Virus Prevalence Survey*. Available online at www.icsalabs.com/icsa/docs/html/library/whitepapers/VPS2002.pdf (accessed 14 May 2007).

—— (2004) *ICSA Labs 2003 Virus Prevalence Survey*. Available online at www.icsalabs.com/icsa/docs/html/library/whitepapers/VPS2003.pdf (accessed 14 May 2007).

—— (2005) *ICSA Labs 2004 Virus Prevalence Survey*. Available online at www.icsalabs.com/icsa/docs/html/library/whitepapers/VPS2004.pdf (accessed 14 May 2007).

Ignatieff, M. (2000) *Virtual War. Kosovo and Beyond*, London: Chatto and Windus.

—— (2004) *Virus Report Status for 2004*. Available online at www.ipa.go.jp/security/english/virus/press/200412/virus2004.html (accessed 14 May 2007).

Information Technology Promotion Agency IPA (2005) *Virus Report Status for 2005*. Available online at www.ipa.go.jp/security/english/virus/press/200512/virus2005.html (accessed 14 May 2007).

Ingles-le Nobel, J.J. (1999) 'Cyberterrorism hype', *Jane's Intelligence Review*, 21 October 1999.

Jacoby, L. (2003) 'Current and Projected National Security Threats to the United States', Statement for the Record of Vice Admiral Lowell E. Jacoby, USN, Director, Defense Intelligence Agency before the Senate Select Committee on Intelligence, 11 February 2003.

Jepperson, R.L., Wendt, A., and Katzenstein, P.J. (1996) 'Norms, identity, and culture in national security', in Katzenstein, P.J. (ed.) *The Culture of National Security: Norms and Identity in World Politics*, New York: Columbia University Press, pp. 33–75.

Jertz, W. (1999) Major General Jertz at the Press Conference by Mr Jamie Shea, NATO Spokesman and Major General Walter Jertz, SHAPE, 28 May 1999, updated 28 May 1999, NATO HQ, Brussels.

—— (2001) *Krieg der Worte, Macht der Bilder. Manipulation oder Wahrheit im Kosovo-Konflikt?* Bonn: Bernard & Graefe.

Johnson, S.E. and Libicki, M.C. (1995) *Introduction to Dominant Battle-Space Knowledge: The Winning Edge*, Washington, DC: National Defense University.

Johnston, H. (1995) 'A methodology for frame analysis: From discourse to cognitive schemata', in Johnston, H. and Klandermans, B. (eds) *Social Movements and Culture*, London: UCL Press.

Joint Chiefs of Staff (1996) *Joint Vision 2010*, Washington, DC: U.S. Department of Defense.

—— (1998) *Joint Publication 3–13, Joint Doctrine for Information Operations*, Washington, DC, U.S. Department of Defense, 9 October 1998.

Joint Security Commission (1994), *Redefining Security: A Report to the Secretary of Defense and the Director of Central Intelligence*, Washington, DC: US Government Printing Office, 28 February 1994.

Joint Staff (1992) C4 Architecture & Integration Division, *C4I for the Warrior*, Washington, DC: Joint Staff, 12 June 1992.

Jones, E.E., Kannouse, D.E., Kelley, H.H., Nisbett, R.E., Valins, S. and Weiner, B. (eds) (1972) *Attribution: Perceiving the Causes of Behavior*, Morristown: General Learning Press.

Kabay, M.E. (1998) *ICSA White Paper on Computer Crime Statistics*. Available online at www.icsa.net/html/library/whitepapers/crime.pdf (accessed 14 May 2007).

Kahn, D. (1967) *The Codebreakers: The Story of Secret Writing*, New York: Macmillian.

—— (1996) *The Codebreakers: The Comprehensive History of Secret Communication from Ancient Times to the Internet*, New York: Scribner.

Katzenstein, P.J. (ed.) (1996) *The Culture of National Security: Norms and Identity in World Politics*, New York: Columbia University Press.

Kelly, K. (1995) *Out of Control: The Rise of Neo-Biological Civilization*, Menlo Park: Addison-Wesley.

Kennedy, J.F. (1963) *National Communications System*, Presidential Memorandum, Washington, DC, 21 August 1963.

Keohane, R.O. and Nye, J.S. (1998) 'Power and interdependence in the information age', *Foreign Affairs* 77, 5 (September/October) pp. 81–94.

Kerrey, B. (1998) 'National security and information technology', *1998 Congressional Debate*, Senate, 12 October 1998. Available online at www.fas.org/irp/congress/1998_cr/s981012-info.htm (accessed 14 May 2007).

King, G., Keohane, R.O., and Verba, S. (1994) *Designing Social Inquiry: Scientific Inference in Qualitative Research*, Princeton: Princeton University Press.

Kingdon, J.W. (2003) *Agendas, Alternatives, and Public Policies*, 2nd edn, New York: Harper Collins College Publishers.

Knezo, G. (2003) *Sensitive but Unclassified' and Other Federal Security Controls on Scientific and Technical Information: History and Current Controversy*, Congressional Research Report for Congress, RL31845, 20 February 2003, Washington, DC: Congressional Research Service.

Kolet, K.S. (2001) 'Asymmetric Threats to the United States', *Comparative Strategy*, 20, 3, pp. 277–92.

Kratochwil, F. (1989) *Rules, Norms and Decisions: On the Conditions of Practical and Legal Reasoning in International and Domestic Affairs*, Cambridge: Cambridge University Press.

Krebs, B. (2006) 'Top cyber-security post is filled', *washingtonpost.com*, 18 September 2006. Available online at www.washingtonpost.com/wp-dyn/content/article/2006/09/18/AR2006091800928.html (accessed 14 May 2007).

Krepinevich, A. (1994) 'Cavalry to computer: The pattern of military revolutions', *The National Interest*, 37, pp. 30–42.

—— (2001) 'The Bush administration's call for defense transformation: A congressional guide', *Center for Strategic and Budgetary Assessments*, 19 Juni 2001. Available online at www.csbaonline.org/4Publications/Archive/H.20010619.The_Bush_Administr/H.20010619.The_Bush_Administr.htm (accessed 14 May 2007).

Kristensen, K.S. (forthcoming 2008) '"The Absolute Protection of our Citizens": Critical Infrastructure Protection and the Practice of Security', in Dunn Cavelty, M. and Kristensen, K.S. (eds), *The Politics of Securing the Homeland: Critical Infrastructure, Risk and Securitisation*, London: Routledge.

Krutskikh, A.(1999) 'Information challenges to security', *International Affairs*, 45, 2, pp. 29–37.

Kuehl, D. (2000a) *Statement of Dr. Daniel Kuehl, School of Information Warfare & Strategy National Defense University, for the Joint Economic Committee*, 23 February 2000. Available online at www.iwar.org.uk/cip/resources/senate/economy/kuehl~1.htm (accessed 14 May 2007).

—— (2000b) 'The information component of power and the national security strategy', in Campen, A.D. and Dearth, D.H. (eds) *Cyberwar 3.0: Human Factors in Information Operations and Future Conflict*, Fairfax: AFCEA International Press.

Kushnick, B. (1999) *The Unauthorized Biography of the Baby Bells & Info-Scandal*, New York: New Networks Institute.

Kyriakopoulos, N. and Wilikens, M. (2000) *Dependability and Complexity: Exploring Ideas for Studying Open Systems*, Ispra: Joint Research Centre. Available online at www.delft2001.tudelft.nl/paper%20files/paper1168.doc (accessed 14 May 2007).

Lacey, M. (2000) 'Clinton gives a final foreign policy speech', *New York Times*, 9 December 2000.

Landau, S. (1994) *Codes, Keys, and Conflicts: Issues in U.S. Crypto Policy*, New York: Association for Computing Machinery Press.

LaPorte, T.R. (ed.) (1975) *Organized Social Complexity: Challenge to Politics and Policy*, Princeton: Princeton University Press.

Latham, R. (ed.) (2003) *Bombs and Bandwidth: The Emerging Relationship Between IT and Security*, New York: The New Press.

Levy, S. (1984) *Hackers Heroes of the Computer Revolution*, New York: Anchor Press.

Lewis, J.A. (2002) *Assessing the Risks of Cyber-terrorism, Cyber War and Other Cyber Threats*, Washington, DC: Center for Strategic and International Studies.

Libicki, M. (1994) *The Mesh and the Net. Speculations on Armed Conflict in an Age of Free Silicon*, McNair Paper 28, Washington, DC, National Defense University.

—— (1995) *What is Information Warfare?* Washington, DC, National Defense University.

—— (1997a) 'The small and the many', in Arquilla, J. and Ronfeldt, D. (eds) *In Athena's Camp: Preparing for Conflict in the Information Age*, Santa Monica, RAND, pp. 191–216.

—— (1997b) *Information Dominance*, Strategic Forum No. 132, Washington, DC, National Defense University.

—— (1999) *Illuminating Tomorrow's War*, Mc Nair Paper 61, Washington, DC, National Defense University.

Lloyd, R. Bartlett, H.C., Denny, D., Holman G.P., Kirby, J.M., Lawler, T., Owens, M.T., Freeman, K.E., and Smith, E.F. (eds) (1990) *Fundamentals of Force Planning, Vol. 1: Concepts*, The Force Planning Faculty, Newport: Naval War College.

Loon, J. van (2000) 'Virtual risks in an age of cybernetic reproduction', in Adam, B., Beck, U. and Loon, J. van (eds) *The Risk Society and Beyond: Critical Issues for Social Theory*, London: Sage, pp. 165–82.

—— (2002) *Risk and Technological Culture: Towards a Sociology of Virulence*, London: Routledge.

Machlup, F. (1962) *The Production and Distribution and Knowledge in the United States*, Princeton: Princeton University Press.

Mahnken, T.G. (1995) 'War in the information age', *Joint Force Quarterly*, 10, pp. 39–43.

Mark, R. (2004) 'U.S. cybersecurity chief resigns', *eSecurity Planet*, 1 October 2004.

Masera, M. and Wilikens, M. (2001), 'Interdependencies with the information infrastructure: Dependability and complexity issues', unpublished paper, given at the *5th Inter-*

national Conference on Technology, Policy, and Innovation, Ispra, 26–9 June 2001. Available online at www.delft2001.tudelft.nl/paper%20files/paper1168.doc (accessed 14 May 2007).
Masera, M., Stefanini, A. and Dondossola, G. (2006) 'The security of information and communication systems and the E+I paradigm', in Gheorghe, A.V., Masera, M., Weijnen, M.P.C. and de Vries, L.J. (eds) *Critical Infrastructures at Risk: Securing the European Electric Power System*, Dodrecht: Springer, pp. 85–116.
McClure, S., Scambray, J. and Kurtz, G (1999) *Hacking Exposed: Network Security Secrets and Solutions*, Berkeley: Osborne/McGraw-Hill.
McLuhan, M. (1964) *Understanding Media: The Extensions of Man*, New York: McGraw-Hill.
McLuhan, M. and Fiore, Q. (1967) *The Medium is the Massage*, New York: Bantam.
McSweeney, B. (1996) 'Identity and security: Buzan and the Copenhagen school', *Review of International Studies*, 22, 1, pp. 81–93.
—— (1998) 'Durkheim and the Copenhagen school: A response to Buzan and Wæver', *Review of International Studies*, 24, 1, pp. 137–40.
—— (1999) *Security, Identity and Interests: A Sociology of International Relations*, Cambridge: Cambridge University Press.
McWilliams, B. (2001) 'Suspect claims Al Qaeda hacked Microsoft – expert', *Newsbytes*, 17 December 2001.
Metcalfe, B. (1995) 'Metcalfe's law: A network becomes more valuable as it reaches more users', *Infoworld*, 2 October 1995, p. 53.
Metz, S. (2000a) 'Lessons from the military experience: The U.S. military and the IR: The pitfalls of uneven adaptation', in Copeland, Thomas E. (ed.) *The Information Revolution and National Security*, Carlisle: Strategic Studies Institute, pp. 56–61.
—— (2000b) 'The Next Twist of the RMA', *Parameters*, XXX, 3, Autumn, pp. 40–53.
Metz, S. and Johnson, D.V. (2001) *Asymmetry and U.S. Military Strategy: Definition, Background, and Strategic Concepts*, Carlisle: Strategic Studies Institute.
Metz, S. and Kievit, J. (1995) *Strategy and the Revolution in Military Affairs: From Theory to Policy*, Carlisle: Strategic Studies Institute.
Metzger, J. (2004) 'The concept of critical infrastructure protection (CIP)', in Bailes, A. J. K. and Frommelt, I. (eds) *Business and Security: Public–Private Sector Relationships in a New Security Environment*, Oxford University Press: Oxford, pp. 197–209.
Mihata, K. (1997) 'The persistence of 'emergence', in Eve, R.A., Horsfall, S. and Lee, M.E. (eds) *Chaos, Complexity, and Sociology: Myths, Models, and Theories*, Thousand Oaks: Sage Publications, pp. 30–8.
Minihan, K. (1998) *Statement of Lieutenant General Kenneth Minihan, USAF, Director, NSA to the Senate Governmental Affairs Committee Hearing on Vulnerabilities of the National Information Infrastructure*, 24 June 1998. Available online at www.senate.gov/~govt-aff/62498minihan.htm (accessed 14 May 2007).
Minkwitz, O. and Schöfbänker, G. (2000) 'Neuerausforderung für die Rüstungskontrolle', *telepolis*, 31 May 2000.
Mitnick, K. and Simon, W. (2003) *The Art of Deception: Controlling the Human Element of Security*, New York: John Wiley & Sons.
Molander, R.C., Riddle, A.S., and Wilson, P.A. (1996) *Strategic Information Warfare: A New Face of War*, Santa Monica: RAND.
Moore, G.E. (1965) 'Cramming more components onto integrated circuits', *Electronics*, 38, 8, pp. 114–17.
Moteff, J.D. (2003) *Critical Infrastructures: Background, Policy, and Implementation*,

164 Bibliography

Congressional Research Report for Congress, RL30153, 10 February 2003, Washington, DC: Congressional Research Service.

—— (2006) *Critical Infrastructure: The National Asset Database*, Congressional Research Report for Congress, RL33648, 14 September 2006, Washington, DC: Congressional Research Service.

—— (2007) *Critical Infrastructures: Background, Policy, and Implementation*, Congressional Research Report for Congress, RL30153, 13 March 2007, Washington, DC: Congressional Research Service.

Moteff, J.D., Copeland, C., and Fischer, J. (2002) *Critical Infrastructures: What Makes an Infrastructure Critical?* Congressional Research Report for Congress, RL31556, 29 January 2002, Washington, DC: Congressional Research Service.

Mueller, R.S. (2003) 'War on terrorism', *Statement for the Record of Robert S. Mueller, III, Director Federal Bureau of Investigation Before the Select Committee on Intelligence of the United States Senate*, Washington, DC, 11 February 2003.

Mungo, P. and Clough, B. (1993) *Approaching Zero: The Extraordinary Underworld of Hackers, Phreakers, Virus Writers, and Keyboard Criminals*, New York: Random House.

Mussington, D. (2002) *Concepts for Enhancing Critical Infrastructure Protection: Relating Y2K to CIP Research and Development*, Santa Monica: RAND.

Nadoll, J. (2000) *Diskursanalyse und Außenpolitikforschung*, PAFE-Arbeitspapier Nr. 2, Universität Trier.

Näf, M. (2001) 'Ubiquitous insecurity? How to 'hack' IT systems', *Information & Security: An International Journal*, Volume 7, 2001, pp. 104–18.

Naisbitt, J. (1982) *Megatrends: Ten New Directions Transforming Our Lives*, New York: Warner Books.

National Academy of Sciences (1991) Computer science and telecommunications board, *Computers at Risk: Safe Computing in the Information Age*, Washington, DC: National Academy Press.

National Security Archive (2006) 'Rumsfeld's roadmap to propaganda', *National Security Archive Electronic Briefing Book No. 177*, Posted 26 January 2006. Available online at www.gwu.edu/~nsarchiv/NSAEBB/NSAEBB177/index.htm (accessed 14 May 2007).

Negroponte, N. (1995) *Being Digital*, New York, Alfred A. Knopf.

Nemerofsky, J. (2000) 'The crime of 'interruption of computer services to authorized users' Have you ever heard of it?' *The Richmond Journal for Law and Technology*, 6, 5. Available online at www.richmond.edu/jolt/v6i5/article2.html (accessed 14 May 2007).

NIPC (2002) National infrastructure protection center, 'terrorist interest in water supply and SCADA systems', *Information Bulletin 02–001*, 30 January 2002.

Norman, A.R.D. (1983) *Computer Insecurity*, New York: Chapman and Hall.

Nye, J.S. (1990) 'Soft power', *Foreign Policy*, 80, pp. 153–71.

—— (2002) *The Paradox of American Power: Why the World's Only Superpower Can't Go It Alone*, Oxford: Oxford University Press.

—— (2004) *Power in the Global Information Age: From Realism to Globalization*, London: Routledge.

Nye, J.S. Jr. and Owens, W.A. (1996) 'America's information edge', *Foreign Affairs* (March/April), pp. 20–36.

Office of Technology Assessment (1987) *Defending Secrets, Sharing Data: New Locks and Keys for Electronic Information*, OTA-CIT-310, Washington, DC: US Government Printing Office.

—— (1994) *Information Security and Privacy in Network Environments*, OTA-TCT-606, Washington, DC: US Government Printing Office.
O'Hanlon, M.E. (2000) *Technological Changes and the Future of Warfare*, Washington, DC: The Brookings Institute Press.
—— (2002) 'Rumsfeld's defense vision', *Survival*, 44, 2, pp. 103–17.
OCIPEP (2001) Office of critical infrastructure protection and emergency preparedness, 'Al-Qaida cyber capability', Threat Analysis TA01–001, 20 December 2001.
—— (2003) Office of critical infrastructure protection and emergency preparedness, 'Threats to Canada's critical infrastructure', Threat Analysis TA03–001, 12 March 2003.
Oliver, P.E. and Johnston, H. (2000) 'What a good idea: Frames and ideologies in social movements research', *Mobilization*, 5, 1, pp. 37–54.
Olson, W.J. and Woll, A. (1999) 'Executive orders and national emergencies: How presidents have come to "run the country" by usurping legislative power', *Cato Policy Analysis*, No. 358, 28 October 1999. Available online at www.cato.org/pubs/pas/pa-358es.html (accessed 14 May 2007).
Organski, A.F.K. (1968) *World Politics*, 2nd edn, New York: Alfred A. Knopf.
Owens, W.A. (1995) 'The emerging system of systems', *Naval Institute Proceedings 121*, 5, pp. 35–9.
Papp, D.S., Alberts, D.S., and Tuyahov, A. (1997) 'Historical impacts of information technologies: An overview', in Alberts, D.S. and Papp, D.S. (eds) *The Information Age: An Anthology of Its Impacts and Consequences*, Washington, DC, National Defense University, pp. 13–35.
Parker, D.B. (1976) *Crime by Computer*, New York: Charles Scribner's Sons.
—— (1980a) *Computer Security Management*, Reston: Reston Publishing Company.
—— (1980b) 'Computer-related white collar crime', in Geis, G. and Stotland, E. (eds) *White Collar Crime: Theory and Research*, Beverly Hills: Sage, pp. 199–220.
—— (1983) *Fighting Computer Crime*, New York: Charles Scribner's Sons.
PCCIP, President's Commission on Critical Infrastructure Protection (1997) *Critical Foundations: Protecting America's Infrastructures*, Washington, DC: US Government Printing Office.
Perrow, C. (1984) *Normal Accidents: Living with High-Risk Technologies*, New York: Basic Books.
Poindexter, J. (1986) *Protection of Sensitive, but Unclassified Information in Federal Government Telecommunications and Automated Information Systems*, National telecommunications and information systems security policy (NTISSP) No. 2, Washington, DC, 29 October 1986.
Pollard, N.A. (1998) 'Homeland defense: Threats and policies in transition', *Terrorism Research Center Newsletter*, 15 July 1998.
Pollitt, M.M. (1997) 'Cyberterrorism – fact or fancy?' *Proceedings of the 20th National Information Systems Security Conference*, 1997, pp. 285–9.
Porteus, L. (2001) 'Feds still need to define role in tackling cyberterror, Panelists Say', *govexec.com*, 15 May 2001. Available online at www.govexec.com/dailyfed/0501/051501td.htm (accessed 14 May 2007).
Poulsen, K. (1999) 'Info war or electronic sabre rattling?' *ZDNet*, 8 September 1999. Available online at http://news.zdnet.com/2100-9595_22-515631.html?legacy=zdnn (accessed 14 May 2007).
—— (2003) 'Official: Cyberterror fears missed real threat', *SecurityFocus.com*, 31 July 2003. Available online at www.securityfocus.com/news/6589 (accessed 14 May 2007).

Bibliography

Prasad, R.V. (2000) 'Hack the hackers', *Hindustan Times*, 19 December 2000.

—— (2001) 'Generation gap', *Hindustan Times*, 24 December 2001.

Price, A. (1989a) *The History of U.S. Electronic Warfare: Volume I: The Years of Innovation–Beginnings to 1946*, Alexandria: Association of Old Crows.

—— (1989b) *The History of U.S. Electronic Warfare Volume II: The Renaissance Years–1946 to 1964*, Alexandria: Association of Old Crows.

—— (1989c) *The History of U.S. Electronic Warfare Volume III: Rolling Thunder Through Allied Force–1964 to 2000*, Alexandria: Association of Old Crows.

Prothero, J. (2001) *Cyber-Defense: A Strategic Approach to Defending Our Critical Information Infrastructure*, Hypercerulean White Paper, 18 October 2001.

Putnam, R. (1976) *The Comparative Study of Political Elites*, Englewood Cliffs: Prentice-Hall.

Rasmussen, M.V. (2001) 'Reflexive security: Nato and international risk society', *Millennium: Journal of International Studies*, 30, 2, pp. 285–309.

Rathmell, A. (2001) 'Controlling computer network operations', *Information & Security: An International Journal*, 7, pp. 121–44.

Rattray, G. (2001) *Strategic Warfare in Cyberspace*, Cambridge: MIT Press.

Rawitch, R. (1979) 'Expected bank plot to fail', *Los Angeles Times*, 23 February 1979.

Ray, E. and Schaap, W.H. (2003) *Covert Action: The Roots of Terrorism*, Melbourne: Ocean Press.

Reagan, R. (1982a) *National Security Information*, Executive Order 12356, Washington, DC, 2 April 1982.

—— (1982b) *President's National Security Telecommunications Advisory Committee*, Executive Order 12382, Washington, DC, 13 September 1982.

—— (1984b) *Assignment of National Security and Emergency Preparedness Telecommunications Functions*, Executive Order 12472, 3 April 1984.

—— (1984c) *National Policy on Telecommunications and Automated Information Systems Security*, National Security Decision Directive NSDD 145, 17 September 1984.

—— (1988) *National Security Strategy of the United States*, Washington, DC: US Government Printing Office.

Reus-Smit, C. (1996) *The Constructivist Turn: Critical Theory after the Cold War*, Working Paper No. 1996/4, Canberra: Australian National University.

Rice, C. (2001) 'A mission to build on common challenges', *The Washington Times*, 11 June 2001, p. A15.

Richelson, J. (2005) *Presidential Directives on National Security from Truman to Clinton*, Digital National Security Archive. Available online at www.gwu.edu/~nsarchiv/nsa/publications/presidentusa/presidential.html (accessed 14 May 2007).

Richelson, J. and Evans, M.L. (2001) *Volume I: Terrorism and US Policy*, National Security Archive Electronic Briefing Book No. 55, Available online at www.gwu.edu/~nsarchiv/NSAEBB/NSAEBB55/index1.html (accessed 14 May 2007).

Rittberger, V. (ed.) (1993) *Regime Theory and International Relations*, Oxford: Clarendon Press.

Rona, T.P. (1976) *Weapon Systems and Information War*, Boeing Aerospace Co. Research Report, Seattle: Boeing.

—— (1996) 'Information warfare: An age old concept with new insights', *Defense Intelligence Journal*, 5, pp. 53–67.

Rose, R. and Davies, P.L. (1993) *Inheritance in Public Policy. Change without Choice in Britain*, New Haven: Yale University Press.

Rosecrance, R. (1999) *The Rise of the Virtual State. Wealth and Power in the Coming Century*, New York: Basic Books.

Rosenau, J.N. (1990) *Turbulence in World Politics: A Theory of Change and Continuity*, Princeton: Princeton University Press.

Ross, A. (1990) 'Hacking away at the counterculture', in Penley, C. and Ross, A. (eds) *Technoculture*, Minneapolis: University of Minnesotta Press, pp. 107–34.

Rotenberg, M. (1992) *Letter of the Computer Professionals for Social Responsibility (CPSR) to Representative Jack Brooks, Chairman, House Judiciary Committee*, 11 August 1992. Available online at www2.cddc.vt.edu/www.eff.org/pub/Privacy/Crypto/cpsr_brooks.letter (accessed 14 May 2007).

Rothmayr, C., Varone, F., Serdült, U., Timmermans, A. and Bleiklie, I. (2003) 'Comparing policy design across countries: What accounts for variation in art policy?' in Bleiklie, I., Goggin, M. and Rothmayr, C. (eds) *Comparative Biomedical Policy: A Cross-Country Comparison*, London: Routledge, pp. 228–53.

Ruggie, J. (1972) 'Collective goods and future international collaboration', *American Political Science Review*, 66, pp. 874–93.

—— (1998) *Constructing the World Politics: Essays on International Institutionalisation*, London: Routledge.

Rumsfeld, D.H. (2002a) *DoD News Briefing – Secretary Rumsfeld and General Myers*, 26 February 2002. Available online at www.defenselink.mil/transcripts/transcript.aspx?transcriptid=2798 (accessed 14 May 2007).

—— (2002b) 'Transforming the military', *Foreign Affairs*, 81, 3, pp. 20–32.

—— (2003) (Original signed), *Information Operations Roadmap*, 30 October 2003. Available online at www.gwu.edu/~nsarchiv/NSAEBB/NSAEBB177/info_ops_roadmap.pdf (accessed 14 May 2007).

Ryan, C. (1991) *Prime Time Activism: Media Strategies for Grass Roots Organizing*, Boston: South End Press.

Sabatier, P. (1988) 'An advocacy coalition framework of policy change and the role of policy-oriented learning therein', *Policy Sciences*, 21, pp. 129–68.

Sabatier, P.A. and Jenkins-Smith, H.C. (eds) (1993) *Policy Change and Learning: An Advocacy Coalition Approach*, Boulder: Westview Press.

—— (1999) 'The advocacy coalition framework: An assessment' in Sabatier, P.A. (ed.) *Theories of the Policy Process*, Boulder: Westview Press, pp. 117–68.

Saco, D. (1999) 'Colonizing cyberspace: 'National Security' and the Internet', in Weldes, J., Laffey, M., Gusterson, H. and Duvall, R. (eds) *Cultures of Insecurity. States, Communities, and the Production of Danger*, Minneapolis: University of Minnesota Press, pp. 261–91.

Satchell, M. (1999) 'Captain Dragan's serbian cybercops. How Milosevic took the Internet battlefield', *U.S. News*, 10 May 1999.

Scherlis, W.L., Squires, S.L., and Pethia, R.D. (1990) 'Computer emergency response', in Denning, P. (ed.) *Computers Under Attack: Intruders, Worms, and Viruses*, Reading: Addison-Wesley, pp. 495–504.

Scheufele, D.A. (1999) 'Framing as a theory of media effects', *Journal of Communication*, 49, 1, pp. 103–22.

Schneier, B. and Bansiar, D. (1997) *The Electronic Privacy Papers: Documents on the Battle for Privacy in the Age of Surveillance*, New York: John Wiley & Sons.

Schroeder, G.A. (1982) 'An overview of executive order 12356', *FOIA Update*, III, 3, June 1982.

Schwartau, W. (1994) *Information Warfare. Cyberterrorism: Protecting Your Personal Security in the Electronic Age*, 2nd edn, New York City: Thundermouth Press.

168 Bibliography

—— (1994) *Information Warfare: Chaos on the Electronic Super Highway*, New York: Thunder's Mouth Press.

—— (2002) *Pearl Harbor Dot Com*, Tampa: Inter-Pact Press.

Schwartz, J. (2001) 'Computer network system at risk for terrorism', *USA Today*, 13 September 2001.

Searle, J.R. (1969) *Speech Acts: An Essay in the Philosophy of Language*, Cambridge: Cambridge University Press.

—— (1995) *The Construction of Social Reality*, New York: Free Press.

Seminerio, M. (1999) 'Infowar part of NATO arsenal?' *ZDNet*, 25 March 1999. Available online at www.zdnet.com/zdnn/stories/news/0,4586,2231976,00.html (accessed 14 May 2007).

Serabian, J.A. (2000) *Testimony of CIA Information Operations Issue Manager John A. Serabian Jr. Before the joint Economic Committee on Cyber Threats to the U.S. Economy*, 23 February 2000.

Shannon, C. and Weaver, W. (1949) *The Mathematical Theory of Communications*, Urbana: University of Illinois Press.

Shapiro, A.L. (1999) *The Control Revolution: How the Internet is Putting Individuals in Charge and Changing the World We Know*, New York: Public Affairs.

Shea, D.A. (2003) *Critical Infrastructure: Control Systems and the Terrorist Threat*. Congressional Research Report for Congress, RL31534, 21 February 2003, Washington, DC: Congressional Research Service.

Shea, J. (1999a) Press conference by NATO spokesman, Jamie Shea and Air Commodore David Wilby, SHAPE, Transcript 31 March 1999, updated 31 March 1999, NATO HQ.

—— (1999b) Morning briefing by Jamie Shea, NATO Spokesman, 3 May 1999, updated 3 May 1999, NATO HQ.

Shelby, R.C. (1998) 'Current and projected national security threats to the United States', *Statement of US Senator Richard C. Shelby, Chairman, Senate Select Committee on Intelligence*, 28 January 1998.

Sibilia, R. (1997) *Informationskriegsführung: eine schweizerische Sicht*, Zürich: Institut für militärische Sicherheitstechnik, ETH Zürich.

Sieber, U. (1986) *The International Handbook on Computer Crime: Computer-Related Economic Crime and the Infringements of Privacy*, Chichester: John Wiley and Sons.

—— (1998) *Legal Aspects of Computer Related Crime in the Information Society*, COMCRIME-study prepared for the European Commission, 1 January 1998. Available online at http://europa.eu.int/ISPO/legal/en/comcrime/sieber.doc (accessed 14 May 2007).

Singer, D.J., Bremer, S. and Stuckey, J. (1972) 'Capability distribution, uncertainty, and major power war, 1820–1965', in Russett, B. (ed.) *Peace, War, and Numbers*, Beverly Hills, Sage Publications, pp. 21–7.

Sjursen, H. (2002) *The Transformation of the Nation State: Implications for the Study of European Security*, unpublished paper, given at the NOPSA-Conference, Aalborg, August 2002.

—— (2004). "Changes to European security in a communicative perspective," *Cooperation and Conflict*, 39, 2: 107-128.

Slocombe, W.B. (2003) 'Force, pre-emption and legitimacy', *Survival*, 45, 1, pp. 117–30.

Smith, G. (1998) 'An electronic Pearl Harbor? Not likely', *Issues in Science and Technology*, 15, Fall 1998.

—— (1999a) 'Electronic Pearl Harbor: A slogan for U.S. info-warriors', *Crypt News-*

letter. Available online at www.soci.niu.edu/~crypt/other/harbor.htm (accessed 14 May 2007).

—— (1999b) 'The meaning of eligible receiver', *Crypt Newsletter*. Available online at www.soci.niu.edu/~crypt/other/eligib.htm (accessed 14 May 2007).

—— (2000) 'How vulnerable is our interlinked infrastructure?' in Alberts, D.S. and Papp, D.S. (eds) *The Information Age: An Anthology of Its Impacts and Consequences* (Vol. II), Washington, DC: National Defense University Press, pp. 507–23.

Smith, M.R. and Marx, L. (eds) (1994) *Does Technology Drive History? The Dilemma of Technological Determinism*, Cambridge: MIT Press.

Smith, S., Booth, K. and Zalewski, M. (eds) (1996) *International Theory: Positivism and Beyond*, Cambridge: Cambridge University Press. Excerpt taken from: Viotti, P.R. and Kauppi, M.V. (1999) *International Relations Theory: Realism, Pluralism, Globalism, and Beyond*, 3rd edn, Needham Heights, Prentice Hall, pp. 38–54.

Snow, D.A. and Benford, R.D. (1988) 'Ideology, frame resonance, and participant mobilization', *Social Movement Research* 1, pp. 197–217.

—— (1992) 'Master frames and cycles of protest', in Morris, A.D. and McClurg Mueller, C. (eds) *Frontiers in Social Movement Theory*, New Haven: Yale University Press, pp. 133–55.

Snow, D.A., Rocheford, E.B., Worden, S.K., and Benford, R.D. (1986), 'Frame alignment processes, micromobilization and movement participation', *American Sociological Review*, 51, 4, pp. 464–81.

Solomon, R.H. (1997) 'The information revolution and international conflict management', *USIP Peaceworks*, Keynote address from the virtual diplomacy conference, June 1997. Available online at www.usip.org/pubs/peaceworks/virtual18/inforev_18.html (accessed 14 May 2007).

Stapleton, J.R. (2000) Assistant Secretary for Intelligence and Research Statement before the Senate Select Committee on Intelligence, 2 February 2000.

Sterling, B. (1993) *Hacker Crackdown, Law and Disorder on the Electronic Frontier*, New York: Bantam Books.

Stoll, C. (1989) *The Cuckoo's Egg: Tracking a Spy through the Maze of Computer Espionage*, New York: Doubleday.

Stoneburner, G. (2001) *Computer Security. Underlying Technical Models for Information Technology Security. Recommendations of the National Institute of Standards and Technology*, NIST Special Publication 800–33, Washington, DC: U.S. Government Printing Office.

Strange, S. (1988) *State and Markets: An Introduction to International Political Economy*, New York: Basil Blackwell, pp. 25–31.

Strogatz, S.H. (2001) 'Exploring complex networks', *Nature*, 410, 8 March, 2001, pp. 268–76.

Sundelius, B. (1983) 'Coping with structural security threats', in Höll, O. (ed.) *Small States in Europe and Dependence*, Wien: Braumüller.

Suter, M. (2007), 'Improving information security in companies: How to meet the need for threat information', in Dunn Cavelty, M., Mauer, V. and Krishna-Hensel, S.-F. (eds) *Power and Security in the Information Age: Investigating the Role of the State in Cyberspace*, Aldershot: Ashgate.

Swidler, A. (1986) 'Culture in action: Symbols and strategies', *American Sociological Review*, 51, 4, pp. 273–86.

—— (1995) 'Cultural power and social movements', in Johnston, H. and Klandermans, B. (eds) *Social Movements and Culture*, London: UCL Press, pp. 25–40.

Tainter, J.A. (1988) *The Collapse of Complex Societies*, Cambridge: Cambridge University Press.
Taylor, R. (1999) 'UK: Partisans wage virtual war', *The Guardian*, 22 April 1999.
Technical Analysis Group (2003) *Examining the Cyber Capabilities of Islamic Terrorist Groups*, Institute for Security Technology Studies, Darthmouth College. Available online at www.ists.dartmouth.edu/TAG/ITB/ITB_032004.pdf (accessed 14 May 2007).
Tenet, G.J. (1997) *Statement by Acting Director of Central Intelligence George J. Tenet Before the Senate Select Committee on Intelligence Hearing on Current and Projected National Security Threats to the United States*, 5 February 1997.
—— (1998) 'Vulnerabilities of the National Information Infrastructure', *Testimony by Director of Central Intelligence George J. Tenet Before the Senate Committee on Government Affairs Hearing*, 24 June 1998.
—— (1999) *Testimony by Director of Central Intelligence George J. Tenet Before the Senate Armed Services Committee*, 2 February 1999.
—— (2000) 'The worldwide threat in 2000: Global realities of our national security', *Statement by Director of Central Intelligence George J. Tenet Before the Senate Select Committee on Intelligence*, 2 February 2000.
—— (2002) 'Worldwide threat – Converging dangers in a post 9/11 world', *Testimony of the Director of Central Intelligence Before the Senate Armed Services Committee*, 19 March 2002.
Thompson, L.B. (2005) 'The quadrennial defense review: Are secretary Rumsfeld's priorities valid?' Heritage Lecture #876, 28 April 2005. Available online at www.heritage.org/Research/NationalSecurity/hl876.cfm (accessed 14 May 2007).
Toffler, A. (1970) *Future Shock*, New York: Bantam Books.
—— (1980) *Third Wave*, New York: Bantam Books.
—— (1981) *Power Shift: Knowledge, Wealth, and Violence at the Edge of the 21st Century*, New York: Bantam Books.
Toffler, A. and Toffler, H. (1993) *War and Anti-War: Survival at the Dawn of the Twenty-First Century*, Boston: Little, Brown.
Townson, M. (1992) *Mother-Tongue and Fatherland: Language and Politics in Germany*, Manchester: Manchester University Press.
Tritak, J.S. (1999) *Statement of the Director Critical Infrastructure Assurance Office Before the Senate Judiciary Committee Subcommittee on Technology, Terrorism and Government Information*, 6 October 1999.
Turner, B.A. and Pidgeon, N.F. (1997) *Man-Made Disasters*, 2nd edn, Oxford: Butterworth-Heinemann.
United States Air Force (1995), *Cornerstones of Information Warfare*, Washington, DC: Department of the United States Air Force.
United States Joint Forces Command USJFCOM (2004) United States Joint Forces Command USJFC Glossary. Available online at www.jfcom.mil/about/glossary.htm (accessed 14 May 2007).
US Senate Permanent Subcommittee on Investigations USSPSI (1996) 'Security in cyberspace', *US Senate Permanent Subcommittee on Investigations, Minority Staff Statement*, 5 June 1996. Available online at www.fas.org/irp/congress/1996_hr/s960605b.htm (accessed 14 May 2007).
Vatis, M.A. (1998a) 'National infrastructure protection', *Michael Vatis, Deputy Assistant Director and Chief of the Federal Bureau of Investigation's National Infrastructure Protection Center (NIPC) Before the Senate Judiciary Subcommittee on Terrorism, Technology and Government Information*, 10 February 1998.

—— (1998b) *Statement for the Record, Deputy Assistant Director and Chief, National Infrastructure Protection Center, Federal Bureau of Investigation, Before the Congressional Joint Economic Committee*, 24 March 1998.

—— (1999) 'NIPC cyber threat assessment', *Statement for the Record of Michael A. Vatis, Director, National Infrastructure Protection Center Federal Bureau of Investigation Before the Senate Judiciary Committee, Subcommittee on Technology and Terrorism*, 6 October 1999.

—— (2001) *Cyber Attacks During the War on Terrorism: A Predictive Analysis*, Institute for Security Technology Studies, 22 September 2001.

Verton, D. (2004) 'Nation's cybersecurity chief abruptly quits DHS post: 'I'm not a long-term government kind of guy', says Amit Yoran', *Computerworld*, 1 October 2004. Available online at www.computerworld.com/printthis/2004/0,4814,96369,00.html (accessed 14 May 2007).

Virilio, P. (1995) 'Speed and information: Cyberspace alarm!', *Ctheory*, 18 March 1995.

Vistica, G.L. (1999) 'Cyberwar and sabotage', *Newsweek*, 31 May 1999, p. 22.

Wæver, O. (1995) 'Securitization and desecuritization', in Lipschutz, Ronnie (ed.) *On Security*, New York: Columbia University Press, pp. 46–86.

—— (2002) 'Security: A conceptual history for international relations', unpublished paper, presented at the annual meeting of the British International Studies Association in London, 16–18 December 2002.

—— (2003) *Securitization: Taking Stock of a Research Programme in Security Studies*, unpublished manuscript.

—— (2004) 'Aberystwyth, Paris, Copenhagen. New 'Schools' in security theory and their origins between core and periphery', unpublished paper, presented at the annual meeting of the International Studies Association, Montreal, 17–20 March 2004.

Waldrop, M.M. (1998) 'Is there an information revolution?' in Henry, C.R. and Peartree, E.C. (eds) *Information Revolution and International Security*, Washington, DC, Center for Strategic and International Studies Press, pp. 1–9.

Walker, R.B.J. (1993) *Inside/Outside: International Relations as Political Theory*, Cambridge: Cambridge University Press.

Wallace, C. (2002) 'Internet as weapon: Experts fear terrorists may attack through cyberspace', *ABC News.com*, 16 September 2002.

Walt, S.M. (1991) 'The renaissance of security studies', *International Studies Quarterly*, 35, 2, pp. 211–39.

Waltz, E. (1998) *Information Warfare: Principles and Operations*, Boston: Artech House.

Watson, D.L. (2002) 'The terrorist threat confronting the United States', *Statement for the Record of the Executive Assistant Director on Counterterrorism and Counterintelligence, Federal Bureau of Investigation, Before the Senate Select Committee on Intelligence*, Washington, DC, 6 February 2002.

Webster, F. (1995) *Theories of the Information Society*, London: Routledge.

—— (1997) 'What information society?' in Papp, D.S. and Alberts, D.S. (eds) *The Information Age: An Anthology on Its Impact and Consequences, Vol. I*, Washington, DC: National Defense University Press, pp. 51–71.

Weimann, G. (2004a) 'www.terror.net. How modern terrorism uses the internet', United States Institute of Peace, Special Report 116, March 2004, Washington, DC: United States Institute of Peace. Available online at www.usip.org/pubs/specialreports/sr116.pdf (accessed 14 May 2007).

—— (2004b) 'Cyberterrorism – how real is the threat?' United States Institute of Peace,

172 Bibliography

special report 119, May 2004, Washington, DC: United States Institute of Peace. Available online at www.usip.org/pubs/specialreports/sr119.pdf (accessed 14 May 2007).

Weiner, B. (1974) *Achievement Motivation and Attribution Theory*, Morristown: General Learning Press.

—— (1986) *An Attributional Theory of Motivation and Emotion*, New York: Springer-Verlag.

Weldon, C. (1997) 'Threat posed by electromagnetic pulse (EMP) to US military systems and civil infrastructure', *House of Representatives, Committee on National Security, Military Research and Development Subcommittee*, Washington, DC, 16 July 1997. Available online at www.fas.org/spp/starwars/congress/1997_h/has197010_1.htm (accessed 14 May 2007).

Wendt, A. (1992) 'Anarchy is what states make of it: The social construction of power politics', *International Organization*, 46, 2, pp. 391–425.

—— (1999) *Social Theory of International Politics*, Cambridge: Cambridge University Press.

Wenger, A., Metzger, J. and Dunn, M. (eds) (2002) *The International CIIP Handbook: An Inventory of Protection Policies in Eight Countries*, Zurich: Center for Security Studies.

Werner, W. (1998) *Securitisation and Legal Theory*, COPRI Working Paper 27, Copenhagen: Copenhagen Peace Research Institute.

Westrin, P. (2001) 'Critical information infrastructure protection', *Information & Security: An International Journal*, 7, pp. 67–79.

White House (1999) 'Fact sheet on encryption export policy', Office of the press secretary, Washington, DC: The White House, 16 September 1999.

—— (2001a) *Report of the President of the United States on the Status of Federal Critical Infrastructure Protection Activities*, Washington, DC: US Government Printing Office, 22 February 2001.

—— (2001b) 'Fact sheet on new counter-terrorism and cyberspace positions', Office of the press secretary, Washington, DC: The White House, 9 October 2001.

—— (2001c) 'Remarks by the president in tax celebration event', Des Moines/Iowa, Office of the press secretary, Washington, DC: The White House, 8 June 2001.

Wiener, N. (1948) *Cybernetics, or Control and Communication in the Animal and Machine*, Cambridge: MIT Press.

Wilby, D. (1999) Press conference by NATO spokesman, Jamie Shea and Air Commodore David Wilby, SHAPE, Transcript 5 April, updated 5 April 1999, NATO HQ.

Williams, M.C. (2003) 'Words, images, enemies: Securitisation and international politics', *International Studies Quarterly*, 47, 4, pp. 511–31.

Wilson, C. (2003) *Computer Attack and Cyber-Terrorism: Vulnerabilities and Policy Issues for Congress*, CRS Report for Congress, Congressional research report for Congress, RL32114, 17 October 2003, Washington, DC: Congressional Research Service.

Wilson, T.R. (2000) 'Military threats and security challenges through 2015', *Statement Before the Senate Select Committee on Intelligence Given by Vice Admiral Thomas R. Wilson Director, Defense Intelligence Agency*, 2 February 2000.

Winner, L. (1977) *Autonomous Technology: Technics-Out-of-Control as a Theme in Political Thought*, Cambridge: MIT Press.

—— (2004) 'Trust and terror: The vulnerability of complex socio-technical systems', *Science as Culture*, 13, 2, June, pp. 155–72.

Wohlstetter, A. (1959) 'The delicate balance of terror', *Foreign Affairs*, 37, 2, pp. 211–34.

—— (1961) 'Nuclear sharing: NATO and the N+1 country', *Foreign Affairs*, 39, 3, pp. 355–87.
Wolfe, F. (1999) 'Pentagon analyzing serb attacks on DoD web sites', *www.infowar.com*, 22 June 1999. Available online at www.tla.ch/TLA/NEWS/1999sec/19990622serb.htm (accessed 14 May 2007).
Wood, L. (1999) *Director's Technical Staff, Lawrence Livermore National Laboratory & Hoover Institution, Testimony Before the Military Research & Development Subcommittee Hearing on Electromagnetic Pulse (EMP) Threats to U.S. Military and Civilian Infrastructure*, 7 October 1999.
Wright, L. (2001) *Memorandum for the Chairman, Defense Science Board, Subject: Report of the Defense Science Board Task Force on Defensive Information Operations*, 1 March 2001.
Yates, A. (2003) *Engineering a Safer Australia: Securing Critical Infrastructure and the Built Environment*, Institution of Engineers, Australia.
Young, K. (1977) 'Values in the policy process', *Policy and Politics*, 5, 3, pp. 1–22.
Yourdon, E. and Yourdon, J. (1998) *Time Bomb 2000: What the Year 2000 Computer Crisis Means to You*, Needhman Heights: Prentice Hall.
Zacher, M.W. (1992) 'The decaying pillars of the Westphalian Temple: Implications for international order and governance', in Rosenau, J. N. and Czempiel, E.-O. (eds) *Governance Without Government: Order and Change in World Politics*, Cambridge Studies in International Relations Nr. 20, Cambridge: Cambridge University Press, pp. 58–101.

Index

'414s' Gang 46, 55
9/11 103–4, 117–18, 123–4

Abele-Wigert, I. 6, 117
Acts of Congress 39
Adler, E. 7, 33, 37, 128, 129
advocacy coalition framework (ACF) 127
agenda-setting theory 33–5
Air Force 15, 72
Air Force Information Warfare Center (AFIWC) 80–1
Akdeniz, Yaman 67
Al-Qaida 118–20
Alberts, D.S. 7, 12, 19, 66, 69
Alexander, B. 68, 69
analogies, threat framing through 129–32
analytical framework 8–9
Anderson, R.H. 19, 67, 81, 132
Andersson, R. 141
Andreas, P. 141
Anti-Terrorism Act (2001) 104
Antoniades, A. 58, 128, 129
Aradau, C. 27, 90, 142
Arkin, W.M. 75
Armstrong, J.E. 17
Army Missile Research Laboratory 81
ARPANET 2, 47–8, 67
Arquilla, J. 7, 61, 69–70, 117
Ashby, W.R. 16
asymmetric tactics 68–73
attack, modes of 21–3
attribution theory 32
Austin, J.L. 8, 25
Aviziensis, A. 20
Axelrod, R. 16
Azment, A. 136

Bacon, K.H. 75
Bailey, D. 46

Baird, Z. 67, 136
Ball, D. 44
Bamford, J. 112
Bansiar, D. 51
Barbrook, R. 53
Barlow, J.P. 53
Barnett, M. 7
Bartlett, H.C. 95
Baudrillard, J. 125
Beck, U. 58, 139
Beedham, C. 14
Beer, S. 16
Bellin, D. 41
Bendrath, R. 4, 5, 6, 7, 24, 32, 39, 77, 91, 97, 130, 133
Benford, R.D. 30, 122
Bennett, R. 2, 3
Bequai, A. 45
Berger, P. 7
Berkowitz, B.D. 41, 43, 44, 66
Berman, J.J. 50, 52
Berners-Lee, T. 67
Bertalanffy, L. von 16, 17
Beth, T. 50
Biddle, S. 69
Biggiero, L. 17
Bigo, D. 26, 27, 58, 126, 141
Bikson, T.K. 19
'Black Hand' 77
'Black Hat Hackers' 21
Blank, S.J. 68
Bleiklie, I. 31
Blondell, J. 58
Boeing 44
Boekle, H. 27
Books, J. 50–1
Booth, K. 16
Borger, J. 79
Borgmann, A. 12, 15

Bosch, O. 136
Bowker, G. 17
Bowman, L.M. 101
Brandt, D. 70
Bremer, S. 5
Brenner, S.W. 46
Brewin, B. 77
Brock, J.L. 59, 80
Brodie, B. 43
Brown Report (1996) 110
buffer overflow attacks 22
Burke, E.B. 47
Burns, R. 78
Bush, George H.W. 51–2, 64, 65, 95
Bush, George W. 9–10, 92, 101–8, 113, 118, 120–1, 133, 135
Butts, C.T. 17
Buzan, B. 5, 8, 24, 25, 26, 28, 32, 58, 122, 137, 144

'Californian ideology' 53
Cambel, A.B. 17
Cameron, A. 53
Campbell, D. 7
Campen, A.D. 9, 67, 68–9, 117
Carter, J. 62
Cashell, B. 3
Castells, M. 12, 61
Casti, J.L. 16
Cebrowski, A.K. 117
Center for Strategic and International Studies (CSIS) 78
Center for the Study of Terrorism and Irregular Warfare 4, 103
Central Intelligence Agency (CIA) 119
Cha, A.E. 120
change 13–14
Chapman, G. 41, 67, 139
Chertoff, M. 107
Chilton, P. 130
Clarke, R. 1, 117, 120, 130
Clinton, B. 10, 53, 87, 91–108, 117
'Clipper chip' 53
Clough, B. 45
cognitive level of action 128
Cohen, E. 43, 75
Cohn, C. 130
Cold War 5, 42–4, 68
command and control (C2) 74, 78
command, control, communications and intelligence (C3I) systems 69, 89
command, control, communications, computers and intelligence (C4I) component systems 70, 90

command-and-control warfare (C2W) 72, 73–4
complexity 13–14, 17–19
Computer Crime and Abuse Act (1984/86) 9, 42, 62–3
Computer Emergency Response Team (CERT) 2, 48
Computer Fraud and Abuse Act (1986) 63, 104, 105
Computer Investigations and Infrastructure Threat Assessment Center (CITAC) 94
Computer Professionals for Social Responsibility 51
Computer Science and Technology Board 84–6
Computer Science and Telecommunications Board 56, 82, 90
Computer Security Act (1987) 9, 42, 50–1
computer security as national security issue 44–53
Computers at Risk: Safe Computing in the Information Age, CSTB 84–6, 117
Congressional Research Service (CRS) 109
Connolly, W.E. 23
constructivism 7–8
contextualisation 9–11
Conway, M. 39, 118, 125
Cooper, J.R. 43
Copeland, C. 134
Copeland, T.E. 69, 72
Copenhagen School 8, 24, 25–9, 30, 32
Cordesman, A.H. 73, 78, 79
Cornerstones of Information Warfare, Air Force 72
counter-culture 53
Counterfeit Access Device and Computer Fraud and Abuse Act (1984) 47–8
countermeasures 40; public-private partnerships/changing conditions of securing 132–7
Covert, C. 46
Cox, R.W. 7
'crackers' 21
Crawley, V. 120
Creveld, M. van 54
crime, confronting 45–8
Critical Infrastructure Assurance Office (CIAO) 94
Critical Infrastructure Coordination Group (CICG) 94
Critical Infrastructure Protection (CIP) 134–7; as dominant threat frame 98–101; link to cyber–threats 92–8;

Index

Critical Infrastructure Protection *continued*
overview 91–2; as priority 10–11; review of 102–3
Critical Infrastructure Protection Oral History Project 93
Critical Infrastructure Working Group (CIWG) 91
critical infrastructures 113–21
criticality as systemic/symbolic concepts 135–6
Crutchfield, J.P. 140
cryptology 54; *see also* encryption
CSIS 14
Cuban Missile Crisis 41
Cuckoo's Egg (Stoll) 48
Cuckoo's Egg incident 2, 55, 59
Cukier, K.N. 67
'Cyber Storm' exercise 108
cyber-doom scenarios 2–4
cyber-prefix 16–17
cyber-terror frame 131
cyber-threats 19–23; frames 130–1; linked to CIP debate 92–8; military roles in protection against 84–90
cyber-war: Kosovo 73–80; offensive in 108–13
Czempiel, E.O. 58

Daase, C. 6
Dam, K.W. 49
Dao, J. 111
Data Encryption Standard (DES) 49–50
data, case studies 39–40
David, N.C. 43
Davies, P.L. 36
Davis, Jack 6
Day After methodology 81–2, 114–15
De Wilde J. 5, 8, 24, 25, 26, 28, 32, 58, 122, 137
Dearth, D.H. 9, 67, 69
Debrix, F. 39
Defending America's Cyberspace 97–8
Defense Advanced Research Projects Agency (DARPA) 44, 47
Defense Information Systems Agency (DISA) 89, 97
Defense Science Board (DSB) 70–1, 87–9, 109, 110, 117
Deibert, R.J. 12
Dekker, M. 15
Demchak, C.C. 137
Denial-of-Service (DoS) attacks 115–16
Denning, D. 5, 21, 23, 73, 76, 77, 132
Denning, P. 63, 67

Denny, D. 95
Department of Defense (DoD): civil sector role 88–9; computer-attacks against 80–4, 109; Directive 3600.1 70
Department of Homeland Security (DHS) 105–8
dependent variables, frames as 31–3
Der Derian J. 7, 125
Deutch, J. 91–2, 109–10
Deutsch, K.W. 13
Devost, M.G. 22, 23, 70
Dewar, J.A. 19
diagnostic framing 30
Diffie, W. 49
digitalisation 45–6
Directorate for Information Analysis and Infrastructure Protection (IAIP) 106
discursive dominance 27–9
Dodd, G.S. 47
dominant threat frame, emergence of 98–101
Donati, P. 31
Dondossola, G. 3
Donnelly, J. 120
Douglas, M. 143
Downes, L. 17
Drucker, P.F. 13
Drummond, N. 47
Dunn Cavelty, M. 141
Dunn, M. 4, 6, 10, 21, 22, 72, 73, 74, 77, 94, 106, 113, 117, 136
'Dutchthreat' 77
dynamic framework, study of threat politics 35–40

e-mail 76, 78
EC-130 'Commando Solo' planes 75
Eichin, M. 63
electromagnetic pulse (EMP) debate 43–4
Electronic Privacy Information Centre 50–1, 52, 59, 105
'Eligible Receiver' exercise 82–3, 115
Ellison, R.J. 20, 61, 66, 67
Ellul, J. 13
Elmer-Dewitt, P. 46
encryption 45, 48–53
epistemic communities 125–9
Erickson, J. 21
Eriksson, J. 7, 8, 24, 29, 32, 33, 39, 113, 123
Evans, M.L. 92
Executive Orders (EOs) 49, 93, 104
Export Administration Act (1969) 49
Ezell, B.C. 139

Farr, J.V. 139
Federal Bureau of Investigation (FBI) 46–7, 92, 93, 94, 97–8, 105; Computer Crime Squad 90–1
Federal Computer Incident Response Capability (FedCIRC) 97
Federal Emergency Management Agency (FEMA) 93
Feenberg, A. 13
Feske, S. 6
Field Manual 100–6, Department of the Army 72
Fine, G. 105
Fiore, Q. 53
Fischer, J. 134
Fisher, F.A. 20, 61, 66, 67
Fisher, K. 29, 31
Fisher, U. 14, 132
Fitzpatrick, D. 1
foreign intelligence threat frame 59–65, 80–4
foreign spies 45–8
Forrester, J.W. 18
Foucault, M. 127–8
frame analysis 29–33
frame resonance 30
Fredericks, B. 70
Freedman, L. 113
Freeh, L.J. 53, 83, 91
Freeman, C. 12
Frisch, M. 50
Froehlich, J.N. 63
Froomkin, A.M. 53
Fuchs, D.A. 23
Fulghum, D. 78
Fursenko, A. 41

Galbraith, J.K. 13
Gamson, W.A. 30
Garamone, J. 110
Garreau, J. 13
Garstka, J.J. 117
Gellman, B. 3
General Accounting Office (GAO) 56, 62, 63–4, 70, 80, 81, 83, 101–2, 115, 117
Gertz, B. 82
Giacomello, G. 7, 24, 32, 39, 67
Gibson, D.M. 57, 113
Gilmore, G.J. 102–3, 111
Glickman, D. 46, 50–1
Goff, P. 77
Goldman, E.O. 18
Gomez, P. 17

Goodden, T. 9, 67, 69
Goodman, M.D. 46
Goodman, S.E. 136
Graham, B. 112
Green, J. 3, 4, 19
Gross, G. 107
Gulf War (1991) 68–70
Guzzini, S. 31

Haas, P.M. 7, 33, 58, 128, 129
Hables Gray, C. 41
Hacker News Network 77
hackers: confronting 45–8; types of 21–3
hacktivism 21–3, 77–8
Hahn, R.W. 44
Haimes, Y.Y. 136, 139
Halperin, D. 67, 131
Hamre, J.J. 82, 83–4, 115, 120
Hart-Rudman Commission 105
Hasselbroek, P.B. 136
Hearn, A.C. 67, 81, 132
Hedges, S.J. 112
Heider, F. 32
Hellman, M.E. 49
Henry, R. 16, 54
Herrera, G. 12
Hildreth, S.A. 109
Hinsely, F.H. 41
Hobart, M.E. 12
Hoffmann, L. 78
Holman, G.P. 95
Holmgren, J. 9
Holsti, J.K. 140
Holzner, B. 128
Homer-Dixon, T. 4
Houghton, M.G. 22, 23
Hughes, P.M. 100
Hundley, R.O. 19, 67, 132
Husain, K.N. 68
Huysmans, J. 5, 26, 27

ICSA Labs 2, 117
Ignatieff, M. 75
incidents, nature of 20
information age, concepts and meanings 14–19
Information Architecture for the Battlefield (DSB) 87–8
Information Operations (IO) 72–3
Information Operations Roadmap 111–12
Information Technology Promotion Agency 2
Information Warfare – Defense (IW–D) (DSB) 88–9

Index

information warfare (IW) doctrine: birth of 42–4; development of 68–73; use in Kosovo 73–80
Infrastructure Protection Task Force (IPTF) 93–4
'infrastructure threat matrix' 22–3
Ingles-le Nobel, J.J. 4, 116
international relations (IR), cyber-threats in 6–8
Internet 67, 70, 75–7, 99

Jackson, W.D. 3
Jacoby, L. 119–20
Jenkins-Smith, H.C. 36, 127
Jepperson, R.L. 31
Jertz, W. 74, 76
Jiang, P. 139
Jickling, M. 3
Johnson, S.E. 68, 90, 117
Johnston, H. 29
Joint Doctrine for Information Operations, Joint Chiefs of Staff 72–3
Joint Security Commission (JSC) 71, 86–7, 99–100, 117
Joint Task Force – Computer Network Defense (JTF–CND) 97
Joint Vision 2010, Joint Chiefs of Staff 72
Jones, E.E. 32

Kabay, M.E. 45
Kahn, D. 41, 52
Kannouse, D.E. 32
Katzenstein, P.J. 7, 31
Kelley, H.H. 32
Kelly, K. 13
Kemp III, W.T. 19, 66, 69
Kennedy, J.F. 41
Keohane, R.O. 7, 109
Kerrey, B. 115
KGB, Soviet Union 48
Kievit, J. 54
King, D. 136
King, G. 7
Kingdon, J.W. 33–5, 39–40, 54, 117, 124, 125, 129
Kirby, J.M. 95
Knezo, G. 62
Kolet, K.S. 68
Korean Atomic Energy Research Institute 80
Kosovo 73–80
Kosovo Task Force 76
Kratochwil, F. 23, 140
Krebs, B. 107

Krepinevich, A. 54, 108
Krim, J. 120
Kristensen, K.S. 136
Krutskikh, A. 22
Kuehl, D. 95, 96
Kurtz, G. 21
Kushnick, B. 12, 14, 66
Kyriakopoulos, N. 18

Landau, S. 50, 53
LaPorte, T.R. 4, 13, 16
Laprie, J.-C. 20
Latham, R. 7
Lawler, T. 95
Levy, S. 21
Lewis, J.A. 4, 139
Libicki, M.C. 19, 43, 71, 73, 90, 117
Libutti, F. 107
Lin, H.S. 49
Lincoln Group 112
Linger, R.C. 20, 61, 66, 67
Lipson, H.F. 20, 61, 66, 67
Lloyd, R. 95
logic bombs 22
Longstaff, T. 20, 61, 66, 67
Loon, J. van 6, 13, 139
Louca, F. 12
Luckmann, T. 7

McClendon, D.J. 47
McClure, S. 21
Machlup, F. 14
McLuhan, M. 53
McSweeney, B. 26
McWilliams, B. 119
Mahnken, T.G. 9, 69, 72
Mark, R. 107
Marsh, R. 10
Marshall, A. 68
Marx, L. 13
Masera, M. 3, 18
Mauer, V. 141
Mead, N.R. 20, 61, 66, 67
Merriam–Webster Dictionary 16
metaphors, threat framing through 129–32
Metcalfe's Law 17
Metz, S. 54, 68, 69, 79
Metzger, J. 6, 135
Microsoft 118–19
Mihata, K. 140
military affairs, revolution in 42–4
military roles, protection against cyber-threats 84–90

military: studies in 86–90; transformation of 108–13
Milosevic, S. 74, 75, 78
Minihan, K. 88, 101, 110, 115
Minkwitz, O. 79
Mitnick, K. 44–5, 46
Molander, R.C. 9, 69, 82, 132
'Moonlight Maze' incident 83, 115
Moore's Law 17
Morris Worm incident 2, 47–8, 55, 63–4
Moteff, J.D. 102, 103, 106, 107, 134
motivational framing 30
Mueller, R.S. 120
Mui, C. 17
Mungo, P. 45
Mussington, D. 116

Nadoll, J. 27
Näf, M. 15, 67, 114
Naftali, T. 41
Naisbitt, J. 13
National Academy of Sciences (NAS) 1, 21, 56, 59, 84–6, 88, 124, 133
National Academy of Sciences, Computer Science and Telecommunications Board (CSTB) 56
National Asset Database 107
National Bureau of Standards (NBS) 49–50, 51
National Communications System 41–2
National Cyberspace Strategy 113
National Information Infrastructure (NII) 86–7
National Information Infrastructure Protection Act (1996) 47
National Infrastructure Advisory Council (NIAC) 104
National Infrastructure Protection Center (NIPC) 94, 97–8, 102, 118
National Institute of Standards and Technology (NIST) 51, 59
National Intelligence Council 109–10
National Research Council 56
National Security Agency (NSA): hackers from 82; role of 48–53, 58–9, 110
National Security Decision Directives (NSDDs) 39, 49, 50, 57, 59, 60–5, 92, 112
National Security Incident Response Center (NSIRC) 97
National Security Presidential Directives (NSPDs) 102
National Security Strategies (NSS) 91–2, 94–8

national security: issues 44–53; meaning of 57–9
National Telecommunications and Information Systems Security Policy (NTISSP) No. 2 50
Naval Academy 81
Necromancer (Gibson) 57
Negroponte, N. 13, 17, 45
Nemerofsky, J. 47
networked global information infrastructure as target/weapon 19–23
Neu, C.R. 19
'new' threats 87, 98–100; construction of 5–6
Nisbett, R.E. 32
Noreen, E. 7, 8, 24, 29
Norman, A.R.D. 45
North Atlantic Treaty Organisation (NATO) 68, 73–80, 111
Nye, J.S. 69, 108–9

O'Hanlon, M.E. 69, 112–13
OCIPEP 20, 21, 23, 118
offensive cyber-war 78–9, 108–13
Office of Computer Investigations and Infrastructure Protection (OCIIP) 94
Office of Technology Assessment 51
Oklahoma City bombing 10, 92–3, 113–21, 123–4
Oliver, P.E. 29
Olson, W.J. 39
Operation Allied Force 73–80
Operation Desert Storm 70
Operation Liberty Shield 107
Organski, A.F.K. 5
Owens, M.T. 95
Owens, W.A. 69, 72, 117

Papp, D.S. 7, 12, 19, 66, 69
'Paris school' 26–7, 29
Parker, D.B. 45
Patrick, N. 46
Patriot Act (2001) 104–5, 133
Peartree, E.C. 16, 54
perception management 111–13
Perrow, C. 4, 18
Peters, I. 6
Pethia, R.D. 48
PFF 91
phenomena 14–15
phreaks 45–8
Pidgeon, N.F. 4, 18
Pinter, E.M. 63
Poindexter, J. 50

180 *Index*

policy streams 33–5
policy windows 36–7, 53–7, 124–5
political streams 33–5
political windows 55–7, 113–21
Pollard, N.A. 22, 23, 92
Pollitt, M.M. 131
Porteus, L. 2
Poulsen, K. 2, 103, 130
practical level of action 128–9
Prasad, R.V. 119
President's Commission on Critical Infrastructure Protection (PCCIP) 1, 6, 10, 11, 21, 88–9, 91–4, 97, 99–100, 101, 106, 114–18, 130–2, 134–5
Presidential Decision Directives (PDDs) 91–2, 93, 100
Price, A. 43
Price, R. 141
privacy 51–2
problem windows 36–7, 54–7, 122–5
'professionals of security' 27, 28–9, 125–9
prognostic frames/framing 30, 61–4, 131–2
propaganda warfare 75–7
Prothero, J. 4
Psychological Operations (PSYOPS) 74–5, 112
public–private partnerships 132–7
Putnam, R. 31

RAND Corporation 44, 68, 81–2, 114–15
Randell, B. 20
Rasmussen, M.V. 6
Rathmell, A. 114, 143
Rattray, G. 9, 69, 71, 72
Rawitch, R. 46
Ray, E. 92
re-framing phase 35–6, 123–5
Reagan, R. 10, 44, 49, 50, 59, 60–1, 62, 64, 95
Redefining Security (JSC) 71, 86–7, 117
Reus–Smit, C. 8
Revolution in Military Affairs (RMA) 69–70, 90, 92
revolution, concept of 15–16
Rice, C. 110–11
Richelson, J. 44, 50, 92
Riddle, A.S. 9, 69, 82, 132
Rifkin, Stanley M. 46
risk 84–6
Rittberger, V. 31
Rocheford, E.B. 30
Rochlis, J. 63
Rome Laboratory incident 80–1, 114

Rona, T.P. 41, 44, 58
Ronfeldt, D.F. 7, 61, 69–70, 117
Rose, R. 36
Rosecrance, R. 13
Rosenau, J.N. 14, 58
Ross, A. 46
Rotenberg, M. 51, 52
Rothmayr, C. 31
Ruggie, J. 7, 127–8
Rumsfeld, D. 108, 111–13
Ryan, C. 29

Sabatier, P.A. 36, 127
Sachs, M. 103
Saco, D. 49
safe computing 84–6
Sage, A.P. 17
Salt River Project incident 3
Satchell, M. 75, 76
Scambray, J. 21
Schaap, W.H. 92
Scherlis, W.L. 48
Scheufele, D.A. 30
Schiffman, Z.S. 12
Schmitt, E. 111
Schneier, B. 51
Schöfbänker, G. 79
Schroeder, G.A. 49
Schwartau, W. 117, 130
Schwartz, J. 118
script kiddies 21
Searle, J.R. 7, 8, 25
securing, changing methods of 132–7
securitisation phase 35
securitisation theory 25–9
securitisation/framing actors 37–8
Security Pacific Bank, Los Angeles 46
Security Policy Board (SPB) 87
Seminerio, M. 79
Senate Select Committee on Intelligence (SSCI) 100
'sensitive but unclassified' 62
Serabian, J.A. 132
Serdült, U. 31
Shannon, C. 14, 17
Shapiro, M. 7, 125
Shea, D.A. 4
Shea, J. 74, 75
Shelby, R.C. 110
Shelton, H.H. 75
Sibilia, R. 22
Sieber, U. 45, 46
Simmons, G. 50
Simon, W. 46

Singer, D.J. 5
Sjursen, H. 141
Slocombe, W.B. 113
Smith, G. 5, 83, 124, 130
Smith, M.R. 13
Smith, S. 16
Smith-Mundt Act (1948) 112
'sneakers' 21
'sniffers' 80
Snow, D.A. 30, 122
Softa, J. 9
Software Engineering Institute 47–8
'Solar Sunrise' incident 82–3, 115
Solomon, R.H. 14
speech act theory 25–9, 30
Squires, S.L. 48
Stahl, B. 27
Stapleton, J.R. 110
Stefanini, A. 3
Sterling, B. 47
Stoll, C. 2, 48, 58, 80
Stoneburner, G. 133
Strange, S. 140
Stripp, A. 41
Strogatz, S.H. 114
Stuckey, J. 5
Sun Tzu 54
Sundelius, B. 32
Supervisory Control and Data Acquisition (SCADA) systems 109
Supreme Court 63–4
Suter, M. 142
Swidler, A. 31
system intrusion 22
systems: complexity of 17–19; concept of 16–17

Tainter, J.A. 4
target, networked information infrastructure as 19–23
Task Force on Terrorism (1985) 92
Taylor, R. 76
Technical Analysis Group 5, 118
technological change 45–6, 66–7
technological determinism 12–13
Tenet, G.J. 110, 116, 119
terrorism 98–101
Theodore Roosevelt Dam, Arizona 3
Thompson, L.B. 108
threat frames 38–40, 122–5; changes in 113–21; process of 8–9
threat framing: actors in 57–9; through analogies and metaphors 129–32
threat perception, shaping of 80–4

threats, overstatement of 4–5
Timmermans, A. 31
Toffler, A. & H. 13, 69, 117
Top Secret (directive) PD/NSC 58 44
Townson, M. 27, 55
Tritak, J.S. 94
Trojan horses 21, 80
Turner, B.A. 4, 18
Tuyahov, A. 7, 12, 19, 66, 69

unbounded systems 67
USSPSI (US Senate Permanent Subcommittee on Investigations) 93
USSR, resources of 68

Valins, S. 32
Varone, F. 31
Vatis, M.A. 83, 101, 115, 117, 118
Verba, S. 7
Verton, D. 107
Virilio, P. 12
virises 21–2
Vistica, G.L. 78

Wæver, O. 5, 8, 24, 25–6, 28, 32, 58, 122, 126, 137
Waldrop, M.M. 12
Walker, R.B.J. 7
Wallace, C. 130
Walt, S.M. 8
Waltz, E. 15, 22
War Games (1983) 57
Watson, D.L. 119
weapon, networked information infrastructure as 19–23
weapons of mass destruction (WMDs) 102
Weapons Systems and Information War (Rona) 44
Weaver, W. 14, 17
Webel, B. 3
Webster, F. 14
Weimann, G. 5
Weiner, B. 32
Weldon, C. 2, 3, 43, 130
Wendt, A. 7, 31
Wenger, A. 6
Werner, W. 26
Westrin, P. 4
'White Hat Hackers' 21
White House 53, 102, 111
Wiener, N. 16, 32
Wiese, I. 139
Wigert, I. 6, 10, 94, 106, 117
Wildavsky, A. 143

Wilikens, M. 18
Williams, M.C. 8
Wilson, C. 4
Wilson, P.A. 9, 69, 82, 132
Wilson, T.R. 100
Winner, L. 13
Wittmeyer III, J.J. 63
Wohlsletter, A. 68
Wolfe, F. 78
Wolfowitz, P. 110
Woll, A. 39
Wood, L. 43
Worden, S.K. 30

World Trade Center 92–3
worms 21–2
Wright, L. 109

'Y2K' (Year 2000 problem) 116
Yates, A. 135
Yoran, A. 107
Young, K. 31
Yourdon, E. & J. 116

Zacher, M.W. 12
Zalewski, M. 16
Zeichner, L. 117